Dangerous Freedom

Dangerous Freedom

Fusion and Fragmentation
in Toni Morrison's Novels

Philip Page

University Press of Mississippi
Jackson

Earlier versions of portions of Chapter 7 were published in *African American Review*, volume 26, number 2 (Summer 1992) and of Chapter 8 in *African American Review*, volume 29, number 1 (Spring 1995).

Copyright © 1995 by the University Press of Mississippi
All rights reserved
Manufactured in the United States of America
99 98 97 96   4 3 2 1
The paper in this book meets the guidelines for permanence and durability of the Committee on Production Guidelines for Book Longevity of the Council on Library Resources.

Library of Congress Cataloging-in-Publication Data

Page, Philip.
    Dangerous freedom : fusion and fragmentation in Toni Morrison's novels / Philip Page.
        p. cm.
    Includes bibliographical references and index.
    ISBN 0-87805-860-5 (cloth : alk. paper). — ISBN 0-87805-861-3 (paper : alk. paper)
    1. Morrison, Toni—Criticism and interpretation. 2. Women and literature—United States—History—20th century. 3. Afro-American women in literature. 4. Afro-Americans in literature. I. Title.
PS3563.08749Z82 1996
813'.54—dc20   95-44261
                                                       CIP

British Library Cataloging-in-Publication data available

FOR MY FATHER

CONTENTS

ACKNOWLEDGMENTS

I thank all the students in my classes that included Morrison's fiction, especially those in the courses devoted solely to it. Their insights, questions, and enthusiasm have fueled this study. I extend special thanks to a trio of graduate students—Yvonne Atkinson, Sally-Anne Josephson, and Charlotte Street—for their ideas, support, and patience. I also thank Harry Hellenbrand for his persistent backing and his provocative comments on early drafts of most of these chapters; Susan Imbarrata for her helpful suggestions on the manuscript; and my other colleagues in the English Department at California State University, San Bernardino for their advice and encouragement. I have received consistent support from my campus, in particular from the School of Humanities and its dean, Beverly Hendricks. I thank Barbara Christian for her insightful reading of the manuscript and for her encouragement. I thank Anders L. Thompson for his careful copyediting. I thank everyone with whom I have worked at the University Press of Mississippi, especially Seetha A-Srinivasan. Finally, I thank my wife, Reba, who showed the way and held my hand.

Dangerous Freedom

ONE

The Puzzle of the One-and-the-Many

As Toni Morrison's fiction details the efforts of African Americans to find viable identities in a racialized society, it subtly probes what Ralph Ellison calls "the puzzle of the one-and-the-many" (*Shadow* 164–65). This is the idea that any entity is simultaneously unified yet divided, a whole yet an aggregation of parts. For example, the United States exists as a whole yet as regions, states, subgroups, and individuals; and, even though a discrete self is usually presumed, any individual exists in a multiplicity of roles, traits, and other factors. Similarly, a novel stands as a unified entity but simultaneously exists as a complex configuration of its constituent parts. Since no single English term adequately expresses this concept, I use "fusion and fragmentation," as well as comparable phrases like "plurality-in-unity," to indicate this simultaneous and overlapping unity and differentiation.[1]

This theme of fusion and fragmentation, which underlies my readings of Morrison's first six novels, provides insight into the novels' content, their form, and their contexts. In the novels' depictions of African-American identities, characters' psyches are revealed to be whole yet divided, families oscillate between unity and separation, communities exist yet are always already fragmented, and blacks and whites are always at odds. Present and past and North and South are yoked in a plurality-in-unity, always separate but often bridged through memory and ancestry.

Correspondingly, the forms of the novels fret out the pattern, thereby richly doubling the content. Each novel employs mechanisms in the telling of the story that enact and enhance the novel's themes. The narration is frequently subdivided among multiple points of view so that each novel, while retaining its unity, also projects a collection of perspectives. Plots tend to be circular or spiral rather than linear, as meaning is accreted through repetition and layering and as multiple times are overlaid on each other. By requiring the reader to engage actively, the novels also create a plurality-in-unity between reader, text, characters, narrators, and author.

Although fusion and fragmentation are operative in many contexts that could be applied to Morrison's fiction, three contexts seem particularly germane: American culture, African-American culture, and deconstruction. In both American and African-American cultures, the interplay between a presumed or desired unity and the divided parts within such an entity has been self-conscious and determining. American culture has always been fraught with unresolved tensions between the two, and African-American culture, historically the most prominent subdivision within American culture, in turn illustrates the theme of plurality-in-unity, both in its relationships with the mainstream culture and in its own cultural forms and traditions. Deconstruction reconceptualizes the issue of fusion and fragmentation, for example by calling into question the unitary existence of any entity, by unraveling the presupposed relationships between binary oppositions, and by privileging multiplicity and process over any form of essentialism. These three perspectives provide multiple and overlapping contexts for my readings of Morrison's novels, as all three develop complex dynamics of multiplicity and unity, fragmentation and fusion.

Although every culture, nation, or society can be described in terms both of its wholeness and its internal variations, the United States is particularly characterized by diversity. It embodies the coexistence of multiplicity and unity: *e pluribus unum*. This propensity is evident in such institutional structures as the constitutional balance of powers, bicameral legislatures, and the continual tensions between states' and federal rights. Since its inception American culture has been engaged with divisions and the difficulties of reconciling those divisions. Lawrence Levine claims that "American culture, from the very outset, was a divided one" (*Highbrow* 9), and Robert Spiller concurs that "mobility and diversity are and always have been the controlling factors in forming the American cultural identity" (5). American history can be seen as the alternation between periods of relative unity and relative plurality (Fisher, "Introduction" xii–xiii) or as a shift from a more holistic culture to a more heterogeneous one (Levine, *Highbrow* 171; Varenne 5). Henry Louis Gates, Jr., attests that "ours is a late-twentieth century world profoundly fissured by nationality, ethnicity, race, class, and gender" (*Loose* xv).

Commentators have provided many terms for this paradoxical trait, for example "*concordia discors*" (Grossman 184; Bercovitch, *Rites* 29), "classic polarities" (Bellah et al. 150), and "ambiguous 'double-consciousness'" (Marx, "Pastoralism" 56). Albert Murray defines America as "patently and irrevocably composite," as "incontestably mulatto" (22). For Ralph Ellison America is "a nation of ethical schizophrenics" (*Shadow* 99), and the American individual is in a state of "psychic uncertainty" (*Going* 20). In *The Rites of Assent*, Sacvan Bercovitch contributes a string of such terms for America: it is "infinitely processual" (14), characterized by "dissensus" (22) and "heterogeneity and pluralism" (372), and can be described as "a continual oscillation between harmony-in-diversity and diversity-in-harmony" and by "the continual flow of the one into the many and the many into the one" (373).

Michael Kammen exhaustively delineates this phenomenon, which he calls "biformity" (89). Tracing the idea to the divisions in seventeenth-century England that the first settlers brought with them, Kammen delineates the manifestations throughout American culture of this pattern of "paradoxical coupling of opposites" (89) or "strange sorts of hybrids" (90). For example, American culture, symbolized by the contrasting icons of Uncle Sam and the Statue of Liberty (108), is marked by conservatism but liberalism (92), by

5

individualism but conformity (108), by pragmatism but idealism (116), by isolation but sociability (179). Similarly, as Eric Sundquist contends, American literature is dominated by plurality-in-unity, encompassing multiplicity and tolerating dissonance, but not necessarily splintering. He formulates the "paradox that 'American' literature is both a single tradition of many parts *and* a series of winding, sometimes parallel traditions that have perforce been built in good part from this inherent conflict" (18).

Such theories of the plurality-in-unity of American culture parallel postmodern theories, which have reshaped traditional perceptions about nearly everything. They have accomplished this reshaping, in part, by calling into question the unity and coherence of all totalizing concepts and presupposed universals. Postmodern formulations of culture, race, gender, or the self, for example, insist on the complex and ever-shifting multiplicity of such concepts. Each concept still exists, but it is unraveled—deconstructed—to reveal its inner contradictions, variability, and indecipherability.[2]

Similarly, postmodern perceptions of the relationships between traditional entities shift from clearly defined (and inevitably hierarchical) bipolar oppositions to more complex fluctuations involving nonunitary entities and the undefinable but crucial differences and similarities between them. Not rejecting the original terms or replacing the traditionally favored one with the unprivileged one, the new perspective seeks a more complex perception of their interrelation. As Barbara Johnson writes: "Instead of a simple 'either/or' structure, deconstruction attempts to elaborate a discourse that says *neither* 'either/or,' *nor* 'both/and' nor even 'neither/nor,' while at the same time not totally abandoning these logics either" (12). That is, one keeps the dichotomy but one blurs the distinction between opposing terms, in recognition of the reality that neither term is self-sufficient, original, privileged or, by itself, knowable. One does not insist on either unity or separation, on fusion or fragmentation, but one maintains all possible relationships in a continuing flux, and one welcomes the open-ended, shifting, and opaque relationships among entities and constituent parts.

Crucial to this formulation is Jacques Derrida's concept of the *différance*, that is, the difference between opposing terms as well as the

6

temporal deferral from one term to the other. By insisting on the space and time between supposedly opposed terms, deconstruction de-emphasizes the original entities with their illusory identities and their unavoidable hierarchy and replaces them with the unresolvable relationships within the structure, which is no longer simply binary. The focus becomes the complex gradations within the opposition, the influences each term has on the other, the similarities between them, and the delicate balance between fusion and fragmentation.

This perspective also accounts for what Fredric Jameson calls "the dialectical reversal" (309). Based on Hegel's recognition that slavery enfeebles the master as well as the slave, many postmodern writers have addressed the reciprocality of influence within so-called binary systems. If any entity x gains hegemony over y, then x is at least partially defined by the distinction, that is to say by y. By becoming the image of what x is not and cannot afford to be, y reminds x of x's identity. In other words, x defines itself in terms of y; in a sense, x becomes y.

Not only does postmodern thinking about American culture reflect fusion and fragmentation, but so do contemporary ideas about texts. Following earlier work in linguistics, M. M. Bakhtin and Roland Barthes altered prevailing notions about written discourse. For Bakhtin, every text is characterized by "heteroglossia": "a set of conditions—social, historical, meteorological, physiological—that will insure that a word uttered in that place and at that time will have a meaning different than it would have under any other conditions" (428). Every text is thus processual and dialogic: "Everything means, is understood, as a part of a greater whole—there is a constant interaction between meanings, all of which have the potential of conditioning others" (426). A text is the result of competing influences, some centripetal, tending toward unity, and some centrifugal, tending toward heterogeneity. Novels especially are comprised of many voices or styles, the languages not only of the various characters or narrators, but the echoes of other styles that creep into every author's language: "dialogization . . . is the basic distinguishing feature of the stylistics of the novel" (263). Like Bakhtin, Barthes sees the text as plural, "a galaxy" (*S/Z* 5), a "cacography" (9), with no beginning or end. The traditional concept of the "work"—a finished, authored product—becomes a "text," a process of ongoing interpretation, in which the reader, inseparable from the text, is as integral as the author ("From Work" 74–79). The text is "fugued," composed of uncountable bits and pieces, forever separate but comprising one text, in which "sequences move in counterpoint" (*Image* 103).

Just as language as a whole and any given text are hybrids consisting of a never-ending multiplicity of parts ambiguously joined in a unity-of-sorts, contemporary ideas about the self are couched in similar terms. A review of contemporary psychoanalytical theories is beyond the scope of this study, but two prevailing ideas are especially relevant. First, most theories imply that the self is formed through separation. This implies that the self is always already linked to other entities (such as language) in complex relationships. Jacques Lacan asserts the connection between language and the self: when the self enters into language, division develops between the speaking "I" and the "I" that the speaker's language represents. Second, most theories deny the traditional idea of a unified self or a fixed identity. Derrida argues that the traditional concept of the unitary self is contradictory and illusory, that no one possesses his or her life, and that every life is always at least double, deriving from the father and the mother. Like the postmodern sense of a text, the sense of self is a complex locus of forces, always in process of becoming, inevitably divided yet somehow an entity.

For the study of the self in literature, Thomas Docherty theorizes that postmodern fiction substitutes much more fluid subjectivities for the fixed notions of character and reader that prevailed in realist fiction. The "rigid logical unity" of the realist's character becomes the "plurality" of the postmodernist's characterization (265): "the conceptual notion of Character is replaced in post-Modern fiction by the process of Characterization, the continual re-creation or re-position of character as a 'becoming' rather than as an 'essence' (268). Fixed unities are unraveled into fluid collocations of fragments, a process that releases the reader as well as the characters: "through the process of de-centering the consciousness of the speaking characters, and the subsequent impersonal form of narration, the reader can be given the subjective authority of a first-person I or we" (109).

Feminist theory has focused particular attention on questions of identity, especially since for women the traditional binary opposition of man/woman has carried the stigma of inferiority. In the patriarchal system, as Simone de Beauvoir writes, "He is the Subject, she is the Other" (xvi). For Beauvoir and many other women, "she" has a reciprocal claim but suffers the conflict between her human aspirations to be a subject/self and her social status as an object/other. This produces an "odd feeling" (297) of being both self and other, both inside and outside the system. Virginia Woolf describes such a feeling: "Again if one is a woman one is often surprised by a sudden splitting off of consciousness, say in walking down Whitehall, when from being the natural inheritor of that civilisation, she becomes, on the contrary, outside of it, alien and critical" (97).

One response to this sense of doubleness is to embrace it, to assert the values of doubled consciousness and insider/outsider status. By so doing, one accepts oneself as a dynamic interplay of forces, whose blurred boundaries become potential strengths rather than absolute liabilities. Luce Irigaray argues that duality is essential for women, that women constitute a "disruptive excess" ("Power" 6) that includes the reversal of anything posited. Woman is "everywhere elsewhere," always displaced, and plural ("Volume" 53). Similarly, Rachel DuPlessis celebrates the "both/and vision" of the female aesthetic as opposed to the traditional Western male's either/or dichotomizing vision (276). For her, everything in women's experience leads to doubleness—doubled consciousness, doubled understandings (278), and a "double dance" in and out of culture and society (284). Women gain not an exclusionary wholeness (279) but the holistic sense of life, becoming "(ambiguously) nonhegemonic" (284).

If women's consciousnesses tend to be split, a remarkably similar phenomenon is attributed to African Americans.[3] Beauvoir notes the "deep similarities between the situation of women and that of the Negro" (xxiii), in particular the equal but different status of women and the separate but equal status of African Americans, and DuPlessis writes that "négritude has analogues with women's aesthetic practices" (285). The language of splitting and doubleness in feminist rhetoric recalls W. E. B. Du Bois's famous formulation: "It is a peculiar sensation, this double-consciousness, this sense of always looking at one's self through the eyes of others, of measuring one's soul by the tape of a world that looks on in amused contempt and pity. One ever feels his twoness,—an American, a Negro; two souls, two unreconciled strivings; two warring ideals in one dark body" (5). Many African Americans have expressed similar feelings. For example, Ralph Ellison describes the Negro as "that sensitively focused process of opposites" (*Shadow* 26), who is forced to become a "negative sign" (48) in the black/white dichotomy.[4]

For both marginalized groups, relegation to otherness leads to an awareness of doubled consciousness, in both cases the sense of plurality-within-unity is thereby heightened, and in both cases the perspective shifts toward the postmodern. Just as many women extol the positive effects of their doubleness, so do African Americans. Du Bois, in the midst of decrying the ill effects of racism in America, nevertheless claims that the Negro is "gifted with second-sight in this American world" (5) and that being forced to the other side of the veil is "a peculiar sensation," one that creates a new sensibility. Demonstrating his both/and vision, Ellison concurs that the Negro's position in America has caused untold disruption *and* has forced him to come to grips with life and self (*Shadow* 112), giving him a "special perspective" (131). Being a Negro "imposes the uneasy burden *and* occasional joy of a complex double vision, a fluid, ambivalent response to men and events which represents, at its finest, a profoundly civilized adjustment to the cost of being human in this modern world" (131–32, emphasis added). According to Houston Baker, Jr., double-consciousness led to forms of discourse such as the blues, whose "matrix avoids simple dualities" and which is built upon "a fluid and multivalent network" (*Blues* 9). African Americans, denied the ordinary sense of self, learned to privilege the unseen and the intangibly personal in complex forms and levels of discourse, a process illuminated by Derrida's privileging of absence as the means by which a system of signs conveys meaning (Baker, *Workings* 39–42, 55–56).[5]

For African Americans, the shift to a doubled perspective can be traced to traditional West African cultures.[6] West African culture contrasted pervasively with Euro-American culture, and those contrasts, along with the slaves' subjugated status, forced African Americans into doubleness—African by tradition but American by necessity. One

10

principal dimension of contrast was the shift from the traditional African sense of harmonious unity to the Euro-American focus on competitive differentiation. Adebayo Adesanya finds in African thinking "a coherence or compatibility among all disciplines" (qtd. in Jahn 96) and claims that the disciplines "all find themselves logically concatenated in a system so tight that to subtract one item from the whole is to paralyse the structure of the whole" (97). In the African world view, there are no clear demarcations between life and death (Asante 99; Barthold 11; Jahn 107), sacred and secular (Smitherman 93), or spiritual and material (Smitherman 75). Instead, the focus is on the reconciliation of oppositions in which the cosmos, as well as every community, is a "balanced force field" (Smitherman 108) and in which harmonies, coherence, compatibility, and equilibrium are the highest goals (Asante 65). The individual is not in competition with other individuals or with the larger community, as in the Euro-American mode, but instead attempts to achieve selfhood in balance with others. Society is a microcosm of universal order, and harmony in each depends on individuals accepting their places and respecting the places of others (Roberts 76). As Asante puts it, "One becomes human only in the midst of others" (185).

Another contrast between African and Euro-American views involves conceptions of time. For Africans time is cyclic and synchronous, as opposed to the linear, diachronic Euro-American sense of time (Asante 18; Barthold 6; Smitherman 75). In African thinking, past, present, and future are composite, and the individual lives "in time" rather than worrying about being "on time" (Smitherman 75). In this conception, as in the conception of harmony, the African view privileges fusion, whereas the Euro-American view tolerates and even values fragmentation.

A third element of contrast is the African emphasis on the spoken word versus the Euro-American privileging of the written word. In the African world view, the spoken word, *nommo*, represents the life-force, "a unity of spiritual-physical fluidity, giving life to everything, penetrating everything, causing everything" (Jahn 124). According to Roberts, "Africans viewed the spoken word as the embodiment of an individual's life-force in that it represented not only the means by which human beings communicated with each other but also the

11

means by which they interacted with all other forces" (77). Through "the magic power of the word" (Jahn 121; Smitherman 121), human beings give life to otherwise dead objects and materials. Even human babies are mere things until they are named (Asante 73; Jahn 125). Because of the power of *nommo*, any recounting, whether of experienced event, vision, or prophecy, causes what is told to be true.

Instead of assimilating African Americans, as it did virtually every other minority, white American culture used this most prominent subgroup to help define itself. James Baldwin maintains that "at the root of the American Negro problem is the necessity of the American white man to find a way of living with the Negro in order to be able to live with himself" (*Notes* 172). Ellison agrees that mainstream American culture has used the Negro to resolve its dilemmas (*Shadow* 28), and he claims that the otherness of blacks provided European immigrants with the reassurance that, in contrast to the excluded other, they truly were Americans (*Going* 111).[7] In *Playing in the Dark*, Morrison extends such ideas to her concept of "an American Africanism" (38), an image of the unimaginable other that white Americans created as a way of defining themselves: "the process of organizing American coherence through a distancing Africanism became the operative mode of a new cultural hegemony" (8).

Consequently, of the innumerable rifts in American culture, the black/white racial schism was and still is the most fundamental. During slavery, American culture developed racial barriers into an almost unbridgeable gap. According to Kammen, slavery has always constituted "an underlying moral and social contradiction" (189) and, in idealistic America, that contradiction led to the concept of the black slave as "a model of what white Americans must never become" (191). For Ellison, race "made for a split in America's moral identity that would infuse all of its acts and institutions with a quality of hypocrisy" (*Going* 333) and "became a major cause, form, and symbol of the American hierarchical psychosis" (336). Stating that even today "slavery . . . is the overarching American issue" (11), Sundquist contends that American culture is inherently multicultural and biracial, built upon "the complex dialectic between 'white' and 'black' cultures" (2).[8]

Not only is African-American culture split off from but still part

12

of the dominant American culture, it is itself a pluralistic entity. By definition, African-American culture is a combination of African and Euro-American elements. Levine examines how the African world view interacted with and was transformed by Euro-American views (*Black* 5). The resulting African-American culture is a "syncretic blend of the old and the new, of the African and the Euro-American" (135) and the result of "a dual process of creation and re-creation, of looking both without and within the black community for the means of sustenance and identity and survival" (189).

African-American culture, simultaneously part of and separate from white American culture, developed a variety of expressive forms, for example Black English, the oral tradition, and musical forms such as spirituals, the blues, and jazz. One oral trope that is particularly noticeable in Morrison's fiction is call and response, in which statements by the individual and the group alternate.[9] Besides ritualizing the individual/group interrelationship, call and response embodies fusion and fragmentation. Since the complete utterance requires the completion of both constituent parts, it is a dialectic form featuring the dynamic oppositions of its parts within the context of the whole (Byerman 3). For Craig Werner, call and response is not a form of synthesis but a kind of inclusive analysis that allows for multiple voices and perspectives (*Playing* xviii). Similarly, Roger Abrahams sees call and response as an indicator of the simultaneous independence and interdependence of African-American culture. The form affirms through the enactment of opposites as it combines innovation and tradition, invention and initiation (83). Call and response thus replaces single-voiced, authoritative monologue with multistranded, collective voices that merge the individual and the community in mutual harmony.

African-American musical forms, in particular the blues and jazz, also illustrate the pattern of fusion and fragmentation. The traditional alternation between soloist and ensemble in the blues and jazz is a version of call and response in which the ensemble's instruments replace the community's collective voice (Jahn 221). Furthermore, Jahn's point that the blues singer typically expresses the community's experience (223) and Levine's similar point that blues songs are expressions of individual emotion but are designed to be communal

13

(*Black* 235) suggest that the blues singer is a witness/testifier for the community. According to Levine, "black music was a participant activity" (*Black* 232), not only for those who responded to the leader of a field holler or who sang in response to the lead singer but for those who purchased the records, suggested new singers to the record companies, and followed closely the careers of the star performers (217–39). In African-American culture, music has provided one prominent avenue for the mutual fulfillment of both individual and community, thereby exemplifying the African concept of individual/community harmony: "Jazz is an art of the individual, celebrating originality and imagination, and simultaneously a group art, an art of the collective consciousness" (Nisenson 22).

It is a commonplace that African-American music combines African and European elements.[10] According to Levine, the blues "represented a major degree of acculturation to the individualized ethos of the larger society" (*Black* 221). Jazz has been described as a product of African-European cultural dialogue (Hartman 149) and as the embodiment of the melting pot's ideal synthesis of Africa and Europe (Nisenson 269). Leroi Jones (Amiri Baraka) develops the general pattern by which African-American music expresses Negro culture's "adaptation," "fashion[ing] something out of [mainstream] culture for himself" (79), and creating "a brilliant amalgam of diverse influences" (80).[11]

Besides serving as exemplars of the blending of African and European cultures, the blues and jazz themselves are characterized by the seemingly endless mergers and splintering of styles, forms, and groups. African-American musical history reveals the mingling of folk and professional elements, of secular and sacred styles, of the blues and jazz, and of the constant formation and re-formation of performing and recording groups. This fluidity in the history of African-American music reflects the music itself, for example in Ellison's descriptions of jazz as "a texture of fragments, repetitive, nervous, not fully formed" (*Shadow* 202) and as a vernacular flux, "a dynamic *process* in which the most refined styles from the past are continually merged with the play-it-by-eye-and-by-ear improvisations which we invent in our efforts to control our environment and entertain ourselves" (*Going* 139). For Ellison, a jazz group is both a unified whole and isolated individuals who work "in a spirit of antagonistic cooperation" (*Going* 129).

Characterized by these elements of fusion, fluidity, antiphony, and polyphony, African-American music has served a dual function as both a unifying factor within the subculture and as a vehicle and a symbol of the separateness of that subculture from the dominant culture. James Cone states both that "black music is unity music" (5) and that "it affirms the political 'otherness' of black people" (6). This double function of music has its roots in the common double meanings carried by African-American folk songs to deceive whites.[12] By reminding African Americans of their African heritage and at the same time reflecting the adaptation of traditional African forms into new American genres, the blues and jazz symbolize the doubleness of African-American experience and the ironies associated with that doubleness. As Leroi Jones argues, the emerging black middle class in the 1930s and 1940s often attempted to purge itself of anything reminiscent of Africa or slavery, but African-American music inherently remembers those pasts and the ambiguity of African Americans' "self-division, self-hatred, stoicism, and finally quixotic optimism" (136). African American music is both "a music of alienation" (Nisenson 78) and a music of "assimilation" (Murray 60). Like Black English, African-American music is a metaphor for and an instance of the "combination of acculturation and cultural exclusivity" (Levine, *Black* 154). For Ellison, jazz and the blues represent African-American experience—particularly its ambiguity (*Shadow* 246) and the necessity of losing one's identity in order to find it (*Shadow* 234).

One of the most prominent features of the blues and jazz is their improvisational nature. Classically, they have no fixed forms, no written standardized versions. They are "experimentation" (Murray 53), "a radical art form, always in creative ferment" (Nisenson 247), erupting in "playful festival[s] of meaning," "nonlinear, freely associative, nonsequential meditation" (Baker, *Blues* 5). As Ingrid Monson maintains, jazz is thus representative of elements of the African-American experience and is quintessentially postmodern. Both jazz and postmodernism are heterogeneous, doubled, and dialogic, working within yet subverting mainstream culture. Both constitute "two separate worlds clearly demarcated yet inextricably entwined" (286), and both comment on mainstream culture through irony and parody (285–92).

Just as jazz and the blues are open-ended forms, constantly under revision, always in question, denying fixity, so the historical places and roles of African Americans have been necessarily fluid. African-American music is always shifting, always seeking the next variation, just as the African diaspora, the slave trade, the resale of slaves within the United States, the longed-for and sometimes achieved escape to the North, the myth of the return to Africa, and the northern migrations have kept African Americans literally on the move and metaphorically unfixed within the larger culture.

The improvisational nature of the blues and jazz and their role as epitomes of the paradoxical interrelationships between African-American culture and mainstream culture also associate these forms with deconstruction. For Baker, the blues singer is the *x* of the railroad crossing, implying "the multidirectionality of the juncture" (*Blues* 7), ceaseless flux and mobility, the necessity of polyvalent interpretations, the avoidance of "simple dualities" (9), and instead the sign of "a fluid and multivalent network." For Hartman, the jazz soloist puzzles over and re-interprets the prior musical "text," "recontextualizing" it "to expose its allegiances and assumptions" (63), a procedure analogous to a deconstructive reading of a written text. Like deconstruction, African-American musical forms challenge traditional notions of transcendent universals and bipolar oppositions. As Werner writes, "the jazz impulse (grounded in blues and gospel) engages basic (post)modernist concerns including the difficulty of defining, or even experiencing, the self; the fragmentation of public discourse; and the problematic meaning of tradition" (*Playing* xvii). Alan Nadel, stressing "the deconstructive energies of African-American art and culture," insists that the "strategies" employed by African-American music share "with deconstruction the constant undermining and reconfiguring of the audience-text-performer relationship, so as to reveal the instability of the assumptions that give each of those positions its positionality, its center" (qtd. in Werner, *Playing* xix). Just as Derrida insists on the play between and within oppositions, Albert Murray writes that playing the blues is also "*playing with* the blues" (58). Like deconstruction's shift of perspective from the oppositions between paired entities to the complex relationships within them and their pairing, Murray finds that the blues performer "turns disjunctions into continuities" (59).[13]

The blues and jazz thus provide a metaphor for my contention that a similar current runs through American culture, African-American culture, and deconstruction. All are engaged with the dynamics of bifurcation and interplay, differentiation and assimilation, fragmentation and fusion. American culture is a "delicately poised unity of divergencies"; women in this patriarchy must dance the "double dance" of simultaneous inclusion and exclusion; African-American culture, an adaptive hybrid of African and Euro-American influences, floats among the polarities of assimilation and separatism; "the dialogic nature of jazz places it at the American center" (Hartman 149); and through African-American music "the two separate worlds [of black and white America] [are] clearly demarcated yet inextricably entwined" (Monson 288).[14]

Recent theories of African-American literature, particularly black feminist theories, provide another background for the interweavings of fusion and fragmentation in Morrison's fiction. As they reinforce the connection between African-American experience, women's experience, and deconstruction, these theories call attention to four crucial issues in contemporary African-American fiction, all of which are relevant to Morrison's novels: the quest for place, the recovery of the past, the problem of identity, and experimentation with narrative form.

Since the diaspora, African Americans have been on the move, seeking a place within the American geographic and cultural space. In Morrison's novels, characters' journeys from South to North or vice versa are laden with such overtones. Houston Baker declares that slaves' first place was a hole, a coffin, a place of death and rebirth, on the slave-trading ships: "Place as an Afro-American portion of the world begins in a European displacement of bodies for commercial purposes" (*Workings* 108). As opposed to the seemingly limitless spatial potential of America for whites, blacks were consigned to holes, then to rural cabins, and later to urban kitchenettes, not truly their own places because such places were imposed upon them. This historic condition outside mainstream American culture forced African

17

Americans to deconstruct, defamiliarize, and signify within the master discourse ("There" 136–41).

Melvin Dixon and Charles Scruggs extrapolate on this theme of place in African-American fiction. For Dixon, the geographical dislocations of history led to African-American writers' emphasis on issues of shelter, home, and identity and on images of journeys, conquered spaces, and imagined havens (*Ride* 2). Forced into these alternate spaces, marked by dislocation and fragmentation, characters, narrators, and readers become performers who gain some measure of control over themselves and their environments (5–6). Scruggs's apocalyptic theory posits the dialectic in African-American literature between dystopia and utopia, between the city as ash heap and the city as the Beloved Community, civilization, and home (*Sweet* 2–7). African-American writers' portrayal of their struggle within this dialectic figures the quest to find a secure place in American culture (220–23).

The search for place is inseparable from the theme of lost history (Scruggs, *Sweet* 207). As African Americans were denied place, so their African history was denied and their slave past was repudiated. Bonnie Barthold warns of the resulting danger of "temporal dispossession" (17) for African Americans caught in the chaos of time with no meaningful past or future. In a "no man's land" (42), black characters attempting to flee this chaos are led to temporal duality, a split between their inner vision and the world around them (75). Consequently, contemporary African-American fiction often incorporates the forms and values of the past into modern settings (Cooke 208). Unlike white characters who typically want to escape time, black characters seek redemption in the return to community and the ensuing resolution of their inner/outer fragmentation (Barthold 77–80). This yoking of past and present is often accomplished through memory, which "juxtaposes past and present and, to varying degrees, fuses the past of personal experience with the past of a cultural heritage, underscoring the necessity of accepting, rather than attempting to escape, the past" (89).

Black feminist theorists have articulated this need for reintegration of the past as a form of reestablishing community. Historically, black women have constituted the *other* other, the doubly marginalized, op-

pressed by both racial and gender prejudice. According to black feminist theorists, neither the black (male) drive for civil rights and racial
equality nor the (white) feminist drive for gender equality adequately
listened to black women. Michele Wallace contends that during the
battle to ratify the Fourteenth Amendment black women relin-
quished their hopes for equality in order not to jeopardize the vote
for black males (*Black* 152), and she attests to increasing distrust and
hatred between black men and black women since the 1930s (13). In
the civil rights and black arts movements of the 1960s, black women
were again silent, deferring to the male-led drive for equality and
assuming that once racial equality was won they would be granted
sexual equality (14–29). Excluded from the civil rights movement,
African-American women were also ignored by the white-dominated
women's liberation movement. According to bell hooks, this movement diverted attention from black male sexism (*Ain't* 87) and was
designed to insure white women's superior position over black men
(127).

Other contemporary black feminists express the sense of isolation
(M. Washington, "Introduction" xxxii), invisibility (B. Smith 168),
being misunderstood (McDowell, "New" 187), and being victimized
by damaging stereotypes (hooks, *Ain't* 84–85; Wallace, *Black* 152). By
stressing such concerns, black feminist theorists keep attention focused on the complexities in the relations among blacks and whites
and men and women, and therefore on the related questions of plurality and unity in American culture.

In particular, black feminist theorists urge consideration of the special perspectives of black women. For example, Patricia Hill Collins
cites the corrective insights that an inherently postmodern black feminist perspective provides as it insists on "the interdependence of
thought and action": "This dimension of a Black women's standpoint
rejects either/or dichotomous thinking that claims that *either* thought
or concrete action is desirable and that merging the two limits the
efficacy of both. Such approaches generate deep divisions among theorists and activists which are more often fabricated than real. Instead,
by espousing a both/and orientation that views thought and action as
part of the same process, possibilities for new relationships between
thought and action emerge" (28–29).

19

With regard to literature, black feminist theorists also articulate the theme of pluralism-within-unity. Echoing Du Bois's term, Mary Helen Washington sees a thematic parallel between literature by African Americans and by women: "The theme of double-consciousness is found in most literature by Blacks, and the theme of the divided self, woman split in two (which is closely akin to double-consciousness) is found in literature by women, white and Black" ("Teaching" 208–9). Likewise, Hazel Carby outlines the similarities between black feminist criticism and the white feminist movement (16), and Valerie Smith extends the parallels among feminist, African-American male, and black feminist literary theories, all of which attempt to locate and/or reinterpret the writings of members of their groups ("Black").

Furthermore, black feminist theorists claim that black women writers have a different orientation toward their predecessors than is generally acknowledged for other groups. For Washington, because of the African-American oral tradition and the associated strength of mother/daughter bonds, black women writers escape the dread of the patriarchal authority of previous writers ("I Sign" 160). Missy Dehn Kubitschek concurs that black women's fiction features the positive results of the matrilineal lineage for the individual and her community and that coming to terms with African-American history is necessary for black women. Michael Awkward differentiates black women's fiction as a quest for "comm(unity)" that features "self-division," "textual sharing," "double-voiced narration," and "Afro-American female protagonists' efforts to end debilitating psychological disjunction (or double-consciousness) and isolation from the larger black community" (*Inspiriting* 14).

The implicit connection between such theories and deconstruction becomes explicit in the formulations of Mae Henderson and Valerie Smith. For Henderson the "deconstructive function of black women's writing" is "to interpret or interpenetrate the signifying structures of the dominant and subdominant discourse in order to formulate a critique and, ultimately, a transformation of the hegemonic white and male symbolic order" (135). Black women writers "remain on the borders of discourse, speaking from the vantage point of the insider/outsider" and thereby able "to see the other, but also to see what the other cannot see" (137). Before developing her ideas about black feminist theory, Smith analyzes the overlapping among deconstruction, male African-American literature, and Anglo-American feminist theory, arguing that the latter two have been drawn to deconstruction because, like them, it is a destabilizing, oppositional discourse ("Black" 40). Smith warns, however, that deconstruction, which questions the validity of selfhood and which typically takes an ahistorical stance, may undermine the efforts of black males and black and white women to situate their places in American culture: both feminists and African Americans "may betray the origins of their respective modes of inquiry when they seek to employ the discourse of contemporary theory" (43). For Smith the antidote to this danger is the perspectives of black feminists, who can insure that the oppositional discourses remain radical and not tamely institutionalized.

One way for fiction writers to embody the fusion of past and present is through intertextuality. Awkward's thesis is that contemporary black women's fiction is based on the positive, "inspiriting influences" among black women's texts, as opposed to the male competition between texts and writers. The lineage—in Awkward's case, from Zora Neale Hurston to Morrison to Gloria Naylor to Alice Walker—involves complex interrelationships, not simple oppositions, among texts, identities, narrative strategies, and communities (*Inspiriting* 13–14).

Intertextuality as a form of integrating the past is also central to the theories of African-American literature formulated by Robert Stepto and Henry Louis Gates, Jr. For Stepto, "the primary pregeneric myth for Afro-Americans is the quest for freedom and literacy" (*From* ix), which is revealed by the "contrapuntal and dialectical aspects of the relationship" between slave narratives and twentieth-century African-American fiction (xi). His idea of the "immersion narrative" (x), one of his types of slave narratives, relates the hero's absorption of and reabsorption into his or her past. For Gates, *Signifyin(g)* not only refers to the oral art form of indirection and to the propensity for African-American writers to rework their predecessors' texts, but also implies a redoubling of ordinary signification. African-American discourse, the discourse of the excluded other in American culture, signifies within its own traditions and simultaneously, because of its excluded position, comments upon, or shadows, mainstream discourse: "The relationship that black 'Signification' bears to the English 'signification' is, paradoxically, a relation of difference inscribed within a relation of identity" (*Signifying* 45).

Given that space and time in African-American experience have been so problematic and that individual and collective identities have been overriding concerns for all Americans, it is not surprising that "Negro Americans are in desperate search for identity" (Ellison, *Shadow* 297). Baldwin contends that African Americans are unique in American culture because their traditional past was so categorically taken away (*Notes* 169), that consequently African Americans have no acceptable self-image (*Nobody* 80), and that their identity has been achieved only by estrangement from the past (*Notes* 174). The sense of self and of one's role in the larger culture has been caught in the crossfire between such culturally constructed oppositions as exclusion/inclusion, freedom/slavery, and tolerance/prejudice, as well as between the contradictions of white attitudes. Bernard Bell suggests that, instead of the emphasis on the search for innocence in white American fiction, African-American novelists have had to grapple with the central theme of the black/white Manichean drama and the corresponding double consciousness (341). African Americans, forced into a plural identity, have documented in literature their quest to discover that identity and to realize its potential. Since African Americans "were compelled to verify a self's being-in-the-world" (Baker, "There" 136), they often chose such literary forms as autobiography, slave narrative, and essay that lent themselves to exploration of one's personal spirituality.

Typically for African Americans, identity is not only plural but it is never fixed, always in process (Byerman 5). It is necessarily formed in reaction to the controlling mainstream culture, so that there is never any sure reality, only a variation on it (Byerman 5), with the result that one often feels that one "does not exist in the real world at all" (Ellison, *Shadow* 304). One's identity is always a variation, a mask, with the constant danger that the mask will slip or, worse, that the disguise will become reality and any real identity will be lost (Barthold 45).

Perhaps because identity has been an often neglected and even

22

more perplexing issue for black women than for black men, commentators on black women's literature have dwelt on it. One perspective, discussed above, is the promise for identity formation provided by black women's matrilineal heritage. Another theme is the necessity for black women to take control of their own agenda. For Barbara Christian, this means the need "to define and express [their] totality rather than being defined by others" (*Black Feminist* 159), to define the cultural context as African-American, to analyze the interacting forces of racism and sexism, to question traditional definitions of womanhood, and to insist "not only on the centrality of black women to Afro-American history, but also on their pivotal significance to present-day social [and] political developments in America" (180). Also building on the fusion of racial and gender conflicts in black women's fiction, Elliott Butler-Evans sees the fictional texts of Toni Cade Bambara, Toni Morrison, and Alice Walker as "site[s] of dissonance, ruptures, and . . . a kind of narrative violence" (3). The resulting response is "an attempted reconciliation of a fragmented self and a synthesis of racial and gender politics" (4).

With the shift in focus of African-American fiction from the protest politics of the 1960s to more introspective portrayals of personal and community life (Bell 342), the form of the fiction has become more significant and more flexible.[15] In contemporary African-American fiction, traditional conventions are loosened, pushed in the directions of multiplicity, nonlinearity, open-endedness, and orality.

In many contemporary African-American novels, multiple perspectives are necessary to convey the intricacies of characters' responses.[16] As Barthold writes, "point of view in black fiction, with few exceptions, is multiple, at least dual" (79). She sees it specifically as an alternation between characters' inner perspectives and a third-person, outer perspective, an alternation that inscribes the ironic discrepancy between individual and world and that ultimately brings the character, as well as the reader, to a clearer understanding (82–83). Kubitschek connects the multiple perspectives with the "multitextured reality" (6) of African-American experience, particularly the necessity of bringing past female experience to bear on the present (21–22).

Partly as a result of such multiple perspectives, the plots of African-

23

American novels typically do not unfold in a conventionally linear fashion. Instead, differing renditions of the same events overlap like a circle or spiral, a temporal structure reminiscent of West African ideas about time. For example, the events in Toni Cade Bambara's *The Salt Eaters* take place in less than an hour, while Minnie Ransom tries to heal Velma Henry, but that time period is multiply expanded as the impressions and memories of numerous characters are narrated. The forward momentum of the narration is based more on repetition (Byerman 7) than on the linear addition of "new" events or time. In explaining his concept of "the *Timed Book*" (*Workings* 200–203), Baker argues that contemporary black women's fictions are structured on a moment of crisis and then a reworking of that moment to create a newer and healthier time: "[The protagonists'] solutions and sojourns carry them from a static instant of crisis to a new *now*" (201).

As multiple perspectives and nonlinearity suggest, contemporary African-American novels tend also to de-emphasize conventional closure. The immediate crisis is perhaps averted or even transcended, but endings usually leave the characters with their lives still in process, still to be endured. Jacqueline De Weever sees this tendency as a result of the mixtures of cultures and myths affecting contemporary black women's fiction and the corresponding psychological and cultural crosscurrents that control the characters (16). For Kubitschek the openness is a consequence of the novelists' insistence on the continuous process of reabsorbing their cultural past (6), and Byerman associates the open-endedness with the folk sense of the necessity for endurance and improvement rather than for the sense of domination or conflict resolution (8–9).

Kubitschek and Byerman both link the novels' lack of conventional closure to call and response. In that form, there is no closure (Kubitschek 6), no resolution or progress, only return (Byerman 7). Like call and response, the novels are built on the open-ended interplay of multiple voices whose interactions are the point. Because of this dialogic play of characters' and narrators' voices, the texts become "speakerly." That is, they push written language in the direction of spoken language. This happens not only in dialogue but also in the characters' monologues and even in the typical informality of the third-person narrators. One result of this oral quality of the prose is to diminish the distance between text and reader and thereby to invite the reader to participate. For example, when Morrison starts *The Bluest Eye* with "Quiet as it's kept" or *Jazz* with "Sth, I know that woman," the colloquial language suggests that the narrator is speaking directly to the reader and therefore that, as in a conversation, the reader is expected to respond.

The loosening of narrative conventions and forms in contemporary African-American fiction calls into question the traditional discourses of the novel. In Dixon's terms, it creates an alternate space in which not only characters but also authors and readers can perform: "protagonists are engaged in verbal performances *in* narratives that help authors produce performances *of* narratives" (*Ride* 6). For Butler-Evans the disruptive conflicts of race and gender force the texts themselves into fragmentation, into "a discursive formation marked by tensions and dissonance" (39). Byerman and Baker couch the tension in more political terms: for Byerman the African-American text creates an alternate discourse designed to counter the claims of the logocentric order (7); and for Baker African-American texts embody "the incendiary deconstruction, defamiliarization, and signifying within the master discourse" ("There" 141).

Toni Morrison's novels satisfy contemporary readers because they resonate with the disturbing themes of fusion and fragmentation in poststructuralist theories about American and African-American cultures. They satisfy in their rhetoric, especially in their reliance on multiple points of view, in their blurring of conventional distinctions between characters and narrators, and in their requirements for the reader's participation. And they satisfy in their unflinching examinations of both the difficulties and the possibilities of finding livable spaces, of coming to terms with the past, and therefore of achieving workable identities, especially for women, in African-American families and communities set within the racialized conditions of American society. Taking up the challenge posed by these complexities, Morrison's novels enter the interstices of the *différance*, not to resolve the unresolvable but to unravel some of the possibilities, to embrace, plumb, and cherish the rich responses to the collage of African-American experience.

Morrison's Novels as Texts, Not Works

"The trauma of racism is . . . the severe fragmentation of the self" (Morrison, "Unspeakable" 214). Toni Morrison's novels spin out the implications of this assessment by delineating the divisions, displacements, and pressures that skew the formation of African-American identities. This issue, fundamental to African-American fiction, pervades the content and the form of her novels, as the novels refigure American and African-American preoccupations with fusion and fragmentation and as they rework the tensions between bipolar oppositions. Morrison has the courage to open these issues and the skill to hold them open, not to fall back on the closure of fixed positions. As a result, her characters must grapple with the contingencies of a divided and divisive world, while at the same time, through Morrison's creation of an open-ended, multi-voiced discourse, readers, narrators, and author are able to transcend the divisions.

For all the participants in Morrison's fiction, these struggles and potential transcendence are couched in often paradoxical terms. Traditional values such as communal ties, family bonds, and even love become two-edged and ambiguous, and conventional distinctions, for example between characters and narrator or between narrator and readers, are called into question. Underlying Morrison's fiction is the paradox of dangerous freedom. Morrison's most intriguing characters—such as Cholly Breedlove, Sula and Eva Peace, Milkman and Pilate Dead, Son, Beloved, Sethe, Paul D, Denver, Wild, and Joe and Violet Trace—are in varying degrees unconventional, wild. They are relatively free from social norms, free to create themselves, to experiment with identity formation and with relationships with others. That freedom is liberating, certainly preferable to the smothering conformity of such characters as Pauline Breedlove, Helene Wright, and Ruth and Macon Dead, and it enables the "free" characters to avoid paralyzing stasis. Yet simultaneously and necessarily, this wildness is also dangerous, for it forces the characters to rely on themselves for their continuing spiritual growth and their precarious stability, and it throws them into uncharted territories of experimental identities.

At the same time, Morrison's fiction is dangerously free for author and readers. Because Morrison opens and keeps open so many significant issues, readers are given the freedom to enter into the texts, to participate in the constructions of their meanings. But such freedom is also fraught with dangers, dangers that the author will provide too little direction, too much direction, or enigmatically contradictory directions, and dangers that readers will resist or abandon the active role the texts demand. Morrison's fiction thus requires courage, skill, and creativity, not only of the author, obviously of the characters, but also, most importantly, of the reader.

In Morrison's novels, the pattern of fusion and fragmentation usually begins with the presentation of paired entities (such as two characters, contrasting families, and opposed settings). Each novel then differentiates between the entities and/or between the parts of one entity, thereby examining and reexamining the complex relationships between those entities and parts. Always already, the entities and the gaps between them, their differences and their similarities, their distinctness and their inseparability, exist simultaneously in a complex and never-ending flux.

Morrison's characters must struggle for meaning in their lives within the black/white polarity of American society, and their explorations are skewed because that unyielding polarity leads to additional polarities and further displacements, which are manifested in the characters' usually unfulfilled selves and problematic relationships. Morrison's plots place her characters in the gaps between historical, geographical, and cultural forces, where they must negotiate between past and present, North and South, black and white. This plight is symbolized by opposing settings—houses, towns, neighborhoods, states—and is reinforced by such motifs as cutting, splitting, hunting, and questing.

In its investigation of fragmented selves and the factors that contribute to the fracturing, each novel is a *bildungsroman,* but each delineates the attempted identity formation of many characters, not just one: "Toni Morrison's novels are *Bildungsromanen* of entire communities and racial idioms rather than the voice of a single individual" (Dixon, "Like" 137). In these multiple stories, the fragmentations and attempted formations of identities occur in the context of multiple layers: the internal self, relationships with a significant other, nuclear and extended families, neighborhood and community, African-American culture, and white-dominated American society. In each novel, each of these layers is fraught with divisions: psyches are split, relationships are tenuous, families are divided, neighborhoods are threatened, and race relations are tense.

While each character's development is charted on each of these layers, each novel also stresses a particular layer. *The Bluest Eye* concentrates on divisions within the self, especially in Claudia, Cholly, Pauline, and Pecola. *Sula* is dominated by attempted dyads—relationships between a character and a significant other—especially that of Sula and Nel, but also Sula and Ajax, Nel and Jude, and Sula and Shadrack.[1] In *Song of Solomon* Milkman must leave his parents' divided family before he can fulfill himself through immersion in his extended and ancestral family. In *Tar Baby* the domestic group at L'Arbe de la Croix is a divided microcosm of American society, and the difficulties of identity formation (for both blacks and whites) are explored in that broad context. *Beloved* focuses on recurrent attempts to establish or restore family groups, from the Sweet Home men to Baby Suggs-Sethe-Denver to Sethe-Denver-Paul D to Sethe-Denver-Beloved. In *Jazz* the dominant and missing relationships are those between children and parents: Violet's trauma stems from her mother's suicide, Joe desperately seeks Dorcas as a substitute for his un-known mother, and Dorcas and Golden Grey suffer from the lack of one or both parents.

In addition to exploring identity formation through these layers, each character's development is examined through time, specifically the past.[2] The past is necessary because characters can know them-selves only through knowledge of their pasts, but self-knowledge is elusive because characters are almost always divided from their pasts: Nel is cut off from Rochelle, Sethe from Ma'am and Halle, Joe Trace from Wild, and Golden Grey from Henry Lestory. An older or deeper past is often required, for instance the folk past of Solomon and Ryna in *Song of Solomon*, the mythical past of the Isle des Chevaliers in *Tar Baby*, or the historical past of slavery and the Middle Passage in *Be-loved*. Because the African-American (and therefore the American) cultural past has been only partially recognized and inadequately ab-sorbed, Morrison's characters have difficulty finding what they need from their pasts.

This temporal dimension always has a spatial counterpart in Mor-rison's fiction. The present is urban and North, whereas the past is rural and South. The action often takes place in Ohio, where Mor-rison was born and raised, but also, in Morrison's phrase, because of Ohio's "curious juxtaposition" between North and South (Tate 119) and its leading role in the underground railway.[3] As characters in the urban North struggle to create healthy identities, they must come to terms with their own or their ancestors' rural southern pasts by somehow fusing past and present. That past is unavoidable because it is heavily value-laden and emotionally burdened, both positively and negatively. The southern communities and farms in the charac-ters' pasts are idyllic (Willis 94) yet disastrous and shameful. The only place where Cholly Breedlove experiences love and a sense of belonging is his hometown in rural Georgia, but there he also learns alienation and self-hate. Milkman finds his history and his identity in Shalimar, but that is also where he suffers his most severe trials and where Pilate dies. Eloe is Son's only community, yet it is where his wife dies and his displacement begins. For Sethe and Paul D, Sweet Home is the ultimate bittersweet, a place they cannot forget but can barely endure to remember. Vesper County, despite the violence of the dispossession and other acts of blatant segregation, remains the place where Joe and Violet were happy, strong, and associated with "Victory."

This postmodern dialectic between present North and past South provides meaning and structure to Morrison's novels. Characters must negotiate between the poles, but the gaps are formidable. In some cases this negotiation involves physical journeys from South to North or vice versa, journeys that become defining moments (Nel), mythic quests (Milkman), or heroic accomplishments (Sethe and Denver). In all cases the negotiation is psychological, as the characters attempt to find, in the flux between the extremes, workable adjustments to the difficult conditions of their lives. In so doing, they must resist the temptation to latch onto a fixed position, for throughout Morrison's fiction identity formation is only successful when it is a continuing and open-ended process.

The negotiations occur primarily through memory, most prominently in *Beloved*, where the repressed memories of Sweet Home and the South must be remembered, yet must be remembered ever so carefully. Similarly, in *Jazz* both Joe's and Violet's memories of Vesper County must be encompassed and transcended for them to achieve stability. Not only do individual characters conduct such negotiations, but, through the entwined relationships of multiple characters' stories, each novel documents a collective negotiation between present and past. For example, whereas neither Pecola nor Claudia has a South to remember, *The Bluest Eye* as a whole recalls their cultural, southern past through the embedded stories of Cholly, Polly, Geraldine, and Soaphead Church.

The characters' fragmented psyches are figured by the motifs of splitting and cutting. Objects are often split, such as the watermelon, Polly's berry cobbler, and the Breedloves' sofa in *The Bluest Eye*. Body parts are frequently missing or torn off: Pauline's missing tooth, Shadrack's comrade's head, Eva's leg, Sula's fingertip, Pilate's navel, and Beloved's head. The image of the divided corpse of Guitar's father epitomizes the motif: "the two halves, not even fitted together, were placed cut side down, skin side up, in the coffin" (*Song* 226). Even when characters do not lose part of their bodies, the threat of being cut open is common, as when Milkman fights Saul in Solomon's General Store, when Guitar almost strangles Milkman, and when Violet stabs Dorcas's corpse. Besides being cut, bodies are repeatedly violated or invaded—for example, through whipping (Claudia and Sethe), rape (Pecola), or milking (Sethe).

With her exploration of splitness, Morrison renders the dividedness of the American and African-American cultures: objects are split, bodies are split, psyches are split, families are split, neighborhoods are split, a race is split, a nation is split. Given that American culture is externally divided from the "old" worlds of Europe and Africa and given that it is internally divided into multiple fragments, Morrison's novels analyze the consequences of African Americans' external separation from the dominant white culture, and they investigate the internal divisions within that separated community, its families, and its individuals. Morrison's novels examine the predicament in which a divided America places African Americans, thereby delineating the split from white culture, the splits within African-American culture, and the effects of those splits.

In one sense the forms of Morrison's novels seem to duplicate this sense of fragmentation. The traditional third-person narrative voice is often divided into multiple first-person narrators. In *The Bluest Eye* the narration is noticeably fractured among numerous voices. In *Tar Baby* the narrator's purview extends to the alleged sensibilities of the island's flora, fauna, and mythical figures. In *Beloved* characters overlap with the narrator as they tell and retell their past stories. In *Jazz* this division becomes more overt since Morrison's peculiar narrator often "speaks" in the first person and is situated both within and without the fictional world, and since characters, most noticeably Violet and Joe, are allowed extended, direct narrations in the first person.

Yet, even as Morrison's narrative form reenacts the theme of division, it intimates a constructive dimension to the pattern. A tenet of postmodern theory is that, since reality depends on the perceiver, multiple perspectives constitute a more valid form of representation than does a single perspective. As Barbara Hill Rigney (*Voices* 37) and Valerie Smith (*Self-Discovery* 124) claim, Morrison's polyvocalism implies that many voices are required to tell her tales because each tale transcends any one perspective. When the narration is split, the form of Morrison's novels recapitulates the divided nature of American and African-American cultures and the consequently divided natures of individuals, families, and communities within those cultures; in Smith's terms, the form thereby achieves "narrative resonance" with the cultural conditions being described (*Self-Discovery* 124n).

Morrison's comments about her novels emphasize this constructive dimension of their form. Repeatedly, she declares her interest in the ambiguity of presumed dualities,[4] and she insists that her novels remain open-ended, not as final authoritative statements but as maps (Morrison, "Memory" 389) or as texts with plenty of "holes and spaces so the reader can come into [them]" (Tate 25). Her texts thus resemble other African-American art forms, such as jazz and call and response, that require audience response and that privilege improvisation, fluidity, multiplicity, and openness. Instead of focusing on the whole or the center, Morrison tries to develop "parts out of pieces," "prefer[ring] them unconnected—to be related but not to touch, to circle, not line up" (Morrison, "Memory" 388). What is absent is at least as important as what is present. Her role is not to reveal some already established reality but to "fret the pieces and fragments of memory" and to investigate "the process by which we construct and deconstruct reality in order to be able to function in it" (E. Washington 58).[5] In short, Morrison requires that her novels be regarded as unfinished texts, not completed works (Barthes, "From" 74–79).

As Morrison's comments suggest, the forms of her novels are characterized by fusion and fragmentation.[6] The narration, although dominated by an external narrator, usually allows multiple perspectives to be heard directly. Reflecting the influence of the African-American oral tradition on Morrison, characters often become secondary narrators, "speaking" in the first person and thereby creating a Bakhtinian polyvocalism. Storytelling, the finding of one's voice and the articulation of one's inner self, becomes a constructive response and a significant theme.

Thus, on the one hand the novels present the devastating effects of many levels of divisions on the lives and psyches of their characters, but on the other hand that same splitness, as part of the novels' form, embodies a provocative shift to a plural perspective. Morrison posits a split fictional world that reflects the split world around it, and that

32

split into doubleness parallels the movement of the narratives from monologism to dialogism. Trapped by the unyielding conditions of a divided society, most of Morrison's characters cannot move beyond the fracture of the split, but Morrison, working through this split, creates novels that enact the multiple perspectives of a broader vision.

Just as Morrison divides the narration into multiple voices, so she treats time not chronologically, but as a divided, multilayered dimension. Flashbacks and "flashforwards" abound, and a multiplicity of times are narrated. Time is more like circular African time than linear European time, as each novel proceeds in both a chronological direction and a circular or spiral redoubling. Characters' mental time is both interfused with and separated from the external time of events: "inner time is always transforming outer time through memory" and "outer time transforms inner time" (Christian, "Layered" 496). Such interpenetrations of individual sensibility and external reality reflect the characters' attempts to achieve harmony between themselves and the community.

Especially in the last three novels, Morrison develops the technique of suspension, in which an image or a fact is narrated but not fully explained until the narration circles or spirals back to that same incident, explains it further but still not fully, then circles back again, and so forth. Through this technique, each novel self-consciously creates its own past, parts of the text that exist in the reader's memory, which then are remembered and reconsidered, much like the characters' attempts to reconstitute their lives. This technique is apparently necessary because the initial fact or event (such as Pecola's rape and insanity, Sethe's murder of Beloved, or Joe's murder of Dorcas) cannot be fully described at first, is beyond verbal explanation, and/or requires the entire novel to be fully understood. The *what* of the story is known from the beginning but not comprehended, and the rest of the novel is required for an understanding of the *how*, which is therefore made more significant. This structure is also related to the lush texture of Morrison's texts, which, like jazz compositions, are built upon richly evocative motifs that often carry the burden of the additive quality of her style and her stories.[7]

Morrison's fiction is also curiously both realistic *and* mythical. The novels depict the historical realities of African-American experience, from the Middle Passage, through slavery and Reconstruction, to life in the rural South, migration to the urban North, and the civil rights movement and beyond. By doing so, they recapitulate African-American history, as her characters come to symbolize all African Americans. Yet at the same time magic and myth exist alongside the realism: a navel-less Pilate guides Milkman Dead through his hero's quest and toward his final flight; a dreadlocked Son emerges from the sea and disappears into the sentient, myth-laden swamp; a murdered child returns in human form to haunt 124 Bluestone Road.[8]

Instead of creating impossible dissonances or contradictions, these modes of pluralism-in-unity combine to give Morrison's fiction its power. To experience that power, readers are encouraged to abandon the old either/or logic and simultaneously to encompass the both/and, the neither/nor, *and* the either/or. Readers must hold the binary oppositions in abeyance, embracing open-endedness and the coexistence of fusion and fragmentation. They must be patient, waiting for a detail or an image, such as the two tiny lines on Beloved's forehead, to be revisited and clarified. To absorb the complex factors behind characters' actions and conditions, readers must not jump too early to conclusions, must wait for more details to be revealed. Such "holes and spaces" both allow and force readers to participate fully in Morrison's fiction, as the usual distinctions between author, narrator, characters, and readers are called into question. In the final words of *Jazz* this strategy becomes explicit when the narrator confesses her secret love for the reader and urges the reader to "make me, remake me" (229), that is to say to (re)make the novel.

As the foregoing implies, Morrison's novels—including the characters' usually precarious situations, the complexities of the narrations, and the reader's invited role—are quintessentially postmodern, American, and African-American. They are postmodern, not in the sense of extreme self-referentiality or in the mockery of narration, but in their privileging of polyvocalism, stretched boundaries, open-endedness, and unraveled binary oppositions. In her novels, time is nonlinear, the forms are open, multiple voices are heard, and endings are ambiguous because Morrison insists on the necessity of continual and multiple reworkings—for characters, narrators, author, and readers. Forming an identity, authoring a text, telling a story, and reading or listening to a text must be ongoing, not fixed in time, place, or position. Since wholeness is illusory and division is endemic, one must explore the fragmentations through multiple visions.

By insisting on the devastating social and psychological consequences of division, Morrison inscribes the metaphysical split. Her novels thereby articulate both the African-American perspective that privileges double consciousness and the postmodern perspective in which traditional Western insistence on unity is a dangerous distortion that must be replaced by multiplicity, dialogue, and process. Working between, among, and within the terms of such traditional dichotomies as black/white race relations, presence/absence, self/other, and first-person/third-person narration, but not allowing for the closure of their duality, Morrison privileges process over product. By "giving away" the suspense, the "answer," at the start, she urges readers, along with the characters, beyond the simplicity of either/or and into the flux of uncertainty and ambiguity that, from postmodern and African-American perspectives, constitutes life. Her novels truly become texts, not works, operating, circling, and living in the endless play of the *différance*.

Morrison's postmodernism also suggests her political stance. In each novel, she exposes the debilitating effects of white oppression, yet she avoids sentimental praise for African Americans.[9] Instead, she locates her novels in the play between the two races: the novels are about the African-American experience *in* white-dominated America and about how that experience is defined by African Americans' historical and continuing relationships with whites. If whites have defined themselves against the African-American other, Morrison's characters have no alternative but to define themselves against the white presence. In either case, Morrison foregrounds the play between the two entities, not the traditionally privileged entity and not a reactive substitution of the traditionally deprived one.

In *The Bluest Eye* Morrison initially posits the split, the violence and trauma of divided lives, in the bleakest terms. The subsequent novels, assuming the existence of the split, are more varied in tone. As they explore conditions within a divided American society and divided African-American communities, they examine possible means of living within such conditions and varying attempts to ameliorate them—

35

Sula by examining the possibility that pairs of characters can help each other find stability, *Song of Solomon* through the quest to rediscover ancestral and cultural origins, *Tar Baby* by trying to reunite disparate elements of American society, *Beloved* by attempting to reestablish the family as meaningful unit, and *Jazz* by endeavoring to reconcile the absences between children and parents. In some novels, such as *Song of Solomon*, more apparent success is found than in others, such as *Sula*. In all cases, no *solution* is found, but life continues: Claudia must wrestle with her conscience; Nel awakens to grief and responsibility; Milkman may live or die physically but flies spiritually; Son runs headlong into the mythical past while Jadine chooses material success; Beloved is forgotten, Denver is released, and Sethe and Paul D, like Joe and Violet, are freed to pursue their quests for authentic selfhood. No lasting solutions can be found because the cultural conditions that the novels reflect and recreate can only be voiced, not resolved, because solution and resolution, like the unitary self, are illusory, because the African-American perspective is always at least double, and because the American cultural body is always already fragmented, the American consciousness is inevitably multiple, and the human condition is caught in the endless play of alternatives.

THREE

The Break Was a Bad One: The Split World of *The Bluest Eye*

Commentators on Toni Morrison's *The Bluest Eye* generally agree that the novel presents an inverted world: the supposedly idyllic images of Dick and Jane's perfect American family are distorting and distorted; the natural cycle of seasons, growth, and renewal does not function ("there were no marigolds in the fall of 1941" [9]); individuals in the African-American neighborhood of Lorain, Ohio, are isolated and dysfunctional; and the world is convulsed by war. The imposition of white ideals of beauty and romantic love and African-American acceptance of them lead to the inversion of the natural order and the distortion of love, freedom, and growth for African Americans (Christian, *Black Feminist* 52), and the Breedlove family, especially Pecola, is destroyed because the dominant society allows only one standard of beauty and virtue (V. Smith, *Self-Discovery* 123).[1]

By positing such an inverted world, Morrison begins her artistic exploration of fusion and fragmentation. Inversion itself embodies a doubleness, a division between right-side-up and up-side-down, between "up" and "down," between any two representations. In addition to implying that an entity—a neighborhood, a society, a culture—can be split into two versions, it implies a hierarchical contrast between "right" and "wrong." Even though exploration of a split and inverted world involves painful revelations, the exploration is necessary, for in a racialized society the split, the inversion, and the consequent double consciousness are always already present. Exposing the gaps between the dominant standards and the hegemony they impose on the disprivileged members of society is therefore a first step toward understanding the hierarchy and its implications. Such an examination suggests that recognizing the split has creative potential, that it dislodges individuals from worn-out, restrictive, and distorting absolutes, allowing for release into the play of the *différance*.

In this novel, the emphasis is on the fragmentation, as Morrison enters the metaphysical and cultural split. Having postulated it, in subsequent novels she can probe more fully various methods of coping with it. Splitting, the dominant image for the conditions of life in *The Bluest Eye*, renders the destructive distance between white standards and the realities of African-American life, and the theme of a split world echoes cultural divisions in the United States. Conversely, splitting also intimates the potential freedom of release from oppressive conventions, and, especially through Claudia's role, the novel's split, polyvocal form has provocative implications for confronting the inversions.

Everything in *The Bluest Eye* is split open: man-made objects, natural objects, nature itself, individuals, families, community, and society. Such splitting is usually damaging, as it threatens or destroys the entity being split. But some entities need to be split, such as the univocal white standard for family life implied by the Dick-and-Jane text, which, as Morrison says, "was *the* way life was presented to the black people" (LeClair 29, emphasis added). For Claudia, the act of splitting leads to knowledge, as when she splits open her (white) dolls to learn the mystery of their voices, a necessary stage in her discovery of her own voice. Splitting is also technically necessary for the creation of meaning in language, to which Morrison calls attention by running together the Dick-and-Jane segments.

Despite such potential for splitting, "splitness" (to use Rubenstein's term) "is a symptom of emotional or spiritual injury" (137), and this symptom figures the novel's radical disharmony. The most dramatic of these images is a synecdoche for the novel: "And now the strong, black devil was blotting out the sun and getting ready to split open the world. . . . The man swung the melon down to the edge of a rock. A soft cry of disappointment accompanied the sound of smashed rind. The break was a bad one. The melon was jagged, and hunks of rind and red meat scattered on the grass" (107). In this novel, watermelons, like families and individuals, tend to break badly, for it is not a world that a god creates but one that a devil breaks apart. Moreover, since the opened watermelon becomes "an emblem for female sexuality" (Rigney, *Voices* 83), it suggests the novel's focus on the inversion of female sexual initiation.

In this fugal novel, the splitting of the watermelon echoes the human splitting of other natural products.[2] Like forbidden fruit, the berry cobbler at the Fishers' house (86) and the peach cobbler that allegedly kills Cholly's Aunt Jimmy (110) seduce characters into tasting or touching them, with disastrous consequences. Polly's berry cobbler leads to an especially "bad break," for the break brings severe pain, both physical and emotional, to everyone present—Polly, the Fisher girl, Claudia, Frieda, and especially Pecola (Pullin 193). Like the peach cobbler that marks the death of Aunt Jimmy, the berry cobbler marks the emotional death of Pecola through her abandonment by her mother in favor of a blond, blue-eyed, white girl into whom Pecola immerses her identity. The scene also epitomizes Polly/Pauline's fractured life in its unwelcome (for her) intrusion of her black and disprivileged family into her white, privileged, adopted family. The irreparably fractured berries represent the irrevocable split between the Fisher girl's "Polly" and Pecola's "Mrs. Breedlove."

But split-open berries and fruit are not always so harmful. Pauline associates meeting Cholly with "berry picking *after* a funeral" (92, emphasis added), with the berries that "mashed up and stained my hips," and with "that purple deep inside me." Here, the splitting open of wild berries is associated with the pleasure of that first meeting and with subsequent sexual pleasure, as the mixed colors of the berries, the lemonade, and the june bugs constitute the "rainbow all inside" that accompanies Pauline's orgasms (104).[3] Pauline's positive association of crushed berries with sex is matched by the positive-turned-negative imagery of the muscadine grapes in the Cholly/Darlene scene (115–18). In that scene the grapes—their taste, their odor, even their stains on Cholly and Darlene's clothes—first impart a festive, mythical aura to the scene, replete with suggestions of rebirth, as Cholly recovers from his aunt's death in his first sexual encounter (Christian, *Black Women* 148). But with the white men's interruption, Cholly and Darlene's pleasure is inverted into bitterness, more deflating because of the mythic heightening, and is crushed like the grapes and washed away in the ensuing rain.

Claudia and Pecola also experience this motif of split-open food. For Claudia, opening a berry produces joy, including its sexual overtones, as when she introduces the Summer chapter with "I have only to break into the tightness of a strawberry, and I see summer" (146). Pecola's parallel experience is much more ambivalent: after being denied an identity by Mr. Yacobowski, she takes refuge in her candy, the Mary Janes that symbolize the false ideal of beauty that she craves. Even before eating them she anticipates the "resistant sweetness that breaks open at last" (41), and then, when she does break them open, she enjoys "her nine lovely orgasms" (43). She thereby shares the sensory pleasure her mother enjoyed, but her inverted pleasure is displaced by her rejection by the outside world and becomes part of her withdrawal into her private world.

Whereas the watermelon, cobblers, berries, and candy are opened up for some purpose, other objects are split apart for no apparent purpose and with more unambiguously damaging effects. Marie responds to Claudia and Frieda by throwing her root beer bottle at them, which "split at our feet, and shards of brown glass dappled our legs before we could jump back" (83). The split bottle not only ends the conversation but punctuates the jagged gap between the prostitutes and the girls. It also represents the prostitutes' condition, cut off from but simultaneously part of the community, and it suggests the violence—physical and emotional—behind that separation and the racial, economic, and social fragmentations that underlie the separation. Another symbolically split object is the Breedloves' new couch, which arrives already broken: "the fabric had split straight across the back by the time it was delivered" (32). This split, which becomes a "gash" and then a "gaping chasm," deepens into "a fretful malaise that asserts itself throughout the house and limits the delight of things not related to it" (32–33). The very fabric of the Breedloves' lives is split open, torn apart by the fundamental conditions of their existence.

That torn couch modulates to "a sore tooth" that "must diffuse its own pain to other parts of the body" (32), such as Pauline's lame foot and lost front tooth. Her foot was split open when a rusty nail "punched clear through" it (88), and the resulting limp is connected with her psychologically impoverished childhood: her lack of a nickname, her lack of friends, "her general feeling of separateness and unworthiness." Despite this psychic scar, which reemerges in her adult feelings of inferiority, her rural, southern adolescence is pleasant enough as she successfully manages her parents' household in Kentucky. Paradoxically, her injured foot becomes the vehicle for her attractiveness to Cholly, although the vehicle and its attraction are tragically repeated in Cholly's rape of Pecola.[4] The foot is therefore both a liability and an asset, marking her as separate, deficient, scarred, and split, yet simultaneously singling her out for Cholly's affection. That affection in turn has both positive and negative results, leading to Pauline's separation from the South and her parents' home and to her initially happy years with Cholly, but also precipitating the collapse of her life with Cholly and resurfacing in Cholly's rape of Pecola. The foot, like any differentiating mark, is loaded with unresolvable ambivalence: it is a necessary distinction, creating in part the individuality of Pauline that allows her to be a self, to be loved, and to love; yet it is a deficiency, a lack, a vulnerability, an Achilles' heel, and therefore a sign of her subjugation.

Although Pauline's first splitting open, the injury to her foot, has ambivalent consequences, her lost tooth is more clearly damaging. Just as the split-open couch represents the Breedloves' futile attempts to find a viable place in society, Pauline's loss of her tooth is "the end of her lovely beginning" (88). The tooth dies not only because of some literal "brown speck" (92) but because of "the conditions, the setting that would allow [the speck] to exist in the first place" (93). It implies the fragmented economic and social conditions of a racialized society in which the lowest class cannot obtain ade-

41

quate health care: there are no lost teeth in the Fishers' or Dick and Jane's families. Because it is a lost *tooth*, it also suggests the limitations of Pauline's ability to express herself. With her power of *nommo* impaired, she can only fight Cholly, ignore her children, and live a divided life, separated from both the black and white communities. Correspondingly, the narration of her "story" is fragmented between her own voice and the third-person narrator's voice, as if Pauline can tell her story only haltingly, lamely, incompletely (89–104). Split-open couch and split-open mouth are emblems for the conditions of life for the Breedloves: wholeness is impossible, whereas loss, violation, and separation are inevitable.[5]

Pauline's pierced foot and lost tooth echo other images of bodies split open. Some result from violence: Cholly and Pauline repeatedly wound each other, and Claudia associates the coming of spring with "a change in whipping style" (78). At other times, bodies burst open with natural functions: Claudia vomits in bed (13), Pecola menstruates (24), Pecola "sling[s] snot" (25), Aunt Jimmy's slop jar must be emptied (110), and Cholly defecates in his pants (124). Although such bodily functions are necessary and normal, the novel focuses on their negativity: they are painful, confusing, and/or fouling.[6]

This array of split-open objects and bodies coalesces in acts of sexual intercourse. Except for Pauline's rainbow orgasms, copulation is fraught with negatives. Pecola's rape by Cholly is the culmination of her previous fragmenting experiences: her false orgasms with the Lady Janes, her terrifying first menstruation, and her painful breaking open of the berry cobbler. Similarly, the rape completes Cholly's sequence of things split open: just as he consumed the heart of the badly broken watermelon, so he consumes the innocence of his broken daughter; just as he learned self-hate in his first sexual encounter, so he transfers that self-hate to Pecola in her sexual initiation. The destructive sexual lives of these two characters are surrounded by a sexually threatening atmosphere. The three prostitutes use sex as a means of power, and men, except for Mr. MacTeer, are sexual predators, as Mr. Henry's violation of Frieda and Soaphead Church's reputation for fondling little girls anticipate Cholly's rape of Pecola.[7]

These images of the splitting apart of food, objects, and bodies are metaphors for the novel's broken community, broken families, and broken individuals. The fragmentation ripples from layer to layer, while attempts at wholeness are repeatedly frustrated.

The black community of Lorain, Ohio, is characterized by violence. Mr. MacTeer must become "wolf killer" (52) to protect his brood from aggressors like Mr. Henry, and the three prostitutes verbally attack the community's members. The neighborhood attracts Geraldine and women like her, who egotistically feather their nests in adulation of false ideals and in so doing sow the seeds of more violent disintegration, as Junior's wantonness with the cat enacts and predicts. The community also harbors misanthropes like Soaphead Church, whose success in peddling "dread" (136) underscores the community's precarious existence.

This community is also fluid, "so fluid . . . that probably no one remembers" when the Breedloves lived in the old storefront (30–31). In this case the fluidity implies instability, reinforced by the gypsies and the idle, cigarette-smoking teenagers who recently inhabited the building. But the fluidity also connotes an openness and a possibility of change, of liberation from the confines of imposed standards and conventions. It suggests the play between rigid alternatives, a loosening of the rules of the culture, an outlet from the narrow strictures of white values of beauty and love. The opening of that gap is also suggested by the fact that Morrison, the narrator, Claudia, and the reader *do* remember the storefront and the neighborhood. Fluidity, like so much else in Morrison's fiction, is two-edged—the formlessness threatens disintegration but at the same time the openness allows for growth. Neither a fixed fusion nor a completely shattered fragmentation suffices.

Despite its fluidity, the neighborhood cannot absorb the Breedloves. They must be exorcised, first putting themselves "outdoors" (17), which is merely a step on their way to complete removal. As Claudia comes to realize, she and the rest of the community must take responsibility for their eviction. As an adult reflecting on the experience, she understands that she and everyone else used Pecola as their scapegoat: "All of us—all who knew her—felt so wholesome after we cleaned ourselves on her" (159). As the Bottom does with Sula and Shadrack, this community, precarious and threatened,

43

"hone[s] [its] egos" and "pad[s] [its] characters" on its ugliest, low-liest members, and in so doing further splinters itself.

In addition to the community's divisions, families tend to be split apart. The MacTeers are the only secure family, yet Claudia and Frieda are partially alienated, physically beaten and browbeaten, never allowed into the "gently wicked dance" (16) of adult conversation, never really understood, never allowed "to feel something on Christmas day" (21). Even this household is almost broken apart: driven by their precarious economic situation to accept a boarder, "the house was bursting with an uneasy quiet" (78) after Mr. Henry is thrown out. Other families are not so fortunate: Soaphead Church and Velma have long since split up, and Geraldine has no affection for her husband or son. The Breedloves are the extreme case. Their fights, in which Pauline threatens to "split [Cholly] open" (36), symbolize their breaking up of the family and each other. In addition, the different reactions and futures of Sammy and Pecola (who, unlike Frieda and Claudia, cannot help each other) dramatize the splintering of this family. For the Breedloves, fragmentation has no up side, no opening out into growth. For them, disharmony with white standards parallels disharmony with the black community and individual disharmony. The painful irony of their disintegration is apparent in Pauline's displaced devotion to her surrogate white family.

As opposed to these divided nuclear families, the only domestic groups that function well are comprised entirely of women. The three prostitutes have created a strong family unit, the first of Morrison's female triads, and their individual strength of character seems to result from their collective harmony. In contrast to that internal power, their relationship with the neighborhood is dominated by belligerence and mutual hostility—they are strong together but only in their position as tolerated pariahs. They have developed a viable identity and social position through their anger and pride (Samuels and Hudson-Weems 19) and through their lack of self-hatred or guilt (Byerman 60). As Chikwenye Ogunyemi puts it, they "symbolize the helplessness of human beings in life," as suggested by the helplessness of their namesakes in World War II: Poland, China, and the Maginot Line ("Order" 119). They, like Pecola, Cholly, and Pauline, are victims of externally imposed, restrictive standards. Rather than merely accepting victim status, they aggressively project "the vision of an alternative social world" (Willis 106), an alternative that is both inside and outside the black community as well as the dominant white society. Since they are simultaneously outlawed from the main community and endemic to it, they constitute a prime example of concomitant fusion *and* fragmentation. Their in/out position as needed scapegoats corresponds to Pecola's position, and later to Sula's, both of whom are useful outcasts for the communities to "clean [them]-selves on" (159). They are emblems for white society's construction of African Americans, an unalterably other community that is useful to the dominant society as a reminder of the latter's superior position.

In the novel's background are two other idealized groups of women: the women with whom Mrs. MacTeer gossips, and Aunt Jimmy, Miss Alice, and Mrs. Gaines. Mrs. MacTeer's friends provide a comfortable community within which she is "all ease and satisfaction" (14), feelings that she can enjoy nowhere else. In the women's dialogue about the forthcoming Mr. Henry, speakers are not identified, as individual differences merge in the collectivity (14–16). The conversation creates an artistic form, requiring the harmonious intermingling of individual and group: "Their conversation is like a gently wicked dance: sound meets sound, curtsies, shimmies, and retires" (16). Morrison explicitly lauds Aunt Jimmy's group and their peers, women who take everything that whites, black men, and their own children throw at them and, goddess-like, "re-created it in their own image" (109). As Wilfred Samuels and Clenora Hudson-Weems make clear, these three communities of women demonstrate the collective power of women, in contrast to the debilitating isolation of Pecola (19–22) and, I would add, of Pauline. That power derives from the women's preservation of their own traditions and values as opposed to Pecola and Pauline's adoption of imposed and therefore, for them, hollow ones (Christian, *Black Feminist* 49). That female collective power contrasts with the absence of any corresponding male communities and, except for Mr. MacTeer, with the destructiveness or absence of men, especially fathers; significantly, the devil-man who breaks open the world/watermelon is identified only as "the father of the family" (106). It is also significant that in the inverted climate of this novel, the examples of female collective power are relegated to

45

the margins of both the neighborhoods the women inhabit and the book itself.

Another family, less marginalized and less idealized than the female triads but also less prominent than the Breedloves, is the Mac-Teers. Through them, Morrison provides a realistic and practical (Wagner 193) alternative to the stereotypes of the Fishers and the Dick-and-Jane family, to the catastrophe of the Breedloves, and to the idealized groups of women. Not measuring themselves by white standards (Byerman 60–61), the MacTeers cope with harsh economic and social conditions and they receive Morrison's implicit praise, in contrast to the families of Soaphead Church, Geraldine, and the thousands of other women who migrated North.

As both a cause and an effect of the splitting of the community and of families, individuals in *The Bluest Eye* are more fragmented than whole. Without group harmony, characters cannot achieve internal harmony. Soaphead and Geraldine, like Pecola, deny their African heritage and create desiccated half-lives and half-selves characterized by hate for others and a mixture of self-hate and shame (Byerman 59, 62; Wallace, "Variations" 64). Even Claudia, who seems to have become a healthy adult, remains divided in her attitudes toward herself and her past (M. Walker 59). She has taken responsibility for her and everyone else's role in Pecola's tragedy, yet she wants to defer responsibility: she confesses that we "assassinated" Pecola, yet she also places the blame on "the land [that] kills of its own volition" (160). "Land" in this formulation suggests not so much nature as the African-American neighborhood in which Pecola could not flourish, as well as the larger society that creates and enforces the arbitrary standards that lead to such tragedies.

In their former rural, southern lives, both Cholly and Pauline were members of viable families and communities, and their youthful identities were comparatively healthy: despite his lack of parents, Cholly had the comfort of Aunt Jimmy and her friends as well as the surrogate fathering of Blue Jack; and despite her social isolation from peers, Pauline had a satisfying role in her parents' household. But in the infertile soil of the North, each is cut off from meaningful group well-being and so neither can create a stable adult identity.

Pauline finds herself alone ("That was the lonesomest time of my life" [93]), separated from others and herself, needing "things to fill the vacant places." Her artistic love of color and arrangement is side-tracked into a passive infatuation with the idealized white beauty and romance she finds in the movies. Her fragmented self is depicted through her difficulties in expressing herself: like Sula, she is an artist without a medium, "miss[ing]—without knowing what she missed—paints and crayons" (89). Her medium is displaced to the white household to which she devotes her energies and talents: "Here she could arrange things, clean things, line things up in neat rows. . . . Here she found beauty, order, cleanliness, and praise" (101). But in finding her medium in the imposed standards of the white culture, she loses her place in the black culture. Her attempted fusion with white values merely patches over her deep internal fragmentation and prevents her from further working on and through the identity-forming process. Therefore, her self is dangerously divided: "It was time to put all of the pieces together" (100). Temporarily she finds refuge in her children and in a dogmatic religious life, but this make-shift arrangement is based on "a hatred for things that mystified or obstructed her," and she "acquire[s] virtues that were easy to main-tain." As a result, she cannot put the pieces of herself together, and her life becomes increasingly split between her hateful, violent, and black home self and her loving, well-ordered, but white work self. Her process of fusion and fragmentation is arrested, since she can never be a true part of the white world and she has renounced affilia-tion with the black one. She is split away from the latter, unable to fuse with the former, and unwilling to look for opportunities in the spaces between them.

Cholly's process of disintegration is more extreme. Thrown on a dump by his departing mother, his physical existence is a miracle, the result of Aunt Jimmy's efforts to pull together the pieces of his defunct family and self. Then Cholly suffers the triple self-destruction of the death of his aunt, the death of his pride (in the scene with Darlene and the two white men), and his rejection by his father. In all three cases his ties with others are broken, which irrevocably splits his psyche: he loses self-control and thereby self when he defecates in his pants, he tries to retreat to the womb by "remain[ing] knotted there in fetal position" (124), and he experiences "a longing [for Aunt Jimmy] that almost split him open" (125).

What survives is broken and unknowable except through a nonverbal medium: "The pieces of Cholly's life could become coherent only in the head of a musician" (125). In jazz or the blues a complex unity of disparate parts is fused in performance, but Cholly can sense only the fragments. He is like the jazz musician that Ellison describes, "liv-[ing] by an extreme code of withdrawal . . . [and] rejection of the values of respectable society," but he lacks the "technical and artistic excellence" (*Going* 301–2) that enables the musician to thrive in such a milieu. Like Pauline, his process of fusion and fragmentation is halted, in his case in a state of nearly complete disharmony. Unlike Pauline, who responds by adopting the strictures of the church and then the self-imposed strictures of her religious devotion to her employers' households, Cholly responds by embracing the freedom of his nonentity, his non-status. He becomes, like Sula, "dangerously free" (125). He is so free because he has nothing, is nothing: "there was nothing more to lose. He was alone with his own perceptions and appetites, and they alone interested him" (126). He is dangerous because he is unrestrained by any social attachments. As Morrison suggests, he has unlimited potential, free to become what he wants to become: "a free man who could do a lot of things" and "a man who is stretching . . . going all the way within his own mind and within whatever his outline might be" (Stepto, " 'Intimate' " 221). But total freedom and unlimited potential cannot be tolerated by society, especially an inverted and subjugated society. Significantly, Cholly's first act after his descent into hell is to copulate, by which he "aimlessly" reclaims his manhood (125). Temporarily, he finds satisfaction with Pauline, but, having been so broken and then so anarchically freed, he cannot find or build a true self. He therefore drifts aimlessly through mid-life as a marginal worker, a sometime husband, and a non-father, spiraling downward into "despair," a "froze[n]" "imagination," "oblivion," and a self that is "totally disfunctional" (126). Given the single, white standard for beauty and value imposed on all Americans, potentially creative and liberated men like Cholly have no physical or psychic place, cannot keep open the process of becoming, and hence have no group or individual identity.

48

When Cholly stumbles upon Pecola's repetition of the image that endeared him to Pauline, his broken psyche is manifested in the flood of mixed emotions that propel him to the incestuous rape. He hates and loves her, he is revolted and attracted, he is moved by her presumed tenderness for him, but he despises her for loving what he cannot love. He wants union with her in the vain attempt to reconstruct his own identity. Yet his attempted union is expressed by more dissolution: he wants to erupt both by vomiting and by ejaculating, and by imparting to her not only his semen but also "his soul" (128). He wants "to save her from falling," from falling as he has already fallen. His fall is like the fallen watermelon, imposed upon him, unwilled, and resulting in a bad break. In contrast, Morrison's subsequent free characters—such as Sula, Pilate, and Milkman—do take responsibility for their falls, their freedoms, and therefore their self-reconstructions. Cholly's act, though, is a desperate, subconscious attempt to regain a lost connection, a lost moment of hope and tenderness, while at the same time it is the last act in the obliteration of an already fragmented self and an already disintegrated family. Ironically, the fusion of sexual intercourse merely marks the final stage of fragmentation.

But the rape is not quite the last act, for Cholly copulates again with Pecola, a repetition of the act of repeating the initial sexual encounter with Pauline and a repetition of his inverted sexual experience with Darlene. The first scene with Pecola is fraught with almost unbearable pain and pleasure for Cholly, and the repetition suggests that Cholly is struggling with a deeply unresolved self and that, blindly and with a frozen imagination, he nevertheless gropes toward some unformulated and unknowable "(comm)union" (Awkward, *Inspiriting* 14).

Pecola is the most completely split character, not only divided from the social and natural worlds, but ultimately divided between her two selves. She reaches this position through a series of steps that successively cut her off from normal interactions, as her communal isolation parallels her internal fragmentation. Her parents' lack of stable identities and their physical and psychological destruction of a home life drive her away from meaningful familial relationships. Those factors, plus her own tendency toward passive flight, lead her to withdraw, indeed to will herself out of existence: during her parents' fight she "cover[s] herself with the quilt" and whispers to herself, "Please make me disappear" (39). Her relations with her peers are no better: she is rejected as the lowest in the hierarchy, the blackest, the ugliest, and she is mercilessly taunted as the "black e mo" (55). Again, her response, in contrast to Frieda and Claudia's angry retaliation, is passive withdrawal. Pecola's isolation from the adult community is conveyed by her encounters with Geraldine, who exiles her ("Get out" [75]) and denies her a respectable place in the community ("You nasty little black bitch"), and with Mr. Yacobowski, who denies her existence by refusing to see her and by avoiding physical contact with her (Samuels and Hudson-Weems 16–17). As Samuels and Hudson-Weems assert, Mr. Yacobowski's reifying look transforms her from subject to object (17), a look that the Dick-and-Jane text ironically alludes to when the reader is urged to "See Jane" (7), that is, to see Pecola. This latter experience also divides Pecola from the natural world, changing her harmony with the dandelions ("And owning them made her part of the world, and the world a part of her" [41]) to alienation ("[The dandelions] *are* ugly. They *are* weeds" [43]). Her disharmony with herself, her family, and her community becomes a metaphysical disharmony with the cosmos. Both dandelions and Pecola are judged by an external, imposed standard of appearance and are found lacking, a situation made all the more ironic because Pecola herself adopts the judgmental role in dismissing the dandelions. For a moment she is angry at her metaphysical isolation, an anger that in Claudia seems healthy and which the narrator asserts "is better. There is a sense of being in anger" (43). But for Pecola "the anger will not hold," so she subsides into her onanistic world of fantasized white beauty and blue eyes. In her fantasy Pecola logically but pathetically extends Pauline's movie-inspired longings for white beauty and Cholly's alienation from his father, his family, and the community.

Other incidents only drive Pecola further into a divided and isolated self. Her menarche, hurtling her too rapidly from innocence into experience, separates her from Frieda and Claudia; her abandonment by her mother is completed in the scene at the Fishers' house; and the rape by Cholly, her pregnancy, and the loss of the baby not only violate and divide her physically but separate her irrevocably from the community and her shattered family. She is left with her imagination and its fixation on a cure for what she believes is the cause of her isolation: values of white beauty. This fixation is the same as Pauline's transferral of values to white movie stars and her white employers' households, the same as Geraldine's attempts to be as white as possible, the same as the efforts of Soaphead Church and his ancestors to eliminate their blackness, and the same as the community's color-based hierarchy of values that places Maureen at the top and the Breedloves at the bottom.

Pecola is thus driven to the double division of a split personality and a pariah. Since to a lesser degree most other characters suffer the same double division, the novel implies the inevitability of this pattern: intense external forces (especially racial, economic, and familial) severely strain the characters' personalities, and in turn those divisions within characters tend to divide them further from others. No individual can be internally harmonious without a harmonious relationship with the community.

Not only do the novel's images of splitting serve as metaphors for the novel's divided community, families, and individuals, but they also represent the divided natures of American culture and African-American culture. *The Bluest Eye* captures the fundamental rift in American culture along racial lines. It links the displacements and divisions of African-American lives to the imposition of white standards of beauty and romance and to the acceptance of those imposed standards by African Americans. It ties the traumas of twentieth-century African Americans to their historical roots in the South and thereby to slavery. In the South, Cholly and Pauline both have stable identities with connections to an African-American community, connections that they lose in the North (T. Harris, "Reconnecting" 75). In Lorain, Ohio, the surrounding white society subjugates the black community by imposing its standards of beauty; by enforcing the black characters' harsh economic conditions; by wielding overwhelming economic, social, and cultural power (for example, by the Fishers and Mr. Yacobowski); and by the implications of the system of power, values, imagery, and language behind the Dick-and-Jane primer.

Furthermore, both the time during which the novel is set and the time when it was written have special significance for racial divisions in America. As Melissa Walker argues, the novel is set "exactly during the time that psychologist Kenneth Clark's research into the damaging effects of the white aesthetic on black children was a public issue" (56), research based on black and white children's reactions to black and white dolls. By revealing black children's internalized sense of racial inferiority, the doll tests, like the novel, imply the depths to which division and dis-equality permeate American culture. As Walker also demonstrates, the late 1960s, when the novel was written, saw extreme tensions within an America violently divided over racial issues and the Vietnam War (55).[8]

As *The Bluest Eye* examines the predicament to which a divided America relegates African Americans, it also delineates the splits within African-American culture and the effects of those splits as that culture responds to the unyielding pressures of subjugation. It portrays a social hierarchy, primarily of females (from Maureen Peal down to Geraldine and on down to Pecola), based on their approximation of white standards of beauty, behavior, and wealth. In such a hierarchical division, someone is inevitably at the bottom, and the novel shows both the causes that bring the Breedloves to that level and the devastating effects of their placement. The Breedloves, in particular Pecola, represent the possible fates of all African Americans: they suffer the consequences of displacement and ostracism within the novel's community, just as African Americans as a whole have been made to suffer within American culture. Pecola's external/internal divisions recall Du Bois's analysis of his internalization of separation: "From the double life every American Negro must live, as a Negro and as an American, . . . must arise a painful self-consciousness, an almost morbid sense of personality and a moral hesitancy which is fatal to self-confidence" (164).

Through Soaphead Church, Morrison depicts another form of the devastation of racial division. Instead of using his education and talents to help his community, he is a predator—familyless, childless, empty, and bitter. He and his ancestors typify the assimilationist strand of African Americanism and its damaging effects, which results in his alienation from both the majority culture and African-American culture. Moreover, his letter to God links his failed assimilation to the religious and cultural traditions of Europe and white America. According to Michele Wallace, "Through Soaphead Church, Morrison designates one culprit as the European Judeo-Christian patriarchal tradition" ("Variations" 64). The novel thus is split between two failed deities, neither of whom can rectify the inversions: Soaphead's white Victorian God and the black devil-man who breaks open the world.[9]

In one sense the novel's form enacts these themes. Echoing the other splits, the narration is split among multiple voices (Butler-Evans 73): the Dick-and-Jane primer, the older Claudia looking back on the events (most noticeably on pages 9 and 158–60), the younger Claudia, the third-person narrator, Pauline's fragmented monologue on her past life, Soaphead Church's letter to God (139–43), and the direct transcription of Pecola's internal dialogue (150–58).

The novel's language is frequently divided between adults and children, for example when Claudia reflects that the children "do not, cannot, know" (16) the meanings of the adults' conversation. On other occasions, Claudia (and the reader) hear only fragments of adult talk: when Mrs. MacTeer gossips with her friends about Mr. Henry (14–16), when unnamed adults scold Claudia about destroying her dolls (21), and in the "fragments of talk" when adults refer to Cholly's rape of Pecola (147–48). The sounds of the language are split off from its meanings, just as the emotional lives of the children are split off from the adults'.

Furthermore, in the Dick-and-Jane passages, language itself is distorted. In the shift from "Here is the house. It is green and white" (7) to "Here is the house it is green and white" and finally to "Hereisthehouseitisgreenandwhite" (8), some linguistic signifiers—such as punctuation, capitalization, and spaces—are eliminated, while the letters themselves are not fragmented but fused. This suggests that, while splitting is one problem for individuals, families, and community in this novel, separations are nevertheless necessary and total fusion is not the answer. In the typographical fusions of the Dick-and-Jane text, the normally signifying letters, spaces, and punctuation are nearly denied their usual signified meanings, and the third version of the primer's text undercuts the alphabet's power to signify (Wallace, "Variations" 64). Linguistic meaning is strained to the breaking point, just as life's meaning is strained and distorted for many of the characters.[10]

This linguistic fragmentation, this loss of the signifying power of language, redounds especially on Pecola, who is painfully denied a voice. Each "character" in the Dick-and-Jane text has a corresponding section in the novel that inversely depicts a "character" in Pecola's life, but there is no section devoted to Jane/Pecola. This omission suggests that Pecola—unseen by Mr. Yacobowski and wishing to disappear under her blanket—not only loses her status as a subject but becomes neither subject nor object. With no viable relationship to the community or her family, she cannot exist, either in their eyes or in her own. Her only option is to substitute new eyes, to reject external reality, to adopt the imposed standards of white society.

Unlike Claudia, who tears her dolls apart to find their voices and consequently her own voice, Pecola lapses into the silence of internal monologue. The first glimpse of such a monologue, in which Pecola idealizes blue eyes, sadly echoes the primer's text, the symbol of Pecola's displaced cultural values: "Pretty eyes. Pretty blue eyes. Big blue pretty eyes. Run, Jip, run. Jip runs, Alice runs. Alice has blue eyes" (40). Pecola can only think in the language of the imposed white system. Then, in Pecola's internal dialogue with her imaginary friend (150–58), not only is she split into two consciousnesses, but the relationship between the two is marked by threats (Wagner 196), contention, recriminations, and jealousy. The language of the dialogue is consistently ironic, suggesting both the separate planes of consciousness into which Pecola's mind has been split and the fracturing of the signifying power of language. For example, the "friend" asserts that "Pecola" is "*crazy*" (151), which "Pecola" denies and the "friend" retracts but which, from a perspective outside of Pecola's, is undeniably true. The monologue ends with the "friend's" departure, suggesting the incompatibility of Pecola's divided inner selves. For Pecola, relegated to internal speech but denied the power of the spoken word, splitness becomes absolute and inescapable.

Even though the novel's form thus reinforces the themes of division and distortion, it also suggests a constructive perspective that transcends the characters. The multiplicity of voices and the fragmented language create an overtly polyvocal text. Like the novel's chord-like image patterns, the multiple narrations alternate with each other much like jazz musicians. As Bakhtin, Barthes, and others have argued, every text is inherently polyvocal, and thus to insist openly on the plurality suggests that Morrison deliberately seeks greater validity than one narrative voice can attain. Linda Dittmar maintains that the novel's multiplicity of voices "posits that meanings get constructed dialogically" (141) and that the "dismantling" inherent in the novel's design "foregrounds reconstitution," at least for the reader (143). Even though the voices are divided, they comprise a whole, overseen by an implied consciousness that has survived the fragmentations. This broader perspective also encompasses past and present—for example, the pasts of Cholly, Pauline, and Soaphead, as well as the future of the grown-up Claudia. As Valerie Smith contends, the novel's form implies the interconnectedness of past and present (*Self-Discovery* 126), and the narrative process leads to self-knowledge because it forces acceptance and understanding of the past (122).

From this perspective, the book both mourns the human loss, pain, and divisions suffered by the victims of a divided society and probes the necessity—and the possibilities—of dividedness. Being divided, despite its concomitant suffering, is not merely negative. Just as language requires gaps for coherence, distinctions are necessary in all phases of human life. This novel therefore posits the divisions and examines them for their damaging effects, but also scrutinizes them as a first step toward recognition of the necessity for a pluralistic perspective and a more profound sense of the play between fusion and fragmentation.

Morrison's examination of splitness is illuminated by Derrida's metaphor of the breach. The breach is the gap between oppositions, both a location of violence and displacement and the hinge or articulation that allows one to know and therefore to escape the death-like fixity of a unitary position. Derrida borrows the notion of the breach from Freud, who uses the term *bahnung* to describe how neurons in the brain store memories by simultaneously reacting to an impulse and remaining constant. For Derrida this action, literally a "pathbreaking," becomes a "metaphorical model": "Breaching, the tracing of a trail, opens up a conducting path. Which presupposes a certain violence and a certain resistance to effraction. The path is broken, cracked, *fracta*, breached" (*Writing* 200). Despite its power, for Derrida this action of breaching is not a sufficient explanation, either for the actions of neurons or for his model, for it is the differences between breaches that allow both to function: "there is no pure breaching without difference" (*Writing* 201).[11] Although *The Bluest Eye* assumes the violent breach of a split world and documents the tragic effects of that fragmentation, it also explores the breach, attempting to understand it, to find the conducting paths, to differentiate among the causes and effects of the divisions, the violence, and the articulations. It embraces the postmodern acceptance of an always already disunified condition and attempts to voice that condition and its attendant problems and possibilities.

In positing and probing the breach, the structure of division, as the given of the inverted experience of African Americans, Morrison stakes out the initial problem for her fiction: the multiply divided nature of contemporary African-American lives. Although Morrison's next move does not come until *Sula*, it is anticipated in Claudia.

Critical interpretations of Claudia have been curiously divided. One position sees her as failing to come to grips with what she has learned and with the person she has become. Michael Awkward labels her a "questing marginal" ("Roadblocks" 61), who achieves partial but ultimately unsuccessful understanding of the effects of white dominance. Similarly, Keith Byerman cites her failure to live in her demystified knowledge (62), and Rigney feels that she doubts her own authenticity (*Voices* 22). For Otten she is somewhat like Nel, too accommodating and arriving too late at the truth (*Crime* 25), a position similar to Melvin Dixon's claim that her confession of her complicity in Pecola's tragedy comes too late (*Ride* 117). In contrast, more laudatory readings of Claudia focus on her roles as storyteller (Christian, *Black Feminist* 49) and as deconstructer of white standards. Rubenstein sees Claudia's examination of her white dolls as the dismemberment of inauthentic and degrading external standards (129), and Samuels and Hudson-Weems view that examination as her effort to overcome external definitions of herself (22). Both Rubenstein and Samuels and Hudson-Weems suggest that this active role leads to Claudia's development of inner strength and continuing growth. Melissa Walker, noting that Claudia, like Morrison, is brought up in Lorain, Ohio, by loving, economically struggling parents (48), elevates her to the status of "the moral register of the novel" (55) who takes responsibility for her role in Pecola's downfall (53).[12]

Claudia's rebellious role in the deconstruction of imposed white standards of beauty and self is fundamental to Morrison's exploration of fragmentation. Unlike other characters' acts of splitting, Claudia splits things to demystify them, to assuage her curiosity about life's mysteries and inequities. She idly "split[s] the stems of milkweed" (78) while reflecting on "ants and peach pits and death and where the world went when [she] closed her eyes." Her childhood is characterized by her propensity to tear apart her dolls (always white, blond, and blue-eyed) and by the intensity of her desire to know what is inside them, to know the secret of their alleged beauty and power, and specifically to learn the mystery of their voices. Unlike each of the Breedloves, she initiates the splitting open, becoming in a constructive sense the victimizer, not the victim. Willed examination of the divisions—black/white, child/adult, self/other—is healthy, whereas unwilled reaction to such splits is not. She splits things open to gain strength, rather than being split open in weakness. Therefore, she keeps open the process of fusion and fragmentation, of identity formation, of the quest for knowledge about oneself and one's situation, rather than becoming locked in a fixed and unitary position. She finds the breach in which she can continue to explore the binary oppositions and to validate the play between them and between their wholeness and their parts.

In doing so, she finds the mystery behind the doll's voices and, more importantly, gains her own voice—actually two voices—as child and as retrospective adult. That doubleness is further split since as adult narrator she has a double perspective: she accepts responsibility for her role in Pecola's tragedy, but she blames "the earth, the land . . . the entire country" (160). Although Melissa Walker worries that she "seems torn between two positions" (59) of self-blame and condemnation, her internal division marks her embodiment of the novel's split world: she is both innocent and guilty, both young and old, both character and narrator, in both past and present. Pinning down an interpretation of her is therefore impossible; she is an example of

Miller's "double blind" (22), for which no single explanation can suffice. This ambiguity is part of Morrison's point: in a divided world, the best recourse is to embrace the divisions, to accept unresolvability, to remain dialogic. If Claudia clearly succeeded or failed, she would seem to have a unitary self and a one-dimensional position, and, given the authority Morrison allots her, both character and author would slip into monologism.

Claudia is not conscious of this liberating but dangerous move, but Morrison places her close to the author's own childhood and allows her to become, like Morrison and the third-person narrator, a spokesperson.[13] As spokespersons, Claudia, the narrator, and Morrison reach parallel conclusions: Claudia realizes that she and everyone else defined themselves by scapegoating Pecola, the other; the narrator documents the depersonalizing effects of the imposition of white standards, for example through Cholly and Pauline's stories, Soaphead Church's misdirected life, and the Dick-and-Jane text; and Morrison oversees all the voices as they delineate how African Americans have been forced to define themselves against white American culture.[14]

As a narrator, Claudia enacts the novel's polyvocalism by being double-voiced: as the innocent, younger child, she tells her part of the story with naiveté and directness; but as the retrospective adult reflecting on the traumatic events of 1941–1942, she narrates with self-consciousness, knowledge, and eloquence. For example, here is Claudia's childish voice: "Our house is old, cold, and green. At night a kerosene lamp lights one large room. The others are braced in darkness, peopled by roaches and mice" (12). In contrast, here is the adult Claudia's language: "And fantasy it was, for we were not strong, only aggressive; we were not free, merely licensed; we were not compassionate, we were polite; not good, but well behaved" (159). These two contrasting voices are left unresolved, like Claudia's youthful rebelliousness and her later conformity, for resolution, in a divided culture, in the postmodern sensibility, is a false hope, a "fraudulent love" (22). Much like Claudia and Frieda, who "piece a story together" by "properly plac[ing]" "the fragments" of talk about Pecola and Cholly (147), all Claudia—and Morrison—can do is present the problem, characterize the divisions, and juxtapose the fragments. Enduring the fragmentations that characterize her culture and herself, Claudia, like Morrison, embraces the breach, narratively reassembles the scattered pieces, and tries to live with her double-consciousness.

In doing so, Claudia anticipates Morrison's development. Just as Claudia must live as best she can within her tragically divided world, Morrison in her subsequent novels explores the conditions within the breach, within a racialized America. Like Claudia's double perspective of child and adult, in the ensuing novels Morrison relies on narrative reassemblies of multiple voices and perspectives. Unlike Claudia, who is still caught in the fragmentation, barely able to realize its potential, Morrison increasingly broadens her perspective above and through the split. In *Sula* she begins to focus more closely on ways of coping with the problematics of creating and maintaining a viable identity in a divided society.

Shocked into Separateness: Unresolved Oppositions in *Sula*

Like *The Bluest Eye*, *Sula* is based on the underlying condition that fragmentation and displacement are the fundamental barriers to the formation of African-American identities. Whereas the first novel probes the pernicious effects of the imposition of external standards on the black community, in *Sula* Morrison more explicitly constructs a system of binary oppositions and simultaneously unravels it. Here, Morrison becomes overtly deconstructive, writing "what the French call *différance*, that feminine style that opens the closure of binary oppositions and thus subverts many of the basic assumptions of Western humanistic thought" (Rigney, *Voices* 3). By moving into the split, Morrison scrutinizes the ambivalent counterforces of fusion and fragmentation.

In this novel, the most important of the oppositions is between self and other. Displaced as they are by the racial dichotomy, characters in *Sula* are drawn into the traditional Western misconception that assumes the existence of a unitary self and that privileges self over other. They assume that they must have an originary self and/or that they can acquire it with or through an other. Morrison thereby directs attention to one potential response to the characters' fragmentation: fusion with another person in the attempt to solidify one's identity. Whereas the characters in *The Bluest Eye* tend to fold inward in their attempts to define themselves, the characters in *Sula* look outward to relationships with significant others. Such pairs involve parent and child, heterosexual couples, and peers—most fully the relationship between Sula and Nel.

In *Sula* Morrison depicts a rigidly bipolar world, one in which the falsifications and privileging are so extreme that the tensions between opposed terms are overwhelming, as attested by the novel's numerous deaths. As the novel documents this bipolarity and the concomitant tensions, however, it undercuts that system and privileges a fluid, open, and liberating perspective. Sula, forced to become exile and then pariah, personifies this new freedom that dares to reject the old dichotomies and to create a new kind of identity. Both the character and the novel become representative of divisions within the American and African-American cultures.

As in *The Bluest Eye* the world in *Sula* is inverted and the mode is ironic, but in *Sula*, as Deborah McDowell asserts, Morrison strikes a more elegiac chord (" 'self' " 85n). The dedication to Morrison's two sons looks ahead to their mother's sense of loss after their departure: "This book is for Ford and Slade, whom I miss although they have not left me." The epigraph from Tennessee Williams's *The Rose Tattoo* also evokes the pathos of loss, the loss of "glory," both for oneself and in the eyes of others: "Nobody knew my rose of the world but me. . . . I had too much glory. They don't want glory like that in nobody's heart." In the novel's first sentence, the narrator grieves for the loss of the Bottom: "there was once a neighborhood" (3). Every chapter includes the physical or spiritual death of at least one African American (Reddy 29), and the plot culminates with Sula's death and the tunnel disaster. As the novel spans the destructive years from World War I through the Depression to the threshold of World War II in 1941 (the year in which *The Bluest Eye* is set) to 1965 and the civil rights movement, it becomes an elegy for the victims of war, poverty, and racial violence.[1] Morrison refers to "the nostalgia, the history,

61

and the nostalgia for the history" in this novel ("Unspeakable" 222), and Melissa Walker describes it in terms of "late sixties nostalgia for a lost but not so distant world" (120). After Sula's death, the mourning becomes more poignant, first when Shadrack grieves for his lost friend: "She lay on a table there. It was surely the same one. The same little-girl face, same tadpole over the eye. So he had been wrong. Terribly wrong. No 'always' at all. Another dying away of someone whose face he knew" (157–58). Then the mourning escalates further when Nel cries for her lost friendship with Sula: "We was girls together. . . . O Lord, Sula . . . girl, girl, girlgirlgirl" (174). Like many contemporary African-American novels, *Sula* eulogizes a lost community and a lost past.

The displacements begin with the novel's setting, which begins with the first sentence: "In that place, where they tore the nightshade and blackberry patches from their roots to make room for the Medallion City Golf Course, there was once a neighborhood." As Morrison explains, this lost world is fragmented into oppositions: place/neighborhood, they/neighbors (and implicitly whites/blacks), nightshade/blackberry, roots/Medallion, houses/golf course, and past/present ("Unspeakable" 221). The larger community is divided between town and Bottom, and the division is ironic, based on the fraud of the "nigger joke" (4) that initiated the racial division of the land, which exemplifies Ellison's "joke at the center of the American identity" (*Shadow* 54).[2]

In *Sula* many issues are depicted in terms of opposing values or terms. The present is directly contrasted with the past, and female and male roles are opposed. The Wrights, the Greenes, and the Bottom itself are studies in social conformity, which is set against the individual freedom of the Peaces. The story of Nel and Sula becomes an investigation of the meanings of good and evil,[3] the values associated with monogamy and promiscuity, and the relevance of innocence and experience. By what it leaves out as well as by what it includes, the novel contrasts presence and absence. And, especially through Sula's meditations on her identity, the novel explores the relationship between self and other.[4]

The novel is thus posited on a binary structure. Its setting is divided between the Bottom and Medallion, a black community and an anonymous white town, a neighborhood and a golf course. Its plot chronicles the lives of two opposed characters who grow up in two opposed houses managed under two opposed theories of child-rearing. The character pairings of Nel and Sula are doubled in the pairings of their contrasting mothers (Helene and Hannah) and grandmothers (Rochelle and Eva). As opposed to the differences in these female pairs, the men in Nel and Sula's lives are similar but also paired: each woman lacks a brother or male friend, each has an absent father, and each has her most significant heterosexual relationship with a self-doubting man who departs abruptly (Jude and Ajax). The plot opposes the highly individualized black characters and the nameless, featureless white characters who hover on the fringes. It opposes the sane residents of the Bottom and the insane Shadrack, whose well-ordered cabin represents a further dichotomy with his disorderly behavior. It sets children in opposition to adults, most notably in mothers' lack of love or liking for their children. It contrasts meaningful employment, such as construction work, and demeaning labor in hotels and white homes.

To reinforce this pattern of binary opposites, *Sula* is divided almost exactly into halves, a dyadic structure that is reinforced by the nearly palindromic pattern in which the introduction of characters in Part I is reversed in the dispensation of characters in Part II (Grant 95). In addition, the novel is split between a linear structure, implied by the inexorable march of years in the chapter titles, and a circular one, suggested by the narrator's frame that starts the discourse after the Bottom has already disappeared.

The narrative form of this novel, in contrast to *The Bluest Eye*, also reveals a binary pattern. Whereas in Morrison's first novel the conventional distinction between external narrator and character breaks down in the polyvocal narration, in *Sula*, except for two paragraphs in which Nel narrates directly (105, 111), the distinction between external narrator and characters is maintained. Moreover, the narrator/character distinction is underscored by the opening section, which highlights the narrator's historical knowledge and vast distance from the characters' perspectives.

Correspondingly, the conventional distinction between an external narrator and the reader is forcefully maintained in *Sula*. This narrator, unlike Morrison's chatty narrator in *Jazz*, establishes her credentials and her distance from the reader in the opening chapter and maintains that separation throughout.[5] The narrator rarely permits dialogue between characters, thus retaining tight control over the telling of the story.[6] The narrator manipulates readers, forcing the story onto them, shocking them with sudden violence, making them question their responses to such characters as Eva and Sula, delaying crucial information (such as Jude's adultery with Sula), leaving frustrating gaps between years, omitting important scenes (such as Plum's and Hannah's funerals), not reporting what happens to Eva or Sula when they leave the Bottom, and not relating what happens to Jude or Ajax after they depart. The narrator also shocks readers with mysterious beginnings of chapters (such as "It was too cool for ice cream" [49] or "Old people were dancing with little children" [79]) and teases them by reversing the normal order of things (as when she reports the *second* strange thing before the first (67). Not only highly controlling, the narrator is also noticeably omniscient, with access not only to many characters' thoughts but also to the collective feelings of the community, for example when she describes the narrow lives of the Bottom's women (122) or the hope that seduces everyone into the last National Suicide Day parade (160).

At the same time that *Sula* is constructed on a system of binary opposites, the novel subverts that structure. Perhaps the clearest example of this deconstructing is the play between linear chronology and circularity. As many commentators have noticed, the novel purports to move steadfastly forward through time, as its chapter titles suggest, but even as it does so, it moves backward and forward, circling or spiraling through time.[7] As Denise Heinze (122–23) and Maxine Lavon Montgomery (128) suggest, the novel's double perspective of linearity and circularity reflects a fusion of Euro-American and traditional African conceptions of time.

This subversion of Western linearity represents Morrison's attack on traditional, white-imposed conceptions. Although McDowell states that "the narrative retreats from linearity" (" 'self' " 86), the strategy is not a retreat but the assertion of an alternative. While *The Bluest Eye* primarily laments the imposition of white, dualistic standards, *Sula* confronts such standards, loosens them, and advocates a nonlinear response. That perspective is suggested by Christian, who argues that the novel is about "the search for self . . . continually thwarted by the society from which Sula Peace comes" (*Black Women* 153), and by Kathryn Bond Stockton, who states that *Sula* confronts "the reign of white gender" that "seduces blacks away from the Bottom's communal bonds into the tight configuration of the couple" (94).

The novel's alternative position leads to its often perplexing openness. Robert Grant documents the novel's emphasis on the lack of a coherent subject and consequently on missing objects (Eva's leg and comb), absent or missed characters (Chicken Little, Ajax, Sula), and objects that evoke missing persons (Sula's belt, Jude's tie) (95–96). These gaps and discontinuities create holes in the text that unhinge any straightforward narration, thereby calling into question traditional means of representation and allowing for greater reader participation. For Grant the novel thereby becomes "a prime 'postmodernist' text whose interpretational difficulties are a function of Morrison's calculated indeterminacies" (94). Similarly, the novel raises but leaves "largely unresolved" the issue of good and evil (Butler-Evans 88), an issue that Morrison has said she deliberately dealt with in a non-Western, that is to say, nonoppositional, manner.[8] Placing this alternative stance in the context of feminine writing, Barbara Rigney claims that the emphasis on absence, ambiguity, multiple perspectives, and fragmentation creates a novel that, "like all of Morrison's works, subverts concepts of textual unity and defies totalized interpretation" (*Voices* 32).

The deconstructive implications of this open perspective are implied by Hortense Spillers, who contends throughout her essay for the creative openness of *Sula*, and are spelled out in detail by McDowell, who quotes Spillers ("No Manichean analysis demanding a polarity of interest—black/white, male/female, good/bad—will do" [" 'self' " 80]). For McDowell, "*Sula* is rife with liberating possibilities in that it transgresses all deterministic structures of opposition." "The narrative insistently blurs and confuses . . . binary oppositions" and "glories in paradox and ambiguity" as it creates "a world that demands a shift from an either/or orientation to one that is both/and, full of shifts and contradictions" (" 'self' " 79–80).

Like a jazz composition, *Sula* sounds a traditional Euro-American motif, a structure of binary oppositions. Simultaneously, it plays on that motif, modifying it, refiguring it, subverting it, fusing it with non-Western values. The result is a complex doubling, or multiplying, of perspectives, content, and form that embodies and challenges both Euro-American and African-American standpoints and that enables Morrison to fret out the fragments in a simultaneously fused and unfused whole.

Whereas *The Bluest Eye* examines isolated individuals who are split from meaningful relationships with community, family, or friend, in *Sula* characters respond to their bipolar world by attempting to create personal meaning through intimacy with another person. Such attempted dyads allow the characters temporary relief from their isolation and thus help them endure the frustrations of their marginalized and divided lives, but they provide no lasting solution.

As this novel focuses on potential paired characters, it noticeably lacks emphasis on larger groups. There is no triad of intimate women, like the three prostitutes in *The Bluest Eye*, Pilate-Reba-Hagar in *Song of Solomon*, or Sethe-Beloved-Denver in *Beloved*. The corresponding group is Eva-Hannah-Sula, but these three women constitute a much less cohesive unit than the other triads, as evidenced by the negation in their relationships (Eva had no time to love Hannah, Hannah does not like Sula, and Sula exiles Eva to the county home). Though tied by blood in a direct matrilineal line, they are a dis-unit, a deconstructed unit. The tensions between their unity and their separateness figure the pervading tensions in *Sula* between *any* structure and its decomposition. The only united triad is the deweys, but their unity is achieved at the expense of each boy's individuality, as suggested by their namelessless. Their stunted physical and mental growth attests to the parodic and inverted nature of their relationship and thus symbolizes the lack of viability of such groups in this novel.

Pairs of characters in *Sula* frequently attempt unions—most noticeably between parent and child, in heterosexual couples, and between peers—but such unions are often short-lived and always problematic. As a result, like the frozen blades of grass during the ice storm, the characters remain "shocked into separateness" (152). At the end of the novel, Nel senses the isolation: "Now there weren't any places left, just separate houses with separate televisions and separate telephones and less and less dropping by" (166).

One type of attempted pair is mother and child (men are so consistently absent that no father/child relationships exist).[9] Daughters, such as Hannah and Sula, desire closer relationships than their mothers can provide: Eva has no time or energy to love Hannah, and Hannah in turn, like her friends, expresses her dislike for her daughter. Mother-daughter relations are even more insecure in Nel's family, where Helene and her mother Rochelle are permanently estranged, where Helene's version of motherhood is to mold Nel (literally by trying to reshape her nose and figuratively by eliminating her individuality) into her own concept of white respectability, and where Nel looks upon her own children as a burden. Throughout the Bottom, except for the artificial period when people use their fear of Sula's alleged evil to rally behind each other, mothers (such as Teapot's Mamma) treat their children as difficult objects rather than as loved human beings. Nevertheless, although mother-daughter relationships appear to lack closeness and love, they do so only in comparison to a traditionally white ideal. As in *The Bluest Eye*, where imposed white standards of beauty and value are set against contrasting black standards, here white stereotypes of parent-child harmonies are implicitly contrasted with more fluid communal values. Mothers may not love or like their daughters in the ideal of the Dick-and-Jane myth, but through belief in communal values, even though such values are not ideal, mothers endure, holding their households and the community together.

Mother-son relationships are just as problematic. Like Sethe's murder of Beloved, Eva must murder Plum out of love, when the alternative for him is worse than death, in his case because he has lost his selfhood. Three Bottom sons—the deweys—are divorced from their mothers, adopted by Eva, and in the process lose their individuality and chance for maturity. Although they are fused with each other, like Plum they are isolated from themselves and society. Another Bottom son, Jude, tries to establish a motherly relationship with his wife Nel, and another son, Ajax, does love his mother, but their overpowering relationship (he "worship[s]" her [126]) seems to prevent him from forming a lasting commitment to anything except airplanes:

"This woman Ajax loved, and after her—airplanes. There was nothing in between." As Baker writes, Ajax "is properly understood . . . not as 'his own man,' but as the offspring of his mother's magic" (*Workings* 153).

Characters also attempt significant relationships as heterosexual couples. Except for the marriage between Helene and Wiley (which presumably lasts because Wiley is so seldom at home), all such pairs (Eva-BoyBoy, Nel-Jude, and Sula-Ajax) are temporary.[10] More successful are Hannah's brief, unthreatening, and mutually satisfying affairs with the Bottom's husbands. More viable is Eva's household and her role as mentor for young married couples. More enduring is the community itself, which provides an alternative form of integration to the couple.

The attempted fusion with another person is most fully exemplified in Sula and Nel's relationship. Critics agree that the two are nearly fused,[11] the critical agreement deriving from the textual evidence of Sula and Nel's near merger into one consciousness. In her pubescent dreams each one fantasizes the presence of the other, a sympathetic female presence with whom the romantic adventure can be shared (51). When they actually meet, their psyches are already half-united: they are instantly like "old friends" (52), they share "their own perceptions of things" (55), and they are "joined in mutual admiration." Later, they have "difficulty distinguishing one's thoughts from the other's" (83), they share one eye (147), and Eva alleges that "never was no difference between [them]" (169).

Despite this near fusion, Sula and Nel are almost opposites, as suggested by their mutual fascination with the other's house and family. As Baker notes, their fantasies betray their opposing destinies (*Workings* 146–47): Nel passively "wait[s] for some fiery prince" who "approached but never quite arrived" (51), whereas Sula "gallop[s] through her own mind on a gray-and-white horse tasting sugar and smelling roses" (52). Fulfilling those early fantasies, Nel never leaves the Bottom, but Sula travels widely, and Nel becomes the model of community respectability as opposed to Sula's unconventional behavior. For Nel "Hell is change" (108), but for Sula "doing anything forever and ever was hell." They are like the poles of two magnets, both irreconcilably repelling and absolutely attracting. After years of separation each regains a glimpse of their lost unity: in Sula's moment of afterlife consciousness she thinks of sharing her experience of death with Nel (149), and the final words of the novel depict Nel's epiphany of lost union with Sula (174).

This rich and ambivalent relationship between Sula and Nel suggests that Morrison is experimenting with alternative conceptions of selfhood and friendship. Their closeness calls into question the traditional notion of the unitary self, and their enduring yet strained relationship also questions the stereotype of undying friendship. According to Rigney, they "represent aspects of a common self, a construction of an identity *in relationship*" (*Voices* 50). Such a construction further probes the issues of unity and separateness, of self and pair.

Although Morrison in her authorial detachment can experiment with their relationship and their identities, both Sula and Nel have trouble resisting the conventional illusion that a relationship with a significant other must be total and all-consuming. Each tries unsuccessfully to find that degree of absorption with her mother and her grandmother. Then, after their momentary union as adolescents, their inevitable differences and social conventions drive them apart. Just as the momentary physical bond between Sula and Chicken Little cannot hold, Sula and Nel slip farther and farther apart. That gap begins at the moment when Chicken Little "slipped from [Sula's] hands" (60), and the gap develops into "a space, a separateness" at Chicken's funeral (64). Nel then attempts to substitute an all-consuming relationship with Jude, but this attempt, in its disequilibrium, is shallow. Nel, cautious and conforming, repeats her mistake with Sula, trying to create her identity in fusion with another's. Sula, more active and nonconformist, embarks on a quest, but her quest is similar to Nel's marriage, for she seeks another Nel (Reddy 36), a friend who will be "both an other and a self" (119), and after her return she seeks union, first with Jude and then with Ajax. Both Sula and Nel seek totalizing unions with significant others, but when such unions do not last, their only recourse is isolation. The counterpart to symbiosis is division (Rubenstein 137).[12]

One consequence of the characters' attempts to find meaning in a relationship with another person is that they have difficulties in

69

maintaining workable self-concepts. Their senses of self become entangled with their quests for fulfilling relationships with another, and in the process their identities, their relationships, and their communal ties all suffer.

The women of the Bottom are remarkably able to endure nearly impossible conditions, but in doing so their balance between self and other is skewed. As a result, like the characters in *The Bluest Eye*, they need "to clean themselves" on such scapegoats as Shadrack, Sula, and even their own children. Helene loses her self in her need to disassociate herself from her prostitute mother, and she endlessly repeats that loss in such acts as her self-denying smile of humiliation on the train. To compensate for such identity loss, she becomes a complete assimilationist, outdoing Pauline in her self-serving refuge in social superiority, rigid Christianity, and self-denying emulation of the white middle class. Like Geraldine (Baker, *Workings* 139) and Ruth Dead, she effaces her funky self, as Helene Sabat becomes the watered-down, whitened Helen Wright, trying in her self-*right*eousness always to be considered "right." Such conforming characters, lacking a core self, disintegrate into fragments. They are examples of the black middle class whom Leroi Jones (Amiri Baraka) describes as determined "to become *citizens*": "They did not even want to be 'accepted' as *themselves*, they wanted any self which the mainstream dictated, and the mainstream *always* dictated. And this black middle class, in turn, tried always to dictate that self, or this image of a whiter Negro, to the poorer, blacker Negroes" (130). Hannah comes closer to a healthy accommodation between self and other, meeting her own needs for male companionship without sacrificing her dignity or making unrealistic demands, but, like the other adults, she too can make no permanent relationships and is estranged from her child.

Eva is forced by her isolation and poverty to take such ultimate risks as abandoning her children and sacrificing her own leg. One-legged, she tries to stand alone, without a significant other, but in doing so, like Baby Suggs and Sethe in *Beloved*, she overdoes her independence and willfulness, assuming a goddess-like imperialism that privileges the righteousness of her self and her will at the expense of others.[13] She "creates" the deweys, rescuing them from potentially

70

worse fates but denying them full identity and augmenting her own selfhood at their expense. Similarly, she saves Plum from further despair, but her act of murder is also motivated by her desire to protect herself from the shame and grief of his loss of self. Eva is so busy surviving that she has no energy for the conventional (white) mother-daughter love, and that lack is also a consequence of her over-reliance on self and her lack of recognition, not to mention compassion, for others. Then, her inability to save Hannah from the fire, a reoccurrence of the fire in which she burns Plum, is part of the price she has to pay, a price she pays again when Sula, also ego-bound, rejects her.

The males in *Sula*, displaced by their inferior racial status, never achieve stable selfhood.[14] Tar Baby, Plum, and the deweys lose their identities. They are like Shadrack, whose sense of self and other is shattered in the war. He, however, can provisionally control his fear of disintegration through his obsessively well-ordered cabin and his ritual of National Suicide Day, measures that parallel the Bottom's collective ability to control its traumas by incorporating whatever evils confront it. Other men—BoyBoy, Jude, and Ajax—are more capable of coping with life, but they never attain full integration of self and other. With no meaningful work, they lack confidence and therefore cannot remain in what they feel are half-emasculated roles. Symbolized by Ajax's fascination with planes, each of these eligible males therefore flies from the burden of a permanent role as husband and father.

Neither Jude nor Ajax can mature fully because each remains too attached to his need for a mother. Jude does not want an equal partner in Nel but someone who will mother him (Lounsberry and Hovet 128; Reddy 34). He is still a child whose selfhood is ever frail, overwhelmed by the weight of the oppressive economic and social conditions of the male work world and taking refuge in self-pity and the desire to be worshipped. He lacks the psychic resources to resist Sula or to face the consequences with Nel. Denied a complete identity by the white system's refusal of satisfying work, he wants "a someone sweet, industrious and loyal to shore him up" (83). Unable to find or become a self, he chooses Nel in the delusion that "the two of them together would make one Jude." His choice of Nel is a displacement, a vain attempt to replace his mother, to replace his own absent identity, to find "someone to care about his hurt, to care very deeply" (82).[15] Ajax appears to be more secure in his selfhood: hero-like, he bears gifts of life, such as milk and butterflies, and he enjoys a temporary equality with Sula. But his close ties to his conjuring mother do not allow him to make lasting commitments to anyone else. Like Jude, his selfhood and self-confidence are frail, so at the first sign of possessiveness on Sula's part, he takes to the air, and his identity is correspondingly deflated from the heroic Ajax to the mundane Albert Jacks.

The course of Nel's efforts to establish an effective balance between self and other is more complex. Her "exhilarating" but "fearful" (28) trip to New Orleans, including her disassociation from her mother's loss of identity on the train and her liberating encounter with her grandmother, at first enables her to find a sense of self: " 'I'm me. I'm not their daughter. I'm not Nel. I'm me. Me.' " This initial spark allows her to become Sula's partner, each fulfilling the gap in the other's imagination. Her flame of independent selfhood gradually burns down, however, under the constant, distorting pressures of racial, gender, and parental influence as well as her own passivity. It falters in comparison to Sula's overwhelming, rebellious selfhood and seems to flicker out with the death of Chicken Little, after which even her relationship with Sula is not the same and for which she denies responsibility for over forty years. By the time she accepts marriage with Jude, the fire is cold, and she becomes the supportive, conforming, self-denying woman her mother tried to construct. Her attempts to fuse herself and Jude are specious, based on assimilated values, and, instead of a healthy unity, she only becomes locked in a fragmentary existence.[16]

Nel's rejection of Sula in favor of a socially acceptable role as nurturing wife and mother leaves her with few psychic resources after that role is rendered unacceptable. Her unfulfilled self then is reflected in her inability to love her children, in which ironically she again conforms with the rest of the mothers in the community. She is unable to love or feel compassion for anyone, becoming all too much like her mother. That unfocused self is symbolized by the grey ball of fur that lurks just out of her imaginative vision (94). Like the white ring—also round—on Ruth Dead's table, it is the cloud in which she hides her self-knowledge and self-acceptance. Its semi-presence suggests that she at least senses that she is denying herself and therefore all others, unlike such characters as Helene, who have forgotten entirely such denial and such self-knowledge. Although it haunts Nel, the grey ball thus indicates that her quest for selfhood is not dead but merely dormant, waiting to be revived by Eva's uncanny divination of the truth of her responsibility for Chicken Little's death and therefore of her responsibility for her own life. At the end of the novel, too late for Nel to reestablish her intimacy with Sula, she dissolves the grey ball and regains a self, her relation to the other, and the deep, humanizing sorrow that accompanies the revelation.[17]

More than any of the other characters, Sula suffers from the dislocations of self and other. The narrator is explicit: "The first experience [Hannah's denial of liking her] taught her there was no other that you could count on; the second [Chicken Little's death] that there was no self to count on either" (118–19). But, unaware of any other choices, "she had clung to Nel as the closest thing to both an other and a self, only to discover that she and Nel were not one and the same thing" (119). Neither aided by the usual models for self-development nor checked by the usual restraints, and finding that she can neither find an identity in the other nor form her own (either in conjunction with or separate from that other), she drifts into the attempt to make herself. Given the confining conditions of life in the Bottom and given the paralyzing conventions for identity in both the mainstream society and the black community, making oneself is a positive and promising choice. Pilate Dead does achieve a healthy, self-made identity, but Sula must struggle, perhaps because, despite her aggressive self-confidence, she has "no ego," "no center, no speck around which to grow" (119). Unlike Pilate, who knows she must guide Milkman, Sula has no defining project, no focus; she is an "artist with no art form" (121). Along with this lack, the defining moments in Sula's development are negative (Byerman 196; Spillers 202). Just as Cholly's dangerous freedom and fragmented self result from the triple deaths of Aunt Jimmy, his masculinity, and his dream for a father, so Sula's undirected self follows from the triple negation of

73

her mother's rejection, her "murder" of Chicken Little, and Nel's preference for marriage.

Part of Sula's problem is that she cannot live anywhere but the Bottom, where her only communal role is that of the pariah. She can exist only in the eyes of others, only as the nonprivileged member of another destructive opposition, but she cannot conform because that would eliminate her visibility and hence her existence. Unlike Pecola, who becomes what she perceives, Sula becomes what she is perceived to be. Thus, her birthmark continually changes shape and color, because, like Sula herself, her mark is what others see it to be.[18] When she does lapse into conformity with the community's role of "wife," her independent selfhood, which Ajax sees and appreciates, vanishes in his eyes, and she becomes nothing to him and to herself. Sula is unable to join herself with any other, yet she is unable to exist independently. As in all of Morrison's fiction, neither fusion nor fragmentation suffices.

It is tempting to fall into the trap of praising or blaming Sula. Deborah Guth lines up previous critics into those who find Sula triumphing and those who find her failing (577n), and Guth herself compares Sula unfavorably to Eva. But such attempts at judgment are misdirected, for, like Claudia, Sula cannot be pinned down to one reading or one value judgment. Spillers articulates the required open-endedness: "We would like to love Sula, or damn her, inasmuch as the myth of the black American woman allows only Manichean responses, but it is impossible to do either. We can only behold in an absolute suspension of final judgment" (202). Like her birthmark, Sula remains open for interpretation.

Sula's resistance to any fixed interpretation parallels her own role in resisting the narrow formulations of self, woman, or black. She strives to remain free of convention, and correspondingly she must remain free of reader's fixed formulations. For Henderson, Sula is a representative of "the self-inscription of black womanhood" (131), an avatar of an alternative identity and role for African-American women. In Henderson's terms, via "disruption and revision" Sula rereads and repudiates "black male discourse," and I would add all conventional discourse, black and white, female and male. Spillers agrees in principle, arguing that Sula is "a literal and figurative *break-*

74

through toward the assertion of what we may call, in relation to her literary 'relatives,' new female being" (181), who "overthrows received moralities in a heedless quest for her own irreducible self" (185), declaring her independence in her "radical amorality" and "radical freedom" (202).

By this reasoning, Sula is the locus for the creativity of the novel. Like Morrison's text, Sula cannot be fully known, as Morrison creates her with unending play between interpretative possibilities. As the novel posits a world governed by binary oppositions and exerts sustained pressure against that structure, Sula personally opposes the binary world, tries to escape it, experiments with subverting it, and finally yields to it.[19] Both novel and character, by questioning the system and by groping toward alternative responses, make themselves up and concomitantly deconstruct the status quo. *Sula* and Sula remain open, for to finalize an interpretation is to close the book and end the process. Sula thus retains her hermeneutical richness; she is the title character, inviting our interpretations, and/but she is offstage for at least half the book, again inviting but not finalizing our readings. Her birthmark is a synecdoche for this role, like her and like the novel, open for interpretation, mediating between the external object and the internal subject. It, Sula, and *Sula* are "free-floating signifier(s)" (Henderson 130).

Sula's self-created self, her role as pariah, and her confusion over self and other double Shadrack's similar status. When he sees his comrade's head blown away, Shadrack loses confidence in the stability of the other and in the order and permanence of the material world. Similarly, Sula's belief in the order of the universe is destroyed by the blank space in the water above Chicken Little's body. Each event also shatters each character's sense of self: Shadrack has to verify his own existence in the imperfect mirror of the toilet bowl,[20] and Sula's course of self-exploration is displaced into her roles as fugitive and witch. Morrison underscores this subconscious bond between Shadrack and Sula, first in the introductory chapter and then in their encounter after the drowning. At that moment she joins him as an outcast from the social order of the community and the psychic order of integrated selves (Baker, *Workings* 149). His ambiguous word, "Always," reinforces the bond between them, implying that always life will be like this, always she and he will be pariahs.[21] On her part she leaves her belt, which further symbolizes the subconscious ties between them. They are a peculiar dyad, linked subliminally by their mutual roles but unable to acknowledge the connection.

As Rushdy notices (" 'Rememory' " 310), just before her epiphany at the end of the novel, Nel encounters Shadrack, who "passed her by" (173), vaguely recalling her but unable to place her. Physically, "Shadrack and Nel moved in opposite directions, each thinking separate thoughts about the past. The distance between them increased as they both remembered gone things" (174). The novel moves from the potential and magical union of Sula and Nel, by way of the subconscious, almost telepathic empathy between Sula and Shadrack, through numerous troubled relationships including Sula and Nel's, to this state of mutual isolation. But in the next sentence "suddenly Nel stopped" because "her eye twitched and burned a little," a trace of Sula's presence in its recall of Sula's birthmark over her eye. The unspoken, unrecognized encounter with Shadrack is the catalyst for Nel's realization that she misses Sula, and Shadrack's presence thereby precipitates her belated mental reunion with Sula, which dissolves her grey fur-ball of guilt and self-denial.

As critics have noticed, Nel's cry is ambiguous. In it she finally finds her voice, but her cry is wordless, void of representational meaning. Margaret Homans contends that the cry "exemplifies the paradox of separatism in language" (193), whereas Keith Byerman finds that the cry's lack of conventional structure makes possible the natural and human order of circles (201). For him Nel achieves true humanity in her cry, but for Spillers, the cry merely expresses remorse and may suggest "the onset of sickness-unto-death" (197). Nel's cry echoes Sula's orgasmic cries—"she went down howling," during which she "met herself, welcomed herself, and joined herself in matchless harmony" (123). Henderson argues that for Sula this "howl, signifying a prediscursive mode, thus becomes an act of self-reconstitution as well as an act of subversion or resistance to the 'network of signification' represented by the symbolic order" (133–34). Each woman's undifferentiated utterance, coming at a moment of internal fusion, constitutes a cathartic release: Sula finds and accepts herself and Nel dissolves her fur-ball, a sign of her self-acceptance and internal harmony. Nel's "fine cry" (174) places her close to Claudia MacTeer's final position—saddened, experienced, self-knowledgeable, and a potential spokesperson.

As in all of Morrison's novels, the ending resists closure. In this novel, destruction and death predominate, and the attempt to create meaning through significant pairs is always problematic. Yet characters do survive, and, strangely and inexplicably, psychic bonds do exist. Shadrack edges slowly toward emotional health through his tenuous relationship with his friend and through his grief for her. Sula, in her moment of post-death consciousness, thinks of Nel: "it didn't even hurt. Wait'll I tell Nel" (149). Nel, after years of repression, self-hate, and isolation, is mysteriously linked to Sula by way of Shadrack, which enables her to rejoin humanity in her "fine cry— loud and long" (174).

Conscious, direct, total union is futile and even destructive, but indirectly, without obsession or compulsiveness, meaningful relationships can endure. Just as the binary opposites are necessary, the independence of each individual must be acknowledged and preserved. The temptation is to think in terms of either/or—either I am separate or I am united, either the oppositions are opposed or they are merged—but this novel and all of Morrison's novels urge that alternative configurations are possible and necessary. Sula and Nel can't know each other's every thought, Nel and Jude can't make one Jude, Sula can't possess Ajax; but Sula's and Nel's lives do intimately affect each other's, and Shadrack can mediate between their souls. Sula, Nel, and Shadrack form a peculiar but compelling triad, subconsciously fused and necessarily fragmented.

From a social and cultural perspective, Morrison's preoccupation with divided entities in *Sula* reflects the endemic divisions within America.[22] The gaps between pairs of characters signify the deepseated fractures between opposed values in the larger society, particularly between blacks and whites. As with other binary pairs, Morrison juxtaposes the two races in direct confrontation, and the racial tension remains simmering, not breaking out into a race riot but contributing to the pervasive violence within the book. The two races constitute another binary pair, and the novel delineates the results of their difficulties in achieving a viable relationship.

This unfolding split is present in the tensions between the black residents of the Bottom and the whites who menacingly surround them. As opposed to *The Bluest Eye*, where the dominating white culture is present only indirectly in such forms as images of white beauty and values, in *Sula* nameless white characters repeatedly appear, always negatively with respect to blacks. The "good white farmer" tricks the gullible ex-slave into accepting infertile land in the hills, and in 1965 nameless whites reverse the trick. Other anonymous whites exert economic and political power over blacks: they withhold meaningful jobs, harass Tar Baby, arrest Ajax, and bury Sula. Enacting that power structure, the four Irish boys make sport of bullying Nel and Sula as they attempt to displace them. Whites abuse their status in their ridicule and humiliation of blacks: the white conductor treats Helene like "the bit of wax his fingernail had retrieved" from his ear (20–21) as he coerces her into mortifying submission. Whites overtly consider blacks as less than human, as when the bargeman who finds Chicken Little's body wonders "will those people ever be anything but animals" (63), and then, ironically, desecrates the corpse. The pervasiveness of his brutality is reinforced by the sheriff's opinion: "whyn't he throw it on back into the water" (64).

Another long-standing division in American culture, still present in the twentieth century, separates the idealized, agrarian past and the industrial present. The American myth promised a new beginning, an Edenic garden where the evils of urbanization and class conflict would be transcended, but the realities of slavery, the Civil War, and increasing industrialization meant the gradual fading of this Jeffersonian ideal.[23] Racial division is fundamental to this failure: a racially segregated society intensifies rather than eliminates class hierarchy; the melting pot fails when cultural islands form (Spiller 16). Despite the fading of the agrarian myth, it retains its force in the twentieth century in the form of nostalgia for an ideal rural past. In *Sula*, Morrison evokes this sentiment by placing the narrator in the near-present, wistfully recalling the old days when the Bottom was a neighborhood, one that, despite its problems and its faults, was preferable to its obliteration. But Morrison is also ironic, for the past that the story recalls is far from idyllic: in contrast to the American agrarian dream, the African-American agrarian past is characterized by violence and hardship. In the Bottom there are no waving fields of grain, no "two chickens in every pot," and, no matter where she travels, Sula finds that "there is no promised land of freedom to look toward" (Reddy 37). Nevertheless, that agrarian past, uncomfortably close to slavery, must be remembered and reclaimed, as Morrison delineates more intensively in *Beloved* and *Jazz*.

The sense of ironic displacement, begun in the novel's preface, deepens as Morrison leads readers to the Bottom via Shadrack. Sent to serve in World War I, "when blacks as a social group were first incorporated into a modern capitalist system" (Willis 85–86), Shadrack is blasted into isolation by experiencing his comrade's decapitation. The dead soldier is physically divided just as Shadrack becomes mentally divided; the soldier's physical loss of his head is transformed into Shadrack's mental loss of contact with the outside world. Together, the physical and mental displacements suggest the displaced situations of blacks: Reddy argues that Morrison's "definition by negation . . . places Shadrack the returning soldier in relationship to his enslaved ancestors" (33). In the Bottom, Shadrack and the other residents are still on the bottom of American society, largely forgotten, and "under erasure" (Gates, *Figures* 202).

The Bottom, even more thoroughly than the Ohio neighborhood in *The Bluest Eye*, inverts the American dream. As Baker claims, it symbolizes "the Afro-American Place," a place that is outside and below history, a place, in contrast to the commemorative implications of the white Medallion, that objectifies the difference between white and black ("When" 254–55). Still, it is a "place," as the novel's first sentence reminds us, a place where neighborhood is possible, where communal values at least exist and can be supportive, where one's double-consciousness becomes an essential ingredient for survival. In the narrator's present time, no amelioration of the inversion has occurred: "Things" only "seemed" "much better in 1965" (163).

The American dream has always been inverted for African Americans: if Europeans were to be regenerated in America (Marx, *Machine* 228), Africans were exiled to it; if America meant freedom to Europeans, it meant imprisonment to Africans; if America promised unlimited mobility to white settlers, the only mobility for slaves was as fugitives; if America meant a new place for Europeans, Africans had no place of their own.[24] R. W. B. Lewis characterizes the new American hero as emancipated from history, undefiled, and able to stand alone (5), none of which applies to the enslaved African American. In Fisher's terms, the existence of slaves and then of ex-slaves rendered inviable the American myth of transparency ("Democratic" 85).

In addition to the double-consciousness that results from being both within and outside mainstream culture, another result of racialization in America is that for African Americans the search for identity has been especially intense, even "desperate" (Ellison, *Shadow* 297). The first major form of African-American writing, the slave narrative, is a response to this need.[25] The theme is also evident in the passing novel, for example James Weldon Johnson's *The Autobiography of an Ex-Coloured Man* and Jesse Redmon Fauset's *Plum Bun*, in which the unsatisfactory choices confronting light-skinned African Americans are examined. The question of identity also dominates most African-American novels of the twentieth century, such as Zora Neale Hurston's *Their Eyes Were Watching God*, Richard Wright's *Eight Men* and *Native Son*, Ellison's *Invisible Man*, and Ernest Gaines's *The Autobiography of Miss Jane Pittman*.

One form that the search for identity takes in American fiction, black and white, is the pattern of escape and return. Typically, the American hero is stifled by the community, must leave it to pursue his or her self-development, but returns to the community with his or her acquired experience.[26] This return, however, is usually problematic, which, according to Marx (*Machine* 363–65), results in the often unresolved endings of American novels in which the hero is unreconciled with or even alienated from the community. Such endings are usually double endings in the sense that the departure/return cycle is fulfilled and yet a loss is inflicted. Hester Prynne is accepted by the Salem community and Pearl is brought into the human community, but in compensation the other "hero," Dimmesdale, and the "villain," Chillingworth, are exorcised. Ishmael returns to tell the tale, but Ahab and the rest of the crew must be eliminated. Huckleberry Finn is integrated into the community but, a kind of double hero, prefers perennial escape. Doubleness especially marks African-American novels. For example, the narrator of *The Autobiography of an Ex-Coloured Man* is torn between the two lives open to him; like Sula,

Janie Starks returns to her community as an outcast, but internally she is fulfilled and serene; and Ellison's invisible man withdraws from the community to a questionable isolation.

Sula extends this rich tradition of white American and African-American heros.[27] Unwilling to subsume her identity into the mold allowed by the black community and the dominant society, she creates her own self, which gains her at least freedom and self-satisfaction ("I got my mind . . . I got me" [143]), but which leaves her isolated and incomplete. Like her chameleon birthmark, she is an optical illusion that varies according to the observer. In Pilate, the mark of difference (the lack of a navel) becomes the germ for a true self, but Sula's birthmark, instead of making her a genuine subject, makes her always an object. Except for her childhood friendship with Nel and her ambiguous relationship with Shadrack, her interactions with other people therefore tend to be negative. She gains a self, but, unable to gain harmony with community and cosmos, she cannot achieve lasting fulfillment. A pioneer, she forges a new path, but, like so many American heros, she cannot be absorbed by the community.

Sula's fate thus resembles that of many African Americans.[28] African Americans are split off from mainstream American culture, and she is split off from the community and the larger society. She has the mobility of all Americans but she has only a marginal place. Neither slave nor free, she is caught in the racial enclosure of negation (Gates, *Figures* 54). Unlike Pauline, Helene, and Nel, she refuses erasure, refuses the impossible attempt to achieve transparency, but in that process, double-consciousness leads, as it does for Pecola, not to health and stability but to a mental state of morbidity and apathy similar to the condition described by Du Bois: "an almost morbid sense of personality and a moral hesitancy which is fatal to self-confidence" (164).

Like other classic American heros, Sula escapes and returns, and, like them, her return is problematic. She has to escape because her first attempt at an identity through companionship fails when Nel chooses the conforming role of housewife. She must return because without the negative self-definition supplied by the Bottom she has no identity, hence the anonymity of the cities she has drifted through. Upon her return, her position is more ambiguous than that of most

American heros, for her place in the community is defined only negatively. Although her self-creation represents a significant advance
over Cholly, who is also "dangerously free" but cannot create his own
self, Sula remains too free, too radical, too resistant to assimilation.
Rejecting assimilation, she opts wholly for the other extreme of nonconformity, not realizing that this too is a bipolar opposition to be
deconstructed, not accepted. She insists on absolute independence,
refusing to negotiate the two extremes, refusing to bend to be ab-
sorbed within the confining limits of community, and finally accepting a fixed position in opposition to convention. But, like one-legged
Eva, she cannot stand alone, so she abandons her attempt at independence when she tries to possess Ajax—in other words when she suc-
cumbs, Nel-like, to the other pole, the social pressures of domestica-
tion.

In a fictional world that emphasizes paired characters, Sula cannot
survive because she finds no enduring relationship with any other
character. That she does not, and that no one else does either, suggests that the quest for identity through such relationships, while
privileged by the dominant society and by the black community, is
impossible in this environment. In the Bottom, external pressures
overwhelm any possibility of Sula and Nel (or of any two people)
working through the convoluted process of forming such a relationship. Similar pressures, plus their own internal needs, disrupt Jadine
and Son's attempt at fusion, whereas Sethe and Paul D and Violet
and Joe Trace are able to build satisfying relationships, even while
both cases document the complex difficulties of such a process.

Like similar antisocial heroes, Sula—radical, funky, anarchistic,
chaotic—must be exorcised for the community to survive. The community endures for twenty-five years but is impoverished by the loss
of this energy, as Nel realizes that post-Bottom, post-Sula Medallion
is spiritually weakened. Without the pariah to clean themselves on,
the members of the community slip into the doldrums. Yet Sula is
not entirely forgotten, as her death is connected to a strange, sad,
nostalgic fruition for Shadrack and Nel.

Although the attempt to find identity through a relationship with
another person is an illusion, that fundamental division between self
and other must be investigated, as Morrison continues to do in her

82

next four novels. The violence of *Sula* is necessary to loosen the rigidity of the bipolar structures. Only by questioning such structures, by accepting the inevitability of separation, and by attempting to bridge the gaps, can one understand the division and therefore one's self. Accepting the grief unblocks the repressed emotion and allows the soul to be reborn and to soar, even if it "howl[s] in a stinging awareness of the endings of things" (123) and even if it soars in "circles and circles of sorrow" (174). For this novel, however, the epiphany comes too late, too late to retrieve what has been lost, too late for Nel or Sula to continue her self-development. Such retrieval, development, and unification is reserved for Morrison's next hero, Milkman Dead.

Putting It All Together: Attempted Unification in *Song of Solomon*

In *The Bluest Eye* images of splitting dramatize a broken community, broken families, and especially broken identities. In *Sula* Morrison focuses on irreconcilable divisions between binarily opposed pairs. *Song of Solomon* initially posits a similarly split world, but this novel moves toward the attempted and ambiguous reconciliation of the divided parts. If *The Bluest Eye* lays out the problem of the creation and maintenance of viable identities for contemporary African Americans, and if *Sula* explores the frustrations of attempting to develop such identities through relationships with a significant other, Morrison's third novel expands that search to a quest for identity and meaning through knowledge of the ancestral and cultural past.[1] As in the first two books, the problem is one of fragmentation—families are "all split up" (291) to the extent that "it's a wonder anybody knows who anybody is" (328)—but here the attempted solution is not to find identity and meaning in a paired relationship, but to unify disparate elements and conflicting clues into a meaningful whole—in short, to "put it all together" (327).

Morrison sets up Milkman's miraculous quest for unity by chronicling the heterogeneity in his environment. His family is divided into two estranged branches, and, within his immediate family, his mother and father barely tolerate each other, and he rarely speaks to his sisters. Simultaneously, he is pulled in contrary directions by Macon, Ruth, Pilate, Hagar, and Guitar. In Part I of the novel, Milkman's response to these pressures modulates from confusion to withdrawal and then to resentment, and yet, particularly through his association with Pilate, there are signs of preparation for his identity-forming quest in Part II. In Part II, Milkman achieves a successful but interrupted integration, a process symbolic of racial schism in American history and of the shift from "Negro" to "black" in African-American culture.

In Morrison's first two novels, characters' immediate families tend not to provide stable bases for individual fulfillment but instead are splintered by unbridgeable gaps between parents and children. In *Song of Solomon* intra-family relations are even worse. The Bains family has been destroyed by the death of Guitar's father and the absence of his mother. The Dead family is indeed spiritually dead; Macon and Ruth's failed individual lives as well as their moribund relationship are reflected in the stagnated lives of their children and in the lack of healthy relationships among them. The household of Pilate, Reba, and Hagar, another of Morrison's female triads, has many positive qualities, but Pilate, who formed her own successful identity despite the violent break-up of her own family, is unable to transmit her strengths to her daughter or granddaughter (Scruggs, "Nature" 322). Both in her personal achievement and in her inability to pass on that achievement, Pilate's case further exemplifies Morrison's questioning of the power of parent/child relationships to foster individual wholeness. Moreover, the extended Dead family seems at first irrevocably split between the two households in their two opposing parts of town, much like the contrasts between the MacTeer and Breedlove households in *The Bluest Eye* and the Peace and Wright households in *Sula* (Barthold 180).

As in the first two novels, the past strongly shapes the disintegration of families and individuals, but for the Dead family the failure to know and incorporate the past is especially disabling. The family's separation from the past is revealed by its misnaming, which, like the "nigger joke" that named and created the Bottom (Christian, *Black Feminist* 51), is an absurd result of racism. Without their name (Solomon) and the wisdom it implies, the Deads are ignorant of their ancestry and hence of themselves, and they are alienated from their community, each other, and themselves. Lacking his spiritual inheritance, Macon substitutes the materialistic ethos of the dominant culture and therefore supposes that his rightful inheritance is the gold. Pilate tries to retain her spiritual connections to her past, in particular to her father, but, not knowing the full story of the past, she makes the erroneous assumption that the bones she keeps are not her father's but those of the white man she and Macon killed. Milkman's task of reintegration requires him to complete Pilate's quest by connecting past and present, thereby rediscovering the family name and converting the false inheritance to a true one.

The past also influences the characters in the form of ghosts, which serve as traces of the past. In this novel, as Freddie urges Milkman, "You better believe" in ghosts (109). For everyone there is the danger of becoming spiritually dead, of becoming, like Hagar, "a restless ghost, finding peace nowhere and in nothing" (127). Guitar's life is determined by the unexorcised ghosts of his parents: the callous response of his father's employer to his father's grisly death motivates Guitar's hatred of whites, and his mother's sycophantic imitation of Aunt Jemima precipitates his mistrust of women.

Each of Milkman's closest parental figures—Ruth, Pilate, and Macon—performs a version of ancestor worship. Ruth, cut off from any meaningful present or future, lives in the memory of her infatuation with her father. "In a way jealous of death" (64), she perpetuates the ghost of her father and the ghost of time past as symbolized by the watermark on her table.[2] Pilate retains the spiritual values of the past, and her close-to-nature lifestyle imitates her childhood life at Lincoln's Heaven. She treasures the signs of that former life—in her earring, her bag of bones, her rocks—but, alone, she cannot complete her quest for understanding of her self and her past. Macon, still suffering from the trauma of his father's murder, erroneously thinks he has successfully repudiated the past: "He had not said any of this for years. Had not even reminisced much about it recently" (51). He can no longer remember his father's real name (Jake) and thus has lost his past and himself. His servile assimilationism (worse than Helene's and Nel's), his accommodation to white standards, his soul-destroying materialism, and his lack of meaningful human contacts all result from his radical disassociation from his past. Having lost all the values of his upbringing in paradisiacal Lincoln's Heaven, he worships gold instead of his ancestors and has substituted material objects (keys, property, cars, money) for people. Having lost the land, he has become a landlord. His desiccated life is a dialectical reversal; he has become the opposite of what he longed to be. Despite his conscious repudiation of his ghosts, he ironically pursues his father's quest for material success and comfort in a white-dominated society.[3]

The persistent presence of Jake's ghost provides one meaningful link with the family past. Three times readers are told of his reappearances after he was blown up: by Macon (40), by Pilate (141), and in a curious third-person flashback allegedly told by Macon to Milkman (169). Presumably also, Jake's ghost is the "figure of a man standing by his friend" (187) that Milkman sees when he and Guitar steal Pilate's bag of bones.[4] Jake's shallow burial, which led to the dumping of his bones in the cave, symbolizes that the past itself needs to be rediscovered and reintegrated into the present. Like Jake, the family past, as well as the African-American cultural and historical past, has been blown apart by the dominant white culture. Like the watermelon in *The Bluest Eye*, the break is a bad one, leading to the "disappointment" and "jagged[ness]" (*Bluest* 107) of an unwilled fragmentation. That disintegration, and its memory, like Jake and his bones, haunt the book like a ghost.

The past is figured in *Song of Solomon* not only in terms of the lost family name, the misdirected inheritances, and the reappearances of ghosts, but also in the novel's narrative form. Its dominant feature is the dozens of flashbacks in which almost a third of the text is narrated.[5] Almost all of these flashbacks are either told or remembered by the characters, not simply by the narrator, which suggests that the characters are endeavoring to regain contact with their pasts. In Part

I, four of the characters who are trying to influence Milkman—Macon, Pilate, Guitar, and Ruth—remember episodes of their past and, more importantly, relate those episodes to Milkman. For example, Macon recounts his childhood at Lincoln's Heaven (51–54) and Ruth's questionable behavior upon her father's death (70–73), Pilate tells Milkman and Guitar her memories of Lincoln's Heaven (39–43), Guitar recalls his early days as a hunter (85), and Ruth tells her story of Milkman's birth (124–26). Milkman, hearing these past stories, is initially not interested. He rejects his family's past just as he rejects responsibility for his own present and future. But, despite his disinterest, the flashbacks provide him with a fragmented sense of his family's past that unconsciously leads to his desire to recover his lost heritage. The embedded stories about Macon and Pilate's childhood also prefigure Milkman's physical journey to Danville and Shalimar, as his quest becomes the effort to make sense of these fragments of time, place, and differing perspectives. He must learn to read correctly the palimpsest of his cultural, familial, and personal pasts.[6] More broadly, the incorporation and transformation of myths similarly imply the need for a broad "reading" of African-American experience in terms of European and African cultural heritages.

In Part II, the primary source of the flashbacks shifts from the other characters to Milkman as he "d[oes] his best to put it all together" (307). For example, he recalls his childhood (267), his whole life (282), Guitar's aphorisms (285), and his rudeness to his family and Hagar (304). He tries to interpret the past through the words of the Solomon song and through the place names on road signs. His quest to find the lost gold becomes his quest for his family's past and his own undiscovered identity.

It is fitting that he seeks the past in a journey to the South, for in Morrison's fiction the South always represents the past. For most of Morrison's characters—such as Pauline and Cholly Breedlove, Sethe and Paul D, or Joe and Violet Trace—the southern past is available only through memory, but Milkman is able to revisit the sites where his ancestors' past took place and thereby to identify himself with these ancestors.[7] As his knowledge of the past increases through the flashbacks and his own travels, his geographical journey expands, duplicating Pilate's geographical collection of rocks from the places she has visited. The stories Milkman collects are like Pilate's rocks: both are fragments of the characters' journeys, reminders of their own pasts and their cultural pasts. Just as the rocks provide the pleasure of connectedness for Pilate, the stories gradually give Milkman self-knowledge, empathy, a sense of place in the African-American culture, and a sense of belonging in the natural world.

Like the juxtaposition of temporal linearity and circularity in *Sula*, this novel simultaneously moves forward and backward in time. From the moment before Robert Smith's suicide on February 18, 1931 (Morrison's date of birth) to Milkman's leap 33 years later, it moves steadily forward, measuring its chronological movement with the stages in Milkman's life. At the same time, the novel spirals backward through the remembered and related flashbacks of the characters, through Milkman's spatial return to the sites of the past, through the evocation of characters from the past such as Circe and Susan Byrd, and through Milkman's unraveling of the secrets of his family's past. The "linear conception of time" is associated with Macon, whereas "Pilate's vision of time . . . is cyclical and expansive" (V. Smith, *"Song"* 280–81). Part of Milkman's task is to fuse these two forms, the first traditionally associated with Euro-American culture and the second with African culture.[8] This double temporal movement creates a circular form, a plurality-in-unity, as the present and past mirror each other in the parallels between Smith's leap and Milkman's, between the singing of Solomon's song at the beginning and at the end, and between Milkman's birth and Pilate's death.[9]

Besides family divisions and the separation from the past, a third form of fragmentation in Milkman's home environment is the acute division between blacks and whites. As in *Sula*, nameless, usually powerful whites surround the black community and treat blacks with cruelty or indifference, for example the nurse who patronizes Guitar (7), the bankers who dominate Macon (20), the drunk Yankee who misnames the Deads (53), and the boss of Guitar's father who dismisses Guitar's mother with forty dollars and Guitar with divinity (61).[10] In *The Bluest Eye* and *Sula* the vise of discrimination remains in the background and relatively peaceful, but here whites murder Jake, Emmett Till, and the four little black girls, and blacks in the Seven Days plan and execute revenge.[11] This underlying principle of violent, racial division and its consequent displacements is symbolized by the image of the corpse of Guitar Bains's father, "sliced in half and boxed backward" (226).

Like the violent divisions in American society, here the black community is also radically divided. As opposed to the relative homogeneity of the black communities in *The Bluest Eye* and *Sula*, the Southside is divided between Macon and Ruth's neighborhood and Pilate's. It is divided politically between the assimilationists, like Macon, and the radical separatists, like the Seven Days.[12] This political division is reinforced by the references to historical events of the 1960s, in particular to the divisions within the civil rights movement between Malcolm X and Martin Luther King, Jr., and between Malcolm X and Elijah Muhammad.[13] The fragmentations within the novel's community thus figure the historic divisions within American culture and within African-American culture. The links between the characters' fragmentations and the fragmented society are suggested by Morrison's allusions to the murder of Emmett Till. This 1955 murder galvanized African Americans, and Milkman most deeply realizes his separation from his community when, ignorant of Till's death, he walks against the crowd (78) and is then chastised by Guitar for his racial apathy (86–89).[14]

The disparity between races is also suggested by the problematic question of "why." In *The Bluest Eye* the grown-up Claudia relinquishes the attempt to explain why things happened: "But since why is difficult to handle, one must take refuge in how" (9). Similarly, in this novel "why" is usually unknowable, which suggests that the causes of the racialized condition underlying the novel cannot be determined. Milkman endures the frustrations of not knowing why other characters behave as they do, for example, why Macon forbids him to visit Pilate's house (50), why Macon hits Ruth (87), or why Guitar wants to kill him (290). But Guitar expresses the general principle: "Listen baby, people do funny things. Specially us. The cards are stacked against us and just trying to stay in the game, stay alive and in the game, makes us do funny things. Things we can't help. Things that make us hurt one another. We don't even know why" (88). This principle applies to all of Morrison's novels: racial oppression leads to displacement and self-destructive behavior whose causes are inexplicable.

Like "why," "not" also articulates the racial disparities in Milkman's urban environment. The Southside community is relegated to denial—on "Not Doctor Street" (3), near "No Mercy Hospital" (4) to which blacks are denied admittance. The pervasive sense of denial of access, hope, rights, and privileges that dominates the black community is expressed in Railroad Tommy's bitter outburst to Milkman about all the things "he ain't going to have" (59).[15] The pernicious effects of this lack, of being the unprivileged members of a divided and hierarchical society, are apparent in the absences that Guitar lives with and that steer his life toward revenge: "Everything I ever loved in my life left me" (311). Hagar also suffers from the absence of things: "a chorus of mamas, grandmamas, aunts, cousins, sisters, neighbors, Sunday school teachers, best girl friends, and what all to give her the strength life demanded of her." The result is that she lives in a state of total absence: "Not wilderness where there was system, or the logic of lions, trees, toads, and birds, but wild wilderness where there was none" (138). Trapped in this nihilism, this dangerous freedom, and unwilling to embrace the wildness like Wild and Golden Grey in *Jazz*, Hagar's only recourse is to try to possess the one thing, Milkman, that she thinks she can possess, even though, as Guitar tells her, "You can't own a human being" (311). Then, upon losing Milkman, Hagar can think only of his absence, of "the mouth Milkman was not kissing, the feet that were not running toward him, the eye that no longer beheld him, the hands that were not touching him" (127).

Collectively, the African-American community can offset the negativity of denial. Not Doctor Street and No Mercy Hospital become "good" in the same sense that "baaad" can indicate its opposite in Black English. According to Roberta Rubenstein, the acceptance of the inverted names indicates the community's resistance to the dominant society (154). Kimberly Benston pushes this point to argue that through the names the Southsiders evade the "monologic violence" (87) of the white society and "protect memory as both continuity and concealment." In other words, the non-names, suggesting the community's subjugation and invisibility, become verbal icons for its internal unity in opposition to white authority. Through these non-texts, the residents signify upon their white oppressors and create meaningful communal identities in opposition to those oppressors.

In two other cases the absence of something becomes the vehicle for positive change.[16] The absence of gold in the cave outside Danville is crucial in shifting Milkman from the moribund materialistic values he acquired from Macon to the spiritual ones modeled by Pilate. Similarly, Pilate's lack of a navel, after causing her anguish and alienation, leads to her self-creation of a viable self (in contrast to Sula who, marked similarly by her birthmark, is less successful in her self-creation). Pilate "began at zero" by symbolically killing her old self by cutting off her hair and then "she tackled the problem of trying to decide how she wanted to live and what was valuable to her" (149). As a result of this self-deconstruction (Mobley, *Folk Roots* 113), she purges herself of fear, develops "compassion for troubled people" (150), "acquire[s] a deep concern for and about human relationships," becomes "a natural healer," stays in close touch with the spirit of her dead father, and becomes Milkman's protector and guide. As Milkman's spiritual guide, his *griot*, she models for Milkman the creation of self that is both within and without the community, she precedes him in her physical journey and her symbolic journey toward love and harmony, and she teaches him the values of a spiritual, Afrocentric, nature-centered, nonlinear perspective as opposed to Macon's material one.[17] Even though she cannot complete her quest until Milkman provides the missing clues, she provides a "template" (Benston 101) for her nephew by fusing disparate forces. As Milkman will pull everything together, Pilate has "deep connectedness" (Guth 581) with people, nature, community, and the past.[18] As Benston puts it, "she asserts . . . the will-to-connection against a world insistent upon definition by division and differentiation" (99). She is Morrison's first character with a well-developed talent for fusion.

The fusion implicit in Pilate becomes explicit in Milkman. Although Sula and Nel are both fascinated by their opposite's house, they remain identified with their irreconcilably different houses and lifestyles; there is no middle ground, no character who straddles the two. In *Song of Solomon*, however, Pilate bridges the gap between the two houses when she abets Milkman's conception and birth, and then Milkman becomes a fully mediating character. He spends time at both houses, he develops significant relationships with characters in both houses, he appreciates the values of his father and his aunt, and he brings about the partial reconciliation of the two families.

At age four having "lost all interest in himself" (9), Milkman becomes vulnerable to the uses of others, becomes the subject of a struggle for his soul between five competing characters: Macon, Ruth, Guitar, Pilate, and Hagar.[19] He is bored with his father's assimilationist and material version of black capitalism, he is disgusted with his mother's necromantic fantasies, and he has no patience for Guitar's political obsession with racial injustice. Although Pilate's natural wisdom and openness intrigue him, they provide no direct route for his personal development, and his affair with Pilate's granddaughter becomes another boring "dead"-end. As Ruth reflects, "he became a plain on which . . . she and her husband fought" (133). All five characters place claims on him to fulfill their own unfulfilled lives, and Milkman is vulnerable to their reification of him because he lacks the will to examine himself and his life.

The influencing characters offer contrasting ideas of love. Guitar tries to convince Milkman of the Seven Days' philosophy of unquestioning love for all African Americans, but that love leads each cult member into the strictures of revenge against whites and pushes Robert Smith over the edge of sanity and Henry Porter to the edge. Instead of love, Guitar becomes co-opted by his hate into the evil practices of the dominant social system he wishes to escape (V. Smith, *Self-Discovery* 152) and therefore, like Macon, Guitar exemplifies the dialectical reversal. In contrast, the love of Ruth and Hagar is personal rather than political, but their version of love is equally unacceptable to Milkman. Ruth indulges herself in worshipping her father and then converts that reifying love into "a passion" (131) for Milkman that denies his identity: "Her son had never been a person to her." Hagar, beset by her own problems, including Milkman's selfish treatment, allows her love for Milkman to congeal into the desire to possess him. Her love, like Beloved's love for Sethe, becomes an "anaconda love" (137) that would as soon kill Milkman as love him and that has devoured everything else within her: "she had no self left, no fears, no wants, no intelligence." Pilate's successful effect on Milkman's spiritual growth derives from her more empathic love. She loves individuals, in particular each member of her and Macon's families, and she unselfishly loves all people: "I wish I'd a knowed more people. I would of loved 'em all. If I'd a knowed more, I would a loved more" (340). Through that love, she achieves and conveys to Milkman the self-fulfillment that results from harmony with community and cosmos.

As Milkman gradually assimilates these varieties of love, he also synthesizes the other characters' attitudes toward the past. Guitar cannot escape the past, obsessed as he is by his father's death and his bitterness toward it. As a result the earth for him is still the "stinking hole" (227) of the outhouse into which he threw his peppermint stick, and his Seven Days' philosophy is his attempt to redress those perceived wrongs. Macon tries to redress the crimes committed against his father, not by killing whites but by outdoing them materially; consequently, he has lost his own spirit and the capacity for love. Ruth does not want to make up for the past but to preserve it, to retain her undying love for her father and to hold on to Milkman's devotion, exemplified by her prolonged nursing of him. She is therefore comforted by the watermark on her mahogany table because it reminds her of her life with her father: "she regarded it as a mooring, a checkpoint, some stable visual object that assured her that the world was still there" (11). First Corinthians provides Milkman with a preferable model when she realizes that her past has not allowed her to become a whole adult and when she exercises her new-found courage by freeing herself from the crushing lies of Miss Graham's sentimentality and the mountains of red velvet. Pilate, again, is Milkman's most helpful guide, for she best combines respect for the past and constructive action in the present.

In addition to the themes of love and the past, Morrison uses multiple images of hunting to articulate the heterogeneous influences on Milkman. Guitar fondly remembers hunting as a boy and teaches Milkman never to hunt a doe, but Guitar's lesson is undercut when he becomes the hunter of people, first his white victims and then Milkman. Hagar resorts to tracking Milkman every thirty days, in her comic/tragic pursuit of something to hold herself together. Milkman becomes the hunter when he trails Ruth to the cemetery, but his purpose is valid, to learn Ruth's story as a counter to Macon's. Milkman's quest to Pennsylvania and Virginia is also a hunt, but a hunt in which the initial prey, the gold, becomes transformed into a search for himself and his ancestral origins. At the climax of that search is the literal hunt for the bobcat, in which Milkman becomes the hunted as well as the hunter (Mobley, *Folk* 124), has his epiphany of oneness with the cosmos, and acquires a new identity.

This pattern of differentiating various characters' orientations toward a value such as love or a mode of action such as hunting suggests the limitations of any single character's approach. Until Milkman begins to fuse the contrasting perspectives, each character tends to use love, the past, the hunt, or any other vehicle for his or her selfish purposes, which consistently fragments him or her from other characters and frequently harms everyone involved. Except for Pilate, the other characters remain trapped in their narrow, fixed, monologic approaches, which denies them the openness necessary for continuing growth.

The inadequacies of individual solutions are evident in individual characters' failures to interpret things around them. Macon widely misinterprets Pilate, thinking of her as a snake who bites the man who feeds it (54). Guitar wrongly concludes that Milkman's desire to go to Danville is designed to betray him and then erroneously assumes that the box Milkman helps load onto the train must contain the gold (259 and 299). Even Pilate, despite her sensitivity, misinterprets her father's ghost when he bids her to remember Sing, and she draws the wrong conclusion about the bones she finds in the cave.

For the first two thirds of the novel Milkman also fails to interpret correctly. Puzzled by his parents' stories, he tries to duck the confusing questions they raise. He ignores his sisters as entities to be interpreted: "He had never been able to really distinguish them (or their roles) from his mother" (68). He is left out of the signifying banter at the barbershop, a result of his isolation from his community and culture. His alienation implies his doubled fragmentation—cut off from the community and internally divided between loyalties to his competing mentors. Once on his quest, he still has difficulties with interpretations, for example wrongly concluding that Pilate took the

95

gold from the cave near Danville (260) and not fully grasping Guitar's threatening message (266) and Guitar's new role as his enemy. For a while, he ignores the possibility that natural and manmade objects are signifiers: he suffers the "city man's boredom with nature's repetition" (228), and he is bored by the highway signs (228) and the "no name hamlet[s]" (262) he encounters.

No one version of love, of the past, of hunting, or of interpretation is adequate, but instead their plurality and their complex and ambiguous combinations are required. This novel is overtly fugal: it presents multiple lines, multiple reactions, and multiple versions of a topic or an entity, demonstrating that no single thread is adequate. It presents "a tough-minded and dynamic interplay of ideas which never come to rest in any simple resolution" but instead probe "the blues-like paradoxes and complexities of modern experience" (Butler 63). In a similar fashion, the novel relies not on just one mythic tradition but fuses elements of at least three: African, classical European, and Christian. As Jane Campbell notes, proper names in the novel "span centuries and hemispheres" (146), thus integrating multiple cultures and traditions. Even the location and identity of Milkman's hometown is a vague mixture (Butler 53–64; Scruggs, "Nature" 319; Imbrie 6), associated with Lake Superior, the Great Lakes in general, and yet with rivers. And the name of Milkman's ancestors' town in Virginia, a town not on any map (Heinze 140), slides among several names: Shalimar, Solomon, Shalleemone, and Charlemagne. By remaining vague and essentially multiple, both towns thus become ritualized places where myth can occur.[20]

Morrison embeds the need for pluralism by insisting on retelling the characters' stories, not only those of the major characters but also of such minor characters as Circe and Reverend Cooper and his friends. Although the novel is unified by a conventional third-person narrator, the characters retell or recall much of the novel's past. As in *The Bluest Eye*, many stories and many viewpoints are needed because no single one is sufficient.[21] The stories gradually create a plurality-within-unity, "a crazy quilt with a sense of pattern" (Fabre 111).

Milkman's role in this structure is to learn his own story, thereby finding his identity in his relation to his past and his community (V. Smith, *Self-Discovery* 136) and thereby becoming the unifying agent.

As Rubenstein contends, he reconciles his two last names (154), and simultaneously he reconciles his two first names. Similarly, Linda Krumholz shows that Milkman's quest constitutes a reinterpretation of "milkman" and "dead," the former name suggesting his connections with nurturance, motherhood, and deliverance, and the latter his ties with his ancestors and his cultural heritage ("Dead" 557–58). He synthesizes the competing lives of his relatives and friends, and he unites the male and materialistic perspective of his father with the female and spiritual one of his aunt. "Milkman's story thus articulates a history of separations and re-connections" (Rubenstein 155) in which the progression moves from the fragmentations to the fusions.

At first, Milkman's reaction to his identity-less and reified situation is marked by confusion.[22] He not only loses interest in himself, but his imagination is "bereft" (9), and he is out of joint with himself and reality. He sits in the family car "riding backward" and feeling "uneasy" (31). As on those tortured family drives, he is "flying blind" rather than with purpose and insight. He is alienated from other children ("He hailed no one and no one hailed him" [32]), is dropped by his mother from the nursing chair, and is routinely scolded by his father. He develops a psychosomatic "short" leg, which results from his disorientation and in turn makes him feel even more out of plumb with the world. For Royster, Milkman is an "unconscious scapegoat," "a victim of his burdensome past, blind to his future, and unable to assert himself in his here and now" ("Milkman's" 431). His nickname, at first a mystery and then a source of shame, creates an odd sense of doubleness: is he Macon or Milkman? This disquieting doubleness is evident in his contemplation of the silver-backed brushes his mother gives him with the monogram *M.D.* and its pun not only on Macon/Milkman but on his initials and on "Doctor of Medicine," with its allusion to Dr. Foster. Milkman's misalignment with the world around him is perhaps best represented by the Poe-like scene in which he walks in the opposite direction from everyone (78), which leads him to wonder "if there was anyone in the world who liked him" (79).[23] Despite the difficulties of Milkman's backward and divided position, this early sense of double-consciousness gives him the perspective of the outsider/insider that eventually aligns him with other African Americans and that subsequently propels him on his quest.[24]

As Milkman learns about his immediate family history, this disorientation phase is followed by a period of withdrawal and denial. Unable and unwilling to assimilate the new information about his parents and his infancy, he becomes passively suicidal: he is bored with everything (90), feels that his life is "pointless, aimless" (107), and desires "above all . . . to escape what he knew," (120) even if that means death at Hagar's hands.

At the same time, however, Milkman begins to resent the conflicting claims on him. Angered by what Macon tells him about Ruth, he "felt put upon; felt as though some burden had been given to him and that he didn't deserve it" (120). After he hears Ruth's side of the story, the feeling goes deeper: "he felt used. Somehow everybody was using him for something or as something. Working out some scheme of their own on him, making him the subject of their dreams of wealth, or love, or martyrdom" (165–66). In his view at this stage, his father, his mother, Guitar, and Hagar are lined up against him, making their "claims" against him.

Milkman's sense of being reified is accurate, but it is also ironic, because throughout Part I Milkman in turn reifies others. Spoiled by his parents and by his attractiveness to women, he blithely assumes the privileges of being cared for without accepting any responsibilities. As Lena accuses him, his misdirected urinations are indicative. Just as he pees on Lena (215), on the newly planted tree (214), and in kitchen sinks (213), he has figuratively "found all kinds of ways to pee on people" (215).[25] His depersonalization of others is evident in the "few and easily chosen" (90) Christmas gifts he buys for people and in his inability to even think of helping his mother in his dream about her and the threatening flowers (105–6). The person he most abuses is Hagar, in his cursory "dear John" letter (126), in his wish for her death (129–30), and in his verbal abuse (130).

Throughout Part I, while Milkman is being used by others and is using them, he nevertheless is being prepared for his quest in Part II. As in the preparation stage of the monomyth of the hero's quest as delineated by Joseph Campbell and Otto Rank, he becomes increasingly uncomfortable with his situation and his unformed identity. He learns from Pilate the mystery of being, symbolized by the egg, and he smells the odor of ginger with its hint of Africa. As he learns more, he is increasingly disquieted and feels more strongly the necessity of breaking away. He receives guidance, direct and indirect, from everyone around him: parents, sisters, community members (such as Freddie and the barbershop group), his spiritual guide (Pilate), and his friend/rival (Guitar). Toward the end of all this preparation, when Guitar yells at him to "live it! Live the motherfuckin life! Live it" (184), Milkman has a preliminary epiphany that anticipates the novel's ending: "All the tentativeness, doubt, and inauthenticity that plagued him slithered away without a trace, a sound" and "he felt a self inside himself emerge, a clean-lined definite self."

To document Milkman's growth, Morrison uses the issue of his fears. At first, like the rest of the family, he is kept "awkward with fear" (10) by Macon. Then he hears how Macon assuaged Pilate's fears after Jake's death, and he learns a valuable lesson from Pilate: "What difference do it make if the thing you scared of is real or not?" (40–41). When Hagar is trying futilely to kill him, Milkman progresses from feeling the fear (113) to controlling it (129), and his fear is replaced by the first stirrings of willpower: "But the fear was gone. He lay there as still as the morning light, and sucked the world's energy up into his own will." At this point, because of his own lack of direction, he can only will negatively—for Hagar to die—but this indication of will and the suggestion of a connection to cosmic energy prefigure his later development. Next, Milkman expresses fear for Guitar, perhaps the first time he feels anything akin to empathy: "Milkman rubbed the ankle of his short leg. 'I'm scared for you, man'" (162). Then, as he thinks about Guitar's self-imposed risks in joining the Seven Days, Milkman realizes that he admires the lack of fear in the three most influential people in his life: "His father, Pilate, Guitar. He gravitated toward each one, envious of their fearlessness now" (178). This experience and his envy of fearlessness lay the foundation for Milkman's transcendence of fear in Part II.

Milkman's quest in Part II enables him to fuse the competing influences, heterogeneous forces, and complex pluralisms in his environment, and from them to find meaning in terms of his identity, his extended family, his community, and his culture. Not only is his development "a movement from a linear to a cyclical perspective on existence" (V. Smith, *Self-Discovery* 136), but it entails the integration of the two perspectives. Like Pilate and unlike the other characters, Milkman transcends individualism and finds himself in a grand harmony with all people and all things.[26]

Milkman's quest enables him to recapture his ancestral and cultural past by embodying the essences of his family ghosts. He reaches the womb of his family (the cave) by embracing the terrifying but guiding Circe, who models Milkman's quest by fusing Western and African-American cultural traditions, life and death, and present and past. He becomes Jake as he rediscovers the lost paradise of Lincoln's Heaven in Shalimar. He then becomes Solomon as he achieves the spiritual equivalent of flying, first in his "dreamy sleep all about flying" (302) and then in his final leap (341).

Milkman also accomplishes this synthesis by partially reconciling the claims of the characters who are battling for his soul. His trip to the South begins as a response to his father's greed but becomes a repetition and extension of Pilate's previous journeys in search of community and self. His discovery of his origins, especially his solving of the mystery of Jake's bones, not only corrects Pilate's assumptions and completes her quest but also symbolically responds to his mother's preoccupation with the ghost of her father. Just as Milkman earlier bridges the gap between Pilate's and Macon's houses, so his quest unites the strengths of Pilate, Macon, and Ruth. His quest for his origins and therefore for his self answers Guitar's longing for love and racial identity as well as Hagar's need for attachment and recognition. In rejecting a present life that had proved intolerable and moribund, Milkman extends the preliminary questing gestures of not only these characters but also of Pecola, Cholly, Sula, Nel, and Ajax.

Milkman's success is most clearly conveyed through his acquiring the power to interpret correctly, to learn to read the layered meanings of texts. His initial inattention to highway signs is transformed into his fascination with them: "He read the road signs with interest now, wondering what lay beneath the names" (333). Guth identifies his "reclamation of the past" as a process of learning a new way of reading and interpreting (579), and Mobley argues that the text creates a "mosaic of narrative" in which "the reader's task is not unlike that of Milkman Dead, who must find the meaning in his complicated life story" (*Folk* 97). In a similar vein, Krumholz develops the intriguing parallels between Milkman's initiation and the "reader's ritual of initiation," which requires the reader, like Milkman, to develop new strategies and sensitivities of interpretation ("Dead" 567–69). As Milkman puts his puzzle together, the reader, like Morrison, must fuse the various pieces.

The primary "text" that Milkman must reinterpret is the actual song about Solomon. Solving the riddle of the song requires interpreting the names of his ancestors and leads to his understanding of his own name and his place in history and the community. The song comes to Milkman, and the reader, as fragments—a blues song, a children's ring game, words and names that suggest but do not clearly name Milkman's ancestors. Milkman's task is to fuse the fragments of the song as well as of the memories of Susan Byrd and others. As Barthold points out (183), the song's allusion to the biblical Song of Solomon conveys the sense of further merger, the marriage of holy bride and bridegroom.[27] The song becomes "the sacred text: a proclamation available to all, and the repository of secrets" (Fabre 113). Like Morrison's novels, the song is appropriately multiple, open-ended, and dialogic: it is "a site of preliterate re-weavings, scène, a fabric of languages alluding to a crazy-quilt of cultures, regions, religions, and affiliations" (Benston 104). In deciphering this text and his own genealogy, Milkman "reconstructs a dialectic of historical transcendence" (Willis 95), finding his own voice in the power of the sung word, literally uniting his maternal ancestor (Sing Byrd) with the song, thereby fusing native American and African-American cultures, and through this complex process synthesizing all the operative oppositions. As Mobley puts it, "As a performed ritual, the song signals a cathartic epiphany for Milkman" (*Folk* 127). Mobley also cites the song's effectiveness not only for Milkman but "as a kind of cultural glue" for the community and "as an illustration of Morrison's folk aesthetic and mythic impulse" for the reader. Since Morrison's maternal grandfather's name was John Solomon, the song is literally the song of Morrison. It is also the song about Solomon, the song that leads Pilate, Milkman, Macon, Ruth, First Corinthians, and Lena to Solomon and thus to their rightful name and place in history.

Milkman's adventure toward harmony reaches its climax when he is alone in the dark woods during the bobcat hunt.[28] Like Milkman's decoding of the song, his earlier boredom with and antagonism toward nature is reversed when he learns in this scene to hear and understand the unspoken language of the natural world: "He tried to listen with his fingertips, to hear what, if anything, the earth had to say, and it told him quickly that someone was standing behind him" (282). This power of interpretation not only saves Milkman's life but marks his integration with the underlying forces of life, establishes the solidity of his identity, and provides him with visionary wisdom. At this moment, he has put it all together, and thereafter he interprets everything with perfect accuracy: "he heard right up close the wild, wonderful sound of three baying dogs who he knew had treed a bobcat" (282) and "his sense of direction was accurate." Simultaneously, he becomes connected with the earth, no longer imagining a tilted, limping relationship: "he found himself exhilarated by simply walking the earth. Walking it like he belonged on it" (284). As a result, everything works for Milkman: he is accepted by the hunters; no longer weighted down with excessive jewelry, the peacock soars (286); and he finds loving companionship with Sweet. Having placed himself in harmony with community and cosmos, Milkman becomes the model human being—he shares the chores with Sweet, he solves the remaining puzzles of the riddle, he feels "connected" (296), he confronts Guitar in "the complete absence of fear" (298), and he revises his attitudes toward his family and Hagar, realizing his previous self-centeredness and lack of empathy. He is transformed, in short, into a hero ready for apotheosis.

Milkman's act of unifying so many disparate elements—himself, the competing claims upon him, self and community, North and South, urban and rural, and present and past—is all the more remarkable because his life and environment are fraught with counterexamples. Rather than achieving spiritual life, many characters suffer spiritual death-in-life: Ruth, Macon, Lena, First Corinthians (for most of the novel), and all the men in Danville, who "as boys . . . began to die and were dying still" (238). Many major characters die tragically, as well as innumerable minor ones (starting with Robert Smith) and many historical figures who are mentioned (John F. Kennedy, Martin Luther King, Jr., Malcolm X, Emmett Till, the four Sunday school girls).[29] In this world where "everybody wants a black man's life" (335), Milkman has cause to feel threatened and displaced: "Who were all these people roaming the world trying to kill him?" (273).

Milkman's ability to fuse everything is also remarkable because in his world people are continually trying to cut each other apart. Several deaths occur by cutting, as when Macon kills the white man in the cave with a knife, when Guitar's father is split in half by a saw, and when a nameless private in Georgia is killed "after his balls were cut off" (156). More murders by cutting are attempted or threatened: Pilate holds a knife to Reba's abuser, Hagar stalks Milkman with a butcher knife, Pilate threatens Macon in the cave with a knife, Milkman is cut with a knife in Solomon's store and in turn cuts Saul with a broken bottle, and Guitar tries to slit Milkman's throat with a wire. Metaphorically, cutting is attractive to Milkman: he is exhilarated to think of Guitar in "proximity to knife-cold terror" (178) and living "on the cutting edge." But it is also repellent: he feels that Guitar "had ripped open and was spilling blood and foolishness instead of conversation" (166). Much like the splitting in *The Bluest Eye*, the motif of cutting conveys the fragility of African-American lives and the difficulties of self-integration.

The cutting motif culminates in the bobcat-skinning scene (284–86), which extends Milkman's epiphany in the woods into his ritual rebirth. In contrast to Milkman's alienation from the black men in the barbershop, here he is initiated into the black male community. Collectively, they skin the cat, each man taking his turn with equal adeptness, as Milkman actively participates as "reader" and initiate. Since the skinning and evisceration of the bobcat eerily hint at "the physical horrors of lynching, castration, and mutilation suffered by black men (Krumholz, "Dead" 563), Milkman is thereby inducted into his racial identity and past. He is then offered the heart, symbolizing his acquisition of a new heart in communion with the natural world of the bobcat, and implying his rebirth as a new man and his penetration to the heart of himself, his ancestry, his community, and his universe. Significantly, in taking the heart he suspends thinking and acts on the intuition he has learned to trust in the woods:

"Quickly, before any thought could paralyze him, Milkman plunged both hands into the rib cage" (285–86).

The cat-skinning scene is narrated by alternating the men's physical actions with Milkman's memories of Guitar's advice. This narrative ingenuity not only heightens the dramatic impact of the scene but also works as call and response, integrating Milkman and the men as well as Milkman and Guitar and pulling into ambiguous juxtaposition competing ideas about life and death and violence and love.[30] The "counterpointed text" (Lee, "*Song*" 70) of the passage and the unresolved oppositions it raises enact the comprehensive, fluid, both/and synthesis that Milkman has attained. His mind now operates dialogically: he is absorbed in the skinning while simultaneously recapitulating his relationship with Guitar. He has achieved double-consciousness and by implication multi-consciousness. Having entered the *différance*, he is wise enough to allow the double voices to remain open, not to insist on final answers to Guitar's and now his own pressing questions: *"Can't I love what I criticize?"* and *"What else? What else? What else?"* There are no further answers to such questions because there is nothing else but love, as Pilate's dying words and Milkman's fusion intimate.

One way of placing in perspective Milkman's quest, as well as Guitar's, is to turn to sociology. William E. Cross, Jr., proposes a model of "Negro-to-Black identity transformation" (158), defined as "nigrescence, the process of becoming Black" (157). Primarily from the late 1960s to the late 1970s, during the time that Morrison wrote *Song of Solomon*, many African Americans modified their "personal identity" and their "reference group orientation" from "Negro" to "Black" (Cross 39). Cross identifies five stages of this transformation: pre-encounter, encounter, immersion-emersion, internalization, and internalization-commitment (190–223). In the pre-encounter stage, Milkman's sense of his race is low and he shares Macon's antipathy for other blacks. Milkman's encounter, as for many blacks a series of episodes (Cross 200), is spread over his truth-revealing conversations with Macon, Ruth, and Guitar and his initiatory experiences in Danville and Shalimar. In Michigan he only experiences these encounters but does not personalize them, and the process leads him to "confusion, alarm, anomie, [and] depression" (Cross 201). In contrast, Gui-

104

tar's encounter stage occurs all at once at the death of his father and is accompanied by his enduring anger toward whites.

The immersion stage, the emotional peak of the transformation, features the substitution of a new identity for the old one (Cross 202). Guitar reaches this stage well before Milkman when he becomes active in the Seven Days. In this "in-between" and emotionally exhilarated state (Cross 202), Guitar is energized by rage and racial pride. He adopts a morally dichotomized view of race and takes the path of militant confrontation (Cross 203–4). In his need to prove his own blackness, he turns inward toward black culture as he seeks the social support of the countercultural group, the Seven Days. Perhaps because of the traumatic origins of Guitar's encounter stage, he cannot progress beyond this "fascist" (Cross 205) position and remains fixed in pain, anger, exasperation, and racial hatred (Cross 208). Like Macon, whose father also died violently when he was young, and like most of the other characters in Morrison's first three novels, Guitar becomes static (Butler 68–69) and rigid (V. Smith, *Self-Discovery* 152), unable to continue the process of fusion and fragmentation.

Milkman's immersion takes the other direction identified by Cross, that of altruism, oneness with his people, and religious feeling (Cross 207). As the object of his quest changes from the materialistic to the spiritual, he undergoes repeated encounter experiences that finally lead him to the immersion stage. Specifically, he immerses himself in the quest for his ancestors, in finding his familial as well as his cultural roots, and in integrating himself with natural forces.

Unlike Guitar's fixation in the immersion stage, Milkman progresses into emersion and internalization. His return to Michigan marks his leveling off from the emotional peak of immersion and his regaining of emotional and intellectual control as he develops a more substantive and textured new self, all of which characterize emersion (Cross 207). Milkman also internalizes his new-found identity, as indicated by such markers as his "resolution of dissonance" (Cross 210); his pride, self-acceptance, and confidence; his inner peace; and his more complex relationships with others (Cross 211).

Despite the success of Milkman's nigrescence, his transformation remains truncated. Left suspended, his flight not completed, he is unable to use his new-found identity and integration to much effect.

He does not proceed to Cross's fifth stage, internalization-commitment, in which one translates one's personal sense of blackness into a plan of action or a general sense of commitment (220). Moreover, his flight, like Solomon's before him, is tainted with ambiguity: are they flights from or to? Solomon left behind Ryna and twenty-one children, and Milkman leaves behind a dead Hagar and a dead Pilate. On the other hand, unlike Robert Smith, who tried to fly *away*, he flies *toward* Guitar (Davis 336), toward a mystical union with his double, who in turn seems to recognize the transcendence of the moment and to embrace his brother, his "main man" (341).

Milkman's transformation and successful hero's quest are miraculous. As he moves from his Michigan hometown to Pennsylvania and Virginia, the novel shifts from realism to myth and magic. Milkman's adventure, associated with mythic parallels, can happen only in myth. His quest works for him, as he works through his fears, creates a new identity, rediscovers his name, integrates with his community and his culture, and completes Pilate's earlier quest.

Milkman's chronicle has parallels with American culture. America has been nearly driven asunder by competing individual agendas, it endured its "knife fight" in the Civil War, and in the 1960s and 1970s it passed through another test of its unity. Despite its motto (*e pluribus unum*), it has always held plurality and unity in a precarious balance. Similarly, *Song of Solomon* details the perils of unquestioned unity (as in Macon's and Guitar's philosophies) and the necessary but arduous process of attaining a viable pluralism (as in Pilate's and Milkman's quests). Like Milkman, American culture has ghosts it tries to mourn and to recognize, riddles it tries to decipher, and a past it tries to rediscover, acknowledge, and appropriate. Like Milkman, it is preoccupied with examining itself to find itself and with learning to love so as to conquer fear. As this novel holds together a decentered subject, a unity inclusive of oppositions, fragments, and tensions, so America tries to recognize and reconcile its disparate voices. In such quests, there can be no final "answer," since final answers mean the closure of death; therefore Milkman lives *and* dies, flies *and* falls, embraces *and* kills Guitar. Similarly, as individuals and as a culture—like Claudia, Nel, and Milkman—Americans continue reading the texts in the necessarily endless process of self-discovery.

Milkman's suspension in mid-transformation underscores the power of his experience, suggesting that it cannot be or need not be brought back into the realm of ordinary life. Such transcendence provides the book much of its power, but it also leaves unexplored the issue of translating the miracle into reality. How can Milkman's mythical experience be approximated by ordinary mortals in ordinary conditions? In *Tar Baby* Morrison makes a second attempt to combine mythical experience with realistic conditions, and in *Beloved* and *Jazz* she examines the difficulties and the possibilities of replicating Milkman's idiosyncratic solution without the aid of mythical power.

Everyone Was Out of Place: Contention and Dissolution in *Tar Baby*

Among Morrison's first six novels, *Tar Baby* is pivotal.[1] In its presentation of divided entities[2] it is like the first three, but stylistically and technically it looks forward to *Beloved* and *Jazz*. In *Tar Baby*, as in *The Bluest Eye* and *Sula*, fragmentation overshadows attempted fusions, but here the scope of fragmented entities is expanded to the societal level, including whites and several socioeconomic levels of blacks. Here also human beings are contrasted with animals and plants, and the mythical is opposed to the realistic. The attempted fusion of the extended Street household is dramatically and irrevocably shattered at the Christmas dinner, and then two of those fragments, Son and Jadine, repeat the process of attempted fusion and ultimate separation. In *Tar Baby* authoritarian control is extremely rigid, and fusion is not a process of self-development from within but a sterile fiat that characters attempt to impose on each other. When the hegemonic power structures are loosened, providing the opening for deeper self-knowledge and possible fusion, characters narcissistically reject the opportunity and instead seek new power in self-serving realignments. Instead of working through the unraveling, the breach, their identity problems, and the past, they revert to new bipolar oppositions.

The spiritual exhaustion and extreme fragmentation in this novel is suggested by the marginal presence of three minor characters with symbolic names. Both Son and Jadine have lost their souls, as implied by their separate snubbings of Alma and by her relegation to cleaning toilets. As opposed to Milkman and Paul D, who have reinforcing interactions with American Indians, Son has severed that connection in his murder of Cheyenne. And, contrary to the recuperative power of the spoken word in *Song of Solomon, Beloved,* and *Jazz,* Nommo, the homeless girl Son briefly rescues in New York, is elusive and unavailing. The characters in *Tar Baby,* lacking *nommo,* cannot retell their stories, and silence often prevails (88, 223).[3]

The setting for the first two thirds of *Tar Baby,* unlike any of Morrison's other settings, is removed from the United States, therefore avoiding the symbolic meanings, in her novels and in American culture, of North or South. Isle des Chevaliers is isolated, at "the end of the world" (7), a kind of laboratory where racial, familial, class, and gender expectations can be tested. It is both within and without the world, not on any map and therefore a potential site for deconstructive unraveling. The island is also confusing. Even its name is disputed: is it Isle des Chevaliers or Isle de Chevalier (40)? That is, does its myth entail many horsemen or one? Are those horsemen one hundred French, white noblemen or one hundred blind, black ex-slaves? What is the status of these horsemen and the swamp women?[4]

Part of the island's confusion is the two faces it presents: the apparently wild, mythic, "back" side with its thick trees and its swamp, and its human, seemingly civilized, "front" side. Nature here is urgently double-edged, explicitly structured in binary oppositions. It is unspeakably beautiful and naturally abundant, a reclaimed Garden of Eden; yet it is threatening, a hell that can physically and mentally destroy one, a "boiling graveyard" (72).[5] Its climate is idyllic, but the messages conveyed by the flora and fauna are decidedly mixed: bees have no sting but also no honey (69); orchids are abundant but the water left in them burns children's fingers (87); fog is ambiguous, like the "hair of maiden aunts" (52). Nature tends to exaggerate everything (Walther 144) as the island "vomits up color" (161). Nature, opposed to human beings on this island, always tries to reclaim its dominance, especially when human beings relinquish their controlling efforts: "Things went back to their natural state so quickly in that place" (80) and the courtyard bricks keep popping out of place (245). Morrison privileges nature, giving sentience to the flora and fauna, whose reported "thoughts" are always critical of human beings: for example, the butterflies "didn't believe" the rumor about Jadine's sealskin coat (74) and the avocado trees think that Jadine misuses the word "horseshit" (108). The implications are that the human order has been crudely imposed on nature and that human dominance is unwelcome and precarious. As a result, chaos is always just around the corner, as "this place dislocates everything" (245). Instead of a constructive loosening of the polarity between nature and civilization, instead of an embrace of a both/and perspective, the commingling of the two results in confusion: the river has become a swamp and the trees' dreams have become nightmares (8).

Similarly, L'Arbe de la Croix is peculiar. Cynthia Edelberg wonders if the name is a variant of "l'arbre de la croix," with its suggestions of the Tree of Life, Paradise, and Christ, and she concludes that instead it is a house of sorrow without Christian transcendence (230–31). It is "a wonderful house" (8), yet it is more like a "hotel" (10, 16) or a "restaurant" (31) than a home. It is a chaos of dysfunction and artfulness: "while the panes did not fit their sashes, the windowsills and door saddles were carved lovingly to perfection" (8). Characters come and go but are uncomfortable: Gideon and Thérèse never venture inside, Valerian retreats to his detached greenhouse, and Son is ill-at-ease either in the main rooms or in the Childs' quarters.[6] In general, "nobody was in his proper place" (167) and "everyone was out of place" (179). The house is described as "unrhetorical" (9), an odd word to use for a house, suggesting that communication within it is garbled and that its own message is unclear. Almost from the beginning, it is "prickly with tension" (122), tension that escalates after the discovery of Son. It becomes a "house of shadows" (202), where the borderline between sanity and insanity is blurred: "We all went crazy" (180).[7] The house is the symbol of Valerian's white, male

110

hegemony over nature, blacks, and females, and its ill effects suggest the damage inflicted by that system. Here, everyone is in limbo, suspended, unable to resolve his or her unfinished pasts (M. Walker 195). It is a place where the subconscious lurks close to the surface, where dreams and night thoughts have disproportionate influence. It is a house of contentions, as predicted by the epigraph, with its allusion to the contentions in the house of Chloe, Morrison's given name. Similar subliminal forces and tensions in Morrison's other novels lead characters to constructive reworking of their psyches, but not here.[8]

Perception in and around this house is problematic. The usually reliable narrator assures readers that "only the bougainvillea" saw Jadine standing naked near the window (77), but Gideon later tells Thérèse that he saw her (91). Normally observant characters, such as the Childs and the Streets, do not realize that every "Mary" whom Gideon brings to work at the house is the same Thérèse. Things sometimes look different at different times or to different characters. For example, the scene of Valerian and Son laughing in the greenhouse is presented three times, first when Jadine sees and overhears them (109), second when she shocks Margaret with the news (110), and third when the narrator reports the scene directly (127). As in the initial discovery of Son in Margaret's closet, there are frequent discrepancies between what characters see, what they report, how other characters interpret the report, and what the narrator later verifies as the truth.[9]

Like Morrison's first three novels, *Tar Baby* addresses the difficulties of divided identities, parent-child relations, and relations between couples, but this novel more explicitly extends the investigation to broader social and cultural dimensions. The extended household at L'Arbe de la Croix consists of four couples, ranging from upper-class whites to lower-class blacks and spanning two generations. It represents a partial microcosm of American culture,[10] and the attempted integration of these four couples, in particular at the Christmas dinner, is a symbolic and forced attempt to integrate whites and blacks. This microcosm stresses the racial and class divisions in American society to the extent that integration is unattainable, as the tensions erupt in unresolvable personal insults and arguments. Margaret exhibits overtly racist attitudes after Son is found in her closet, and Valerian, beneath his gentlemanly pose, is also explicitly racist, referring to Son, Ondine, and Sydney as "these people" (177). Behind the facade, the Street household resembles a stereotypical antebellum plantation, with its aristocratic and bigoted patriarch, its neurotic white lady, its house servants caught between their class superiority over the field hands and their subservience to the whites, and its field hands who surreptitiously fight their ineffectual battles against the prevailing system.[11] Once that patriarchal, white power structure is loosened, instead of seeking fruitful reconstructions of individuals, families, or community, the characters reestablish new hegemonies: after the initial upset caused by the discovery of Son, "the house *locked* back together" (141, emphasis added).

Before Son's disruptive arrival, the residents of L'Arbe de la Croix lead fragmented and unfulfilled lives. Despite the appearance of civility and order, the household is fractured along deeply divisive fault lines of race, class, and gender, and each character is profoundly uneasy. Each is dominated by the repressively hierarchical structure and hence is unable and/or unwilling to continue forming the self, to deepen relationships with others or to renegotiate the past. Each person's fragmentation is implied by the two or more names each goes by, for example, Jade/Jadine, Ondine/Nanadine, Margaret Lenore/ Margarette, Gideon/Yardman (Rigney 43).

The alleged head of the household, Valerian, is, like the candy that was named for him, a flop.[12] He is in self-imposed exile from Philadelphia, further exiling himself to his greenhouse and to impersonal formality. His efforts to produce northern flowers in his greenhouse symbolize his artificiality, his "pseudo-nurturance" (Erickson 296). Blithely sheltered in his convictions of white, male supremacy, he is more interested in ownership and authority, as his emperor's name and his "head-of-a-coin" profile imply. His identity is frozen in the self-congratulatory and ego-fulfilling sterility of monolithic authority. Fearful of dying, he tries to remain a child, "want[ing] his own youth again and a place to spend it" (46) and thinking of himself as only thirty-nine (122).[13] Despite this refusal to acknowledge his age, he is repeatedly associated with death. His first wife is dead, along with their two aborted children. He tries to revive his dead past and to regain his lost innocence (B. Jones, "Garden" 119), for example by asking for ollieballen for Christmas and by communicating with the ghosts of his past (11, 123). He tries to reproduce the washhouse and washerwoman, which remind him of the only time he was able to mourn his dead father. His embrace of Son similarly attempts to regain his own son who is essentially dead to him. Both attempts at fusion only reinforce his isolation, the inadequacy of his unitary self and his blindness to the need to reconstitute his identity and his position. He has no community, no one to talk intimately with, no one with whom to share his life story.

Since Valerian's existence is a false reconstruction of a failed life and a dead past, he cannot tolerate the revelation of Margaret's abuse of Michael, for it demonstrates the falseness of his constructions: "Valerian had received no message, but after waiting so long, to receive, know and deliver its contents, imperceptibly he had made it up. Made up the information he was waiting for. Preoccupied himself with the construction of the world and its inhabitants according to this imagined message. But had chosen not to know the real message that his son had mailed to him from underneath the sink" (209). If his perceptions of Michael were so blind, then his perceptions of everyone, including himself, are no longer reliable. For some of Morrison's characters, the disruption of lifelong beliefs leads to the constructive rebuilding of identity, but Valerian can only excuse himself and the situation by concluding that it "is not the world at all" (202), by denying, in Werner's terms, the "is-ness of the world" ("Briar" 160). Once his myth of male, Euro-American dominance collapses, he withdraws into noncommunication (his stuttering) and incompetence.

Margaret is victimized by the American worship of female beauty. Displaced by her beauty, she is the reverse of Pecola, who is displaced by her lack of and longing for beauty. Like Pecola, she is denied subjectivity by her parents, who cannot believe in her legitimacy. After they "withdrew attention" she withdraws into "separateness" and "loneliness" (48), fragmented from human contact: "she was gone and other people were where they belonged." After Valerian reifies her as the Principal Beauty of Maine, she retreats into a shell of guilt and passive aggression, smooth on the inside but hardened on the outside, "all her tips in shining order" (36). A child thrown into the lion's den of Valerian and his sophisticated circle, she is denied a personal relationship with Ondine and is unable to interact with other adults. The only thing she can influence is her baby, so, as Ruth tries to control Milkman in a similar incest wish (Rubenstein 148), she begins to reify Michael and to control him through abuse. She pricks his body—to deflate him, to prevent him from growing beyond her control and from achieving the selfhood that she was denied, and, as Elizabeth House claims, to retaliate against Valerian's power over her (199). But the repression of this sin pushes her farther away from a healthy self. She settles for surfaces—beauty and beauty products—and she loses the ability to function in her world; driven by Valerian's verbal abuse into near-paranoia, she becomes confused about reality and is driven nearly crazy by the island (159), which to her is "nowhere" (23) and a "graveyard" (72).

After the disruptive Christmas dinner, Margaret surprisingly seems to emerge from her frozen, dysfunctional identity. The revelation of her guilt provides relief and release, allowing her some room to grow and some control over her life. After years of not having "the dream she ought to" (51), she has it (202). She can discuss the abuse with Valerian, she can ask Ondine to forgive her, and she can ask Valerian to punish her. She is stronger and smarter than ever: "Margaret looked flushed and sparkly, her movements directed and sure" (238). She takes advantage of the breakdown of the old order, however, not to embrace the fluidity but narcissistically to reverse it, to substitute her own hegemony for Valerian's: she relishes her new power, becoming "a confident curator" (240). Ironically, despite her revival, Margaret's role remains secondary: as Ondine points out, Valerian is "still the center of everything."[14]

Sydney and Ondine serve their employers flawlessly, but anger over their secondary status simmers just below the surface in Sydney and often above the surface in Ondine. They appear to love their niece and to be proud of her accomplishments, but they expect a "return" from their investment in her, namely that she will take care of them in the future.[15] Sydney is the perfect butler, not only in the sense that he serves flawlessly, but also because he mirrors Valerian's authority. He is smugly self-satisfied, enjoying his status as "one of those Philadelphia Negroes—the proudest people in the race" (51). In his and Ondine's rooms, he shadows Valerian's authority in the larger house, sitting at the head of the table (27), assiduously protecting Ondine from heavy work, and outraged by Son's challenge to *his* household order. Like Margaret, his response to the household fragmentation is not to reinvestigate his identity, but to usurp Valerian's power.

Ondine's life is more complicated because she is doubly displaced as a black woman and because she is burdened with the secret of Margaret's abuse of Michael. Her anger and criticism directed at the Streets have driven her into "psychological disengagement" (Werner, "Briar" 161). She is openly hostile toward Margaret, calling her a "hussy" (31) and "fed up" with her hysteria about Son being in her closet (66). She adopts the role of "ranking officer" (67), which reflects her displaced desire for power and her impatience at not having much of it. Her lifelong struggles, however, have left her "tired" (81) and "uneasy" (82), so that, when Son questions Valerian's authority at the Christmas dinner, Ondine's anger and strength overflow in her verbal and then physical attacks on her employers. She expresses her wish as well as her perception of the actual state of the household when she proclaims, "I am the woman in this house" (180). But she finds less satisfaction in Valerian's downfall than do Margaret and Sydney: "in the mood for death" (240), she realizes that the household still revolves around him. She remains dissatisfied with Jadine, whom she expects to look after her and Sydney, "to care about me" (242). She says that her motive is for Jadine to care about her for Jadine's sake, but her ensuing conversation with her husband reveals her self-centered martyrdom: "[Michael's] okay now. Doin fine. But I'm not responsible for that, no. I'm responsible for not telling nobody. . . . Then I take another one in my heart, your brother's baby girl. Another one not from my womb, and I stand on my feet thirty years so she wouldn't have to. And did without so she wouldn't have to. And she couldn't think of nothing better to do than buy me some shoes I can't wear, a dress I shouldn't, and run off with the first pair of pants that steps in the door" (244).

Until she and Son leave L'Arbe de la Croix, Jadine is also leading a disingenuous life. She is torn between her conscious desire to accept Valerian's patronage, Ryk's sealskin coat, and the worldly success in the white world they promise, and her subconscious anxieties about her race and gender, represented by the woman in yellow, the swamp women, and the night women who haunt her. These women are noticeably dark-skinned, specifically African in the case of the woman in yellow, and they are associated with fertility—the woman's eggs and the night women's bared breasts. The woman in yellow recalls two powerful female elders: Nel's grandmother Rochelle, who wears yellow, and Pilate, who is also associated with eggs. Jadine is divided between glitzy, white materialism and her maternal and racial instincts, and she can only see the two as mutually exclusive choices (Mobley, "Narrative" 290). This schism results in her ambivalent feelings toward the other members of the household. Although she genuinely appreciates Valerian's patronage, she plays a proper but hypocritical role for him and Margaret. She is tolerant of her patrons, finding them "decent" (57), but she is disturbed by Margaret's racism and she is "not interested in" (65) either one, her mind going into "automatic park" while talking with Valerian.[16] She also plays with Sydney and Ondine, talking about opening a shop with them, but knowing that commitment to them conflicts with her career goals.

Jadine's fragmentation is evident in her conflicting traits. She is simultaneously tough, having resolved "never to be broken in the hands of any man" (106), and yet unsure of herself, wavering about whether to tell Valerian about Son's physical advances (107). She wants to let loose her desire for Son, "the small dark dogs galloping on silver feet" (97), yet she must hold firmly to their leash. She is curiously aloof, self-consciously "applying the principles of a survey course in psychology" to Valerian and Margaret (56–57), and yet emotionally involved, admiring Valerian's style ("You had to give it to him. He was marvelous" [78]), trying to please Sydney and Ondine, and both loving and hating Son. This promising multiplicity, recalling Milkman's pre-quest tensions, might have propelled Jadine to enter the deconstructive split and to re-form herself along the lines of Milkman's transformation, but such positive reconstruction does not occur in this novel; instead the tensions merely "jangle" Jadine's nerves (155), and she runs first to Son and then to Paris.

Like Pauline and Sula, Jadine lacks an appropriate art form. As

Keith Byerman points out, instead of becoming an artist, she chose to study art history, and she is the product of art: a model, not a designer (213). Similarly, Rigney notes that Jadine both distances herself from reality when she takes photographs in Eloe and is herself "an 'art object' " (*Voices* 58–59). Lacking the artistic impulse, she, like the other residents at L'Arbe, lacks the creativity needed to live in double-consciousness: she "resists forms of community that draw attention to the gap between the signifier and signified, the forms basic to the African-American tradition" (Werner, "Briar" 163). Consequently, she must rely on Valerian's male, Eurocentric, and materialistic system, and she remains locked in that position.

At the economic bottom of this household is its excluded underclass, Gideon and Thérèse. Denied individual names and therefore identities by the house's rulers, these two try to subvert the order imposed by the main household: Gideon pretends that he cannot read, Thérèse is rehired over and over as "Mary," they break open a window to give "chocolate-eater" access to the house, and they confiscate the prized apples. Gideon is a foil for Son, having attempted to make his fortune in the United States and now content to enjoy the good, albeit poor, life in the islands. Unlike his biblical namesake, he seems not to have been called by God nor to be a deliverer or savior of his people.

Thérèse is like Pilate (T. Harris, *Fiction* 147), a *griot* for the questing hero, connected even more explicitly than Pilate to natural and mythical lore: she can hear the soldier ants, she can feel the ocean currents, and her world is populated with the mythical horsemen and swamp women. Her belief in her own magical breasts associates her with the breast-baring night women who visit Jadine in Eloe. According to Gideon, she is a descendant of the blind slaves who haunt the island and who "s[ee] with the eye of the mind" (131). Although Missy Dehn Kubitschek argues that Thérèse has only a partial perspective that is not necessarily correct (137) and Werner alleges that she has no knowledge of whites ("Briar" 158), her spirituality, her harmony with nature, and her storytelling ability suggest her power. It is no accident that Thérèse's last name is Foucault, which links her with Michel Foucault's questioning of Western systems of discipline and order as well as his privileging of spirituality. Like her namesake, Thérèse constructs a countermyth about Western culture and in so doing lives a richly developed fantasy life.

Thérèse is privileged in several other ways. Her name and her blindness associate her with Tiresias and his wisdom (Hawthorne 100). Just as Morrison praises the real women in the epigraph for knowing "their true and ancient properties," Thérèse criticizes Jadine for having "forgotten her ancient properties" (263; Erickson 304). In addition, in marked contrast to the other characters, she is a story-teller (Erickson 303; Werner, "Briar" 158) and an image-maker. When she invents a scenario to explain Son's presence in the house, she becomes completely involved in her creation: "The more she invented the more she rocked" (92). She thus parallels the narrator and the author as verbal meaning-makers. She also parallels them by inventing epithets for characters: she calls Son "chocolate-eater," Ondine "machete-hair," Sydney "bow-tie," and Jadine "fast-ass," just as the narrator uses epithets like "blue-if-it's-a-boy blue eyes" for Margaret and "savannahs in his eyes" for Son. In the novel's final scene, she replaces the water-lady of the opening scene, in harmony with nature, guiding Son, renewing him in her own image (Erickson 303).

Thérèse (and, through her, Gideon) embody what is absent in the other characters. Living genuine lives, in harmony with themselves, each other, their community, and nature, they possess the constructive fusion so lacking in the others. At home in the islands, they alone are free of the fear and tension that paralyze and confuse everyone else. The implication is that one must be "at home," in harmony with the cosmos, in order to work through the healing process of fusion and fragmentation. Nevertheless, in the fragmented climate of this novel, these relatively fulfilled characters are relegated to minor roles in the wings, as opposed to Milkman, Sethe, Paul D, Joe, and Violet, who occupy center stage in their novels.

In addition to their inability to wrestle constructively with their fragmentations, the inside inhabitants of this chaotic household are beset with several common problems. Like the Wrights and the Deads, their lives are inauthentic, which is conveyed by the motifs of appearances and falsity. As her "frownies" suggest (18), Margaret is more concerned with appearances than reality, and Valerian can present a dazzling but superficial front: "his eyes . . . were all reflection, like mirrors" (62).[17] Margaret tries to lure Michael for Christmas with the bait of a poet, whom Valerian considers a "fake" (65). Valerian is struggling over his diet, which prompts Ondine to rail against the substitutes: "Fake this. Fake that" (30). Jadine is troubled by the superficiality, if not fakeness, of her life, for, as a model, the value of her existence is not her self but her image, an image that is easy to manipulate (37). In her indefinite search for a more authentic existence, she lives a fake one, temporarily "playing store" (41) with her aunt and uncle.

Part of the characters' fragmented lack of authenticity is the transitory nature of their existences. Margaret wants to return to Philadelphia, and Ondine complains about "everything temporary like this" (30). Jadine is in flight, in retreat from her subconscious fears, uncertain what to do about Ryk and her career. After Margaret proposes that she and Jadine run away, Jadine does flee to another transitory life with Son. Jadine frets about being an orphan, and everyone except Gideon and Thérèse is a metaphysical orphan, isolated, not at home.

As in *Song of Solomon*, Morrison uses fear to dramatize her characters.[18] Even though the narrator declares that "in the Caribbean there is no fear" (36), fear permeates the house and the novel. Thérèse senses that Ondine is "subdued—by fear" (89). Jadine, provoked to leave Paris by her fear of the woman in yellow, is awakened by the fear of her dream of large women's hats (37). After Son's arrival she is attracted to him yet fears him and her lust for him. Margaret is terrified when she discovers Son, and her fear remains palpable: when Jadine asks "Are you scared?", she replies, "Not really. Well, sort of" (110); and later when Son comes to apologize to her, she is again startled: " 'I scare you?' 'No. Yes' " (168). As Son detects, everyone except Valerian is fearful: "They are frightened, he thought. All but the old man" (114). Their fear is understandable, but the fact that a stranger has the power to undermine who they are and what they are doing also suggests the precariousness of their identities. Unlike *Song of Solomon*, in which Milkman and Guitar convert fear to inner strength, here characters' fears are immobilizing, because these characters refuse to acknowledge the fear and therefore do not work toward self-knowledge and self-acceptance.

The most pervasive problem for this tense household is the issue of control, which reflects the residents' preoccupations with hierarchy and authority. Valerian is preoccupied with his ability to control things and people. He seeks total control over nature, including the ants and his cyclamens, he tries to control everyone in the household, and he would like to extend his control indefinitely: "A lot of life *is* outside [my control] and frequently it's the part that most needs control" (60). Margaret and Valerian's exchange about the food Ondine prepares illustrates the multiple power battles: Margaret says, "They tell *us* what to eat. Who's working for who?" and Valerian corrects her grammar with "Whom" (19). Thus, while Valerian and Margaret battle their servants, they also battle each other. The latter power struggle is particularly nasty, as Valerian abuses Margaret whenever they are together and especially at the dinner table. But Margaret fights back in her passive-aggressive way, for example relishing her "little victory with the mango" (20).

At the same time that Valerian and Margaret battle each other, Sydney and Ondine struggle to preserve their self-respect by resisting their employers and by asserting their control over Gideon and Thérèse. Ondine exults in her job with its "beautiful surroundings which included her own territory where she alone governed" (82). Later, she is offended when Margaret intrudes on that territory and her rights by insisting on cooking the Christmas dinner. When Valerian treats Son as a guest, Sydney's feelings of power and self-respect are threatened; he laments that he "can't run a house like this with everybody doing whatever comes to mind" (83), and he complains about "letting people run over you." The Childs' middle status is problematic (Werner, "Briar" 157), and it bothers them that first Jadine and now Son are treated as equals by the Streets (85). Such tensions and the Childs' middle status might have enabled them to forge a constructive mediating position or a productive multiplicity, but, like Jadine, they do not take advantage of the opportunity.

Instead of working through the power issue, the characters reduce it to two questions: who owns the house and who is on whose side. Valerian is obsessive about his authority over the house, insisting on "his household" (124) and angrily shouting "Whose house is this?" (177) when Son defies his order to leave. But the characters do not realize that the possession of the house is not an either/or issue. Before Son is discovered, he "owns" it during the nights: "It became his, sort of. A nighttime possession" (119). Sydney, echoing Valerian, also insists on his rights within this house, asserting that "I live here too" (84), contending "But it's my home" (245), and staunchly defending his part of the house when he finds Son talking to Ondine: "What are you doing in my place?" (138). He and Ondine, fearful of the lack of order, can only insist on their narrowly personal needs as they worry about their lack of security and lack of a place, especially when Son's arrival puts the house in turmoil; as Ondine says, "We don't have a place of our own" (166).

These issues of ownership, servitude, and place duplicate the historical circumstances of white hegemony in America. As a microcosm of American culture, the situation on the island exposes the racism, sexism, and classism of the mainstream culture. The Childs, including Jadine, represent the striving African-American middle class, trying to make the best of their secondary status; Son recalls the more militant approach of dispossessed African Americans; and Gideon and Thérèse suggest the spiritually based counterculture developed by African Americans in reaction to white power. Eleanor Traylor associates this fragmentation with endemic divisions within American culture and claims that Morrison, like other African-American writers, reveals the effects of such disconnection and works at possibilities of wholeness (147–48).

Along with the issue of possession, the turmoil in the house raises questions about loyalties. When Ondine questions Sydney's efforts to patrol the house, he challenges her, "Whose side you on?" (86). Ondine reassures him: "Your side, naturally. Our side." The shift from "your" to "our" quickly closes the potential gap between his side and hers. But "our" is problematic throughout the novel, as the question of racial unity conflicts with familial and personal loyalties, and as the characters wrongly assume that others must be either on one's side or against it. When Jadine and Son discuss his "stealing," Jadine says, "It depends on what you want from us" (101), thereby placing herself on the side of the household. Son is disturbed by this alle-

121

giance, taking it as Jadine's racial betrayal: "Us? You call yourself 'us'?" Jadine is quite clear on this ("Of course. I live here"), but her deepest loyalties are to herself alone: "I belong to me." The debate over personal pronouns and their implications continues when Sydney, mollified by Son, argues with Ondine that Son is "one of us" (164). Then at the Christmas dinner Sydney uses "we" to assert his and Ondine's rights when he questions Valerian's inconsistency in welcoming Son but then firing Gideon and Thérèse: "We were slighted by taking in one thief and now we are slighted by letting another go" (176). The "we" refers to himself and Ondine who, in Sydney's view, should have been given authority over the matter: "I just think we should have been informed. We would have let them go ourselves, probably." Sydney and Ondine "probably" would have replicated Valerian's power play on the yard servants, but Sydney insists on his and his wife's prerogative to do so or not to do so. Ondine makes the same point more bellicosely when she attacks Margaret: "She wants to meddle in my kitchen, fooling around with pies. And *my* help gets fired!" (178). When Valerian questions her pronoun, "*Your* kitchen? *Your* help?", she reiterates, "Yes my kitchen and yes my help. If not mine, whose?" Questions of possession, power, and loyalty, questions that the hierarchical system engenders, are repeatedly raised but, based on narrow, polarized assumptions, cannot be answered. In this novel the characters cannot transform the divisions into the bases for new identities.

Into this troubling house with its troubled inhabitants comes the mysterious stranger. Son brings to the surface the repressed secrets, individual problems, and relational tensions of the others.[19] "The center of a primal consciousness" (Berret 277), he has connections to the subconscious, rising out of the sea, trying to manipulate Jadine's dreams (102), and having an unspoken affinity with Thérèse. He has been everywhere and he knows about everything, from war to piano-playing to cures for bunions to ants and cyclamens. Whereas Valerian tries to kill the ants, Son successfully redirects them with mirrors, much as he manipulates the other characters with his opaque facades.

With his multiple identities, Son is a trickster figure, Morrison's most recognizable one.[20] Like the trickster figures described by Lawrence Levine, Son's power is associated with food (chocolate, apples) and sexual conquest (*Black* 108–10). He is like a musician, "a jazz virtuoso" (Berret 278), able to play other people as instruments. He has innumerable names and identities, and he assumes numerous guises, "manag[ing] a face for everybody but [Jadine]" (142). For Valerian he is the affable Uncle Tom, complete with dialect (125–28). For Ondine and Sydney he becomes the self-deprecatory "outlaw" obeying what his "mama" taught him (138). For Gideon and Thérèse he is the conquering hero from the States, a "well-heeled man" (129). Except for Wild, he is the wildest of Morrison's wild characters, free from society's constraints, freer than Cholly, Sula, or Guitar, and, like them, unassimilated and untied. He is one of the "undocumented men" (142), wandering the earth without "things to gather" (1) or ties to bind. Like tricksters, he is both bad and good, bringing bad luck (158) and good luck (161). He befriends everyone in the house but he disrupts it, and he attracts Jadine's love as well as her disgust. He is a pariah, living outside community standards, but, unlike Cholly and Sula, he does subvert the community he enters. He is freer and hence more dangerous than Cholly, Sula, or Guitar.

One dimension of Son's trickster-ness is that he is ambiguously linked to Jesus Christ. His name, his arrival at Christmas, and his harmony with nature mark the association, which is strengthened by his startling effects on the other characters. He is Christlike yet not Christlike.[21] This intermediary and ambiguous status—in the *différance*—is a source of his power as deconstructive agent. A related source is his insider/outsider status, his wildness—like Cholly's, Sula's, and Guitar's before him and Sixo's and Wild's in the novels to come.

Son upsets the household with his outlaw behavior and appearance, then disarms it with his charm, and finally throws it into turmoil with his seemingly innocent but undoubtedly calculated remark at the Christmas dinner: "Too bad Gideon couldn't come" (173). It *is* too bad, but the politics on which L'Arbe de la Croix rest, like those on which the United States rests, do not allow for everyone, certainly not the lowest social rung, to sit at the table. In the ensuing confrontation between Valerian and Son, "the man who respected industry looked over a gulf at the man who prized fraternity" (173).

In spite of his power and freedom, Son, like the others in this novel, has his own problems that prevent him from achieving constructive fusion. Having so many identities that he "did not always know who he was" (142), he is aimless, "trying to think what his next step should be" (118). He is a folk character unable to adapt folk ways to the modern world (Coleman 71). Although committed to his African-American heritage, he has no acceptable past: his family is splintered, he can send money but no words to his father, and life in Eloe is not a realistic option. "He had chosen solitude," but "something had come loose in him" (142) to the extent that he loses his love for Eloe and abandons his soul (Alma) in his pursuit of Jadine (Edelberg 235). He no longer knows where he is going, repeatedly jumping ship as his successive choices do not work out: "each possibility seemed fine and each seemed stupid" (118), and "nothing was clear." He champions fraternity in the duel with Valerian but later he "give[s] up fraternity" (257). Trapped in an unretrievable past and unable to forge a future (Christian, *Black Feminist* 79), he is a fugitive priding himself on his independence, yet he is homesick with no home to return to. He lacks understanding of his own emotions, inexplicably moved to tears by the sight of Gideon's back (119–20) and confused by the depth of his attraction for Jadine. Like the island, the house, and the house's residents, he is "all mixed up" (257).

After the abortive attempt to force the fusion of the household at L'Arbe de la Croix and the resounding fragmentation of that community into its four couples, Morrison follows Jadine and Son in their similarly abortive attempt to force a new unity. Their struggle reenacts many of the same issues that plague the larger household, and like the residents at L'Arbe they are constantly at odds, not able to comprehend themselves or their problems. Fear continues to be a destructive factor, for example in Son's concern for the fear he senses in all the children in New York City (185) and in Jadine's reoccurring fears of the night women. In addition, like the false assumptions in the larger household, Jadine's and Son's assumptions about their relationship are self-serving and therefore inadequate. Each tries to change the other to fit his or her image: " 'Why do you want to *change* me?' 'Why do you want to change *me*?' " (229). Each wants fusion only on his or her prescriptive terms; neither will engage deeply in the process of identity-formation and relationship-building.

For each, changing the other means rescuing him or her.[22] Jadine imagines that she is "rescuing him from the night women who wanted him for themselves" (231), whereas the night women are her problem, not his. Son "thought he was rescuing her from Valerian, meaning *them*, the aliens," that is to say, whites. He concocts a fanciful slave-narrative scenario: "He saw it all as a rescue: first tearing her mind away from that blinding awe. Then the physical escape from the plantation" (189). Son represents the mythical black past and Jadine represents one version of an idealized black future in the white world, but neither can become a place for the other and they cannot find sufficient common ground. In either case, but especially in Son's since he thinks he needs to reform Jadine's mind, they reify each other, making the other fit their need for heroism and leadership. In so doing, each tries to possess the other, to place the other in the proper and subservient role in his or her fantasy. In this way, they merely repeat the "silly game" (179) of the larger household.

Therefore, almost inevitably, their love becomes a power struggle between two new hegemonies, symbolized by the two settings: her New York and his Eloe (Mobley, "Narrative" 289). He reacts to New York with sadness and horror (189), she with giddiness (190). In Eloe, the roles are reversed: he is proud and nostalgic, she is bored and scared. Neither can function in the other's world: no common life, no real communication, no fusion. Like the obvious contrasts between Eloe and New York, Son and Jadine are opposites. According to Morrison, Jadine is committed to the contemporary in disregard for the past, whereas Son is the opposite (B. Jones, "Interview" 138). She is the assimilationist, he the separatist (M. Walker 197); she the insider, he the outsider (Rubenstein 158); she the Euro-American wanting to be "on time," he the African wanting to be "in time" (229). Together, their clash of wills and values creates a dialectic without synthesis (Rubenstein 158), more fragmentation without fusion.

Their power struggle becomes increasingly overt. In Eloe, they feud over how long and where to stay. Jadine fights Son through his friend Soldier, who, as his name suggests, is unrelentingly hostile toward her. He announces that "you can't leave today" (220) because Ernie Paul, "one of us," is coming. "Us," as at L'Arbe de la Croix, is a loaded term, in this case excluding Jadine. Jadine responds to this news in prizefighting terms: "TKO, thought Jadine, but she didn't hang up her gloves." The blows between Jadine and Son become increasingly punitive, especially after they return to New York, where the battle is a mutual struggle for dominance: "Each was pulling the other away from the maw of hell" (232). Each tries to rescue the other because each is positive that his or her view is the only correct one: each knows the truth (227) and "each knew the world as it was meant or ought to be" (232). Despite their physical liberation from the un-healthy mix of depressing fragmentation and forced fusion at L'Arbe, both insist on their fixed, monologic perspectives.

Their battle extends to issues of money, race (notably, Jadine's gratitude toward Valerian), and, most significantly, the past and the future: "One had a past, the other a future and each one bore the culture to save the race in his hands. Mama-spoiled black man, will you mature with me? Culture-bearing black woman, whose culture are you bearing?" (232). Son is homesick for Eloe, for his Old Man, and for his old friends, still grieving for Cheyenne and still feeling guilty about her death. He argues for traditional African-American values and roles, for the "pie-women," for all-black communities like Eloe, for refusing to accept white patronage, indeed for abdicating from the white-dominated system. Unfortunately for Son, the past that he craves is no longer available to him. He cannot bring Chey-enne back, and, despite an enjoyable few days, even he is not content in Eloe, where the conservative sexual mores of his father, Aunt Rosa, and the rest of the town are at odds with his style and his wildness. Significantly, his actions and thoughts in Eloe are rarely reported. Unlike Shalimar, in which Milkman does find unity and community, Eloe remains a dead end of nostalgia for Son. As for all of Morrison's characters, the past cannot be recovered by Son without a prolonged and precarious effort of remembering, retelling, and reintegrating, and Son cannot or will not make such an effort.

In contrast to Son's focus on the past, Jadine directs herself in-creasingly toward the future. She has multiple, albeit conflicting, plans for herself, and she takes over the planning for Son's future.

But this attempt cannot succeed, because Son refuses to accept any planned future, because neither can live in each other's future just as neither can live in each other's past or chosen locale, and because each person must work through his or her own plans and growth. Each appears to have choices, as Byerman argues (211–12), but these choices become less and less mutual as each character clings more tenaciously to a unitary stance and avoids the risk of the breach.

The question of what Son and Jadine will do, which drives the plot after the Christmas dinner, becomes not what they will do together but what each will do separately; the question of fragmentation supersedes the question of fusion. In choosing Paris, Jadine chooses herself, rejecting both Son and her aunt and uncle. She moves inward, becoming "a closed-away orphan" (233) and enjoying being by herself: "Aloneness tasted good" (237).[23] Just as she retreated from Paris and the woman in yellow, she retreats from the complexities of life with Son or with Sydney and Ondine.[24] She chooses the comforting order of her model's life, symbolically smoothing away the rough edge of her fingernail as she runs from the chaos of life with Son (250; T. Harris, *Fiction* 126). She becomes the ant queen, but ants can be tricked by mirrors. She thinks she can be independent of men, "having refused to be broken in the big ugly hands of any man" (237), but she is still disconnected from the feminine in herself. She thinks she can rely only on herself ("She *was* the safety she longed for" [250]), and she is determined to "let loose the dogs, tangle with the woman in yellow—with her and with all the night women who had *looked* at her" (250), but she does not realize the need for community, for telling one's story, for listening to others, for continual reconstitution of the past and the self.

Jadine deludes herself into accepting an either/or choice, which, like most such choices, offers no real solution.[25] Sprung loose from her entrapment, she is momentarily free to reconstitute herself, but she can only conceive of her life in fixed formulations. So, for her, modeling in Paris looks better than fighting with Son or playing with Sydney and Ondine, yet that choice appears doomed since she has not honestly dealt with her demons. Whereas her self-reliance and determination are admirable, the novel's discourse undermines her. In choosing Paris and the white world of material success, she aligns herself against traditional community values and specifically against black women. Twice Morrison privileges exactly what Jadine rejects. The dedication calls attention to the values of maternal relationships, implied by its invocation of women in Morrison's family "and each of their sisters."[26] By making explicit the women's married status, the dedication also privileges traditional female roles. Morrison praises the women because they "knew their true and ancient properties." This powerful phrase is echoed at the end of the novel by Thérèse, whose spiritual wisdom is validated throughout, when she urges Son to forget Jadine: "There is nothing in her parts for you. She has forgotten her ancient properties" (263).

If Jadine's quest is thus devalued, Son's is at best ambiguous. Unlike Jadine, he has the rhetorical backing of Thérèse, who initially associates him with the island's blind horsemen. His journey into myth also seems validated by the narrator's rebirth imagery.[27] He emerges from the sea at the opening of the novel, having yielded to the controlling ocean currents, and at the end he emerges again from "the nursing sound of the sea" (263). First, he "crawled," then he "stood up," then "he took a few tentative steps," then "he walked steadier," and finally, fully grown as it were, "he ran." As in the first scene, nature, normally hostile to and astonished by human beings on this island, is ready to assist him: "The mist lifted and the trees stepped back a bit as if to make the way easier for a certain kind of man" (263–64).

Nevertheless, it is hard to credit Son's accomplishments. Prior to this last scene, he is marked by confusion. In his battle with Jadine, he, much more than she, resorts to meanness, attacking her for her dependence on Valerian and accusing her of becoming a "mammy" if she has a white man's baby (232). After she leaves, he moons over the pictures of Eloe, as if he could still return there (253–54). Despite their obvious incompatibility, he cannot bear the thought of losing Jadine. Then, the sight of Alma Estée throws him into even more confusion about his "original dime," his buddies from Eloe, and his entire life and self: "It was all mixed up. He did not know what to think or feel" (258). His feelings for Jadine also are mixed up: "he had not wanted to love her because he could not survive losing her. But it was done. Already done and he was in it; stuck in it and revolted by the possibility of being freed" (259). Instead of using his freedom to further the process of spiritual identity formation, he is repelled by it. He feels violent and desperate, hardly like a lover: "He wanted to find her but he wanted to smash something too." He is driven, feeling that he has no alternatives: "I don't have a choice. There's nothing else for me to do" (260). So, with a "jaw's harp in his head" (261), he places himself in Thérèse's hands. Upon their arrival at the back side of the island, he keeps asking her, "Are you sure?" (262, 263), meaning not only if she's sure of where they are but symbolically if this is what he should be doing.

Son's "quest" thus becomes unheroic and passive, in some ways a retreat comparable to Jadine's two retreats. Son's flight into the island raises as many questions as it answers, even more so than Milkman's ambiguous leap into myth. Like Milkman's leap, Son's flight remains an idiosyncratic solution, perhaps the best option for him but an option not available to anyone else. Like Sula, his quest is over, but not completed, for both characters realize that they have no place in the community and yet that they cannot tolerate living alone. They represent the free energy of the disruptive pariah, energy that the community cannot contain, and energy that ultimately has no worldly place.

Like the myth of flying home to Africa in *Song of Solomon*, the tar baby myth undergirds this novel. Here, as in the previous novel, Morrison sounds a chord—an apparently one-dimensional allusion to the myth—and then plays the changes on that chord by suggesting endless versions and interpretations of the myth. Taking the conventional white version of the tar baby myth, a first cut indicates that Jadine is the tar baby, a trap constructed by Valerian (the white farmer) to capture Son (the wily rabbit), who manages to escape into the briar patch of the mythical island.[28] As soon as one grasps this initial version/reading, however, other possibilities erupt. For example, the straightforward interpretation of the myth's application leaves open the question of why Valerian would want to capture Son. Morrison herself unravels the issue:

Why was the tar baby formed, to what purpose, what was the farmer trying to protect, and why did he think the doll would be attractive to the rabbit—what did he know, and what was his big mistake? Why does the tar baby cooperate with the farmer, and do the things the farmer wishes to protect wish to be protected? What makes his job more important than the rabbit's, why does he believe that a briar patch is sufficient punishment, what does the briar patch represent to the rabbit, to the tar baby, and to the farmer? ("Memory" 389).

More possibilities emerge because Son seems to be as much an enticing tar baby for Jadine as she is for him,[29] and her flight to Paris can be seen as her escape into her own briar patch (Scruggs, *Sweet* 172). Perhaps, too, the woman in yellow—as well as the swamp women and the night women—is the tar baby for Jadine. Instead of merely one monologic myth, Morrison insists upon multiplicity. In an interview, she calls attention to additional associations with tar: "At one time a tar pit was a holy place, at least an important place, because tar was used to build things. It came naturally out of the earth; it held together things like Moses's little boat and the pyramids. For me the tar baby came to mean the black woman who can hold things together" (LeClair 27). In this sense Jadine becomes the woman who cannot maintain her relationships with Sydney and Ondine, with Valerian and Margaret, or with Son: again according to Morrison, "The tragedy of the situation was not that she *was* a Tar Baby, but that she wasn't" (Ruas 226).[30]

As opposed to the characters' fixed, unitary perspectives, the opening of the tar baby myth into ambiguous multiplicity symbolizes Morrison's fluent, polyvalent position. More radically than in her first three novels, here Morrison does not allow for any tidiness of closure, as no firm conclusions can be drawn about the fate of either major character. Both Son and Jadine can be viewed as retreating into the safety of their respective briar patches, as confidently beginning their lives anew, or as some combination of the two.[31] The underlying myth, the characters' lives, and the novel itself are thus stretched beyond any monologic meaning to become polyvocal, and the characters' narrow essentialism is implicitly devalued. The difference here between *Tar Baby* and Morrison's first three novels is not a difference in kind but in degree. All four works push toward the unraveling and further complicating of binary oppositions and monologic conclusions, but this novel, as Butler-Evans argues, is "essentially interrogative" (162) and comprised of a "plurality of meanings."

Tar Baby also marks a turning point for Morrison because in several additional respects it initiates technical innovations that she develops more fully in *Beloved* and *Jazz*. The narration parallels the characters' fragmentation. It is divided among the multiple settings—the islands, New York, and Eloe. Rather than focusing on a single central character, the narrator presents the separate "thoughts" of the major characters, sometimes during the same time period, for example while they sleep (35–51). The point of view is oddly divided also between the human characters and the island's flora and fauna. The narrator seems omniscient at times, by reporting the butterflies' thoughts, for example, but also at times seems limited, as when characters' names are withheld, for example in the opening chapter.

In this novel Morrison begins to experiment with two verbal techniques that are especially prominent in *Beloved*. The first might be called *suspension*. Like a jazz artist, the narrator drops a hint or suggestion but does not provide sufficient information for the reader to understand the hint until later in the text. For example, the reader first is provided the image of a well-manicured woman's hand (4) but does not know whose hand it is until the image recurs (20). Similarly, the reader learns about the stolen chocolate long before the identification of the chocolate-eater. The reader is left suspended, trying to fuse the fragments into some meaningful array, waiting for the additional information to resolve the uncertainty created by the initial hint.

Related to suspension is Morrison's use of image refrains, phrases that are used repeatedly, like chords or *leitmotifs*. Like suspension they create an internal dialogue within the text, as each iteration of the image, like the completion of the initial hint, is dependent on each other iteration. The reader is required to remember, to make the unwritten connections between the separate iterations, to fuse (at least partially and provisionally) the linguistic fragments. For example, in the early parts of the novel Margaret "did not have the dream she ought to" (51), but after her confession she "had the dream she ought to have had" (202). Some of the refrains are epithets for the characters, such as Margaret's "blue-if-it's-a-boy blue eyes," Valerian's "head-of-a-coin profile," and Son's "savannahs in his eyes." As such, they become synecdoches for the characters, implying the division of the characters into parts. They tend simultaneously to mythologize the characters, to make them larger than life, and to merge them with cultural stereotypes. Sometimes a refrain symbolizes a character's motivation. For example, the leashes with which Jadine holds the "small dark dogs galloping on silver feet" are an emblem for her need to control her sexual desires. Still other refrains are used within a particular scene to heighten its intensity and to emphasize a particular quality, such as "but [or *still*, or *yet*] he insisted on Eloe" (192, 193, 196), which foregrounds the power struggle between Son and Jadine.[32]

These techniques tend to thicken the texture of Morrison's texts,[33] as the novels become increasingly fugal. *Tar Baby* is a polyphonic novel (Butler-Evans 156; Paquet 513) that has multiple centers and central characters (Rigney, *Voices* 32) and in which each character seems to have multiple selves (Kubitschek 132). It suggests that reality is reflected not by any one myth or any one interpretation of a myth but by "a texture of competing myths" (Werner, "Briar" 165), each of which is always likely to change as each "remains subject to eventual deformation" (166). Such multiplicity and flexibility result from the breaking down of traditional fixed entities and allow for the continual growth of the self through an ongoing process. Although the characters in *Tar Baby* are blocked from this rejuvenating process, the novel's discourse opens into greater flexibility, inclusiveness, and harmony. In this novel, Morrison's novelistic techniques outstrip her characters' emotional capacities, whereas in *Beloved* and *Jazz* characters, discourse, and reader fully engage in the complex processes of reconstituting self, past, and meaning itself, as Morrison shifts from the forces that fragment to the recuperative powers of love, memory, and storytelling.

SEVEN

Anything Dead Coming Back to Life Hurts: Circularity in *Beloved*

Thematically, *Beloved* and *Jazz* differ from Morrison's first four novels. The emphasis shifts from external factors that create fragmentation toward internal healing processes that allow for psychic integration. In these two novels, characters' pasts are radically dissociated from their present lives: for Sethe and Paul D, bittersweet memories of Sweet Home, the killing of Beloved, and Alfred, Georgia, cannot be reconciled with their present lives in Cincinnati; for Joe and Violet Trace the rural past in Vesper County, especially the loss of parents, is incompatible with their present existence in New York. In these two novels, however, the characters take advantage of this separation between past and present and the associated fragmentation to engage in extended and intensive reworkings of the past that lead toward their recoveries.[1]

At the same time, as foreshadowed in *Tar Baby*, the form of these latest two novels also shifts. To accommodate the characters' internal quests, more space is allowed for their internal monologues and retelling of memories. Past and present often overlap, not fully distinct from each other. The novels' textures are increasingly cohesive, as image refrains and epithets create unifying repetition and as incidents and scenes are replayed in recurring, circular structures. Moreover, as characters tell, retell, and listen to their own past stories, the reader is drawn into even more active participation as implied listener, which results in the further fusion of author, narrator, characters, and reader.

In each novel, a terrible past event has occurred: Sethe's killing of Beloved and Joe's killing of Dorcas. For the surviving characters to endure, they must bear the truth of that past, by remembering, recounting, and/or listening to it—in any case by accepting it. The novels chronicle this healing process, which, the characters learn, must be based on love. Since the crucial event is known from the beginning, the plots are less concerned with the necessity of a solution, less focused on the events themselves, and more preoccupied with the process of reevaluation. These two novels are more thoroughly postmodern than Morrison's first four, more concerned with process than product, more willing to accept life's mysteries and trade-offs.

Beloved explicitly addresses the issue of fusion and fragmentation. Characters, notably Beloved and Sethe, fear literal fragmentation, which represents their lack of psychic integration. Sethe's word, "rememory," carries the pun of re-member, to put back together the constituent parts. Correspondingly, the novel is written from multiple viewpoints, often with seemingly disconnected imagery, and with one section (200–217) that breaks conventional linguistic rules, as if the text itself were in danger of fragmentation. Thematically, Barbara Rigney argues that in this novel "black history is . . . fragmented into symbols" (" 'Story' " 230). According to Susan Bowers, "*Beloved* is a novel about collecting fragments and welding them into beautiful new wholes" (74), and Scruggs identifies "a recurring figure in the novel, the figure of 'sections,' of a whole seen or felt only as parts" (*Sweet* 192–93). The thematic and formal power of *Beloved* is evident in the patterns of circularity in the novel and in the related issues of revival, storytelling and listening, and overlapping consciousnesses.

The image of circularity controls the crucial scene of *Beloved*. The scene occurs at the end of Part One, in the kitchen at 124 Bluestone, when Sethe tries to explain to Paul D why she had to kill her infant daughter. That shocking act, Sethe's motivations behind it, the memory of it, and Paul D's struggle to understand it form the heart of the novel. As she attempts to tell him about the murder, she nervously circles around the kitchen, around Paul D: "She was spinning. Round and round the room. . . . Once in a while she rubbed her hips as she turned, but the wheel never stopped" (159). And as she "wheel[s]" (160), her confession revolves around the subject, "circling him the way she was circling the subject" (161). Both Paul D and Sethe are aware of her strategy. Paul D thinks, "listening to her was like having a child whisper into your ear so close you could feel its lips form the words you couldn't make out because they were too close. He caught only pieces of what she said—which was fine, because she hadn't gotten to the main part" (161). Sethe is even more explicitly conscious of the circling: "[She] knew that the circle she was making around the room, him, the subject, would remain one. That she could never close in, pin it down for anybody who had to ask. If they didn't get it right off—she could never explain" (163). Gradually, she does close the circle enough to let Paul D know the truth: "I took and put my babies where they'd be safe" (164). As Sethe feared, the shock is too great for Paul D, and he accuses her of over-loving ("Your love is too thick" [164]) and even of being more animal than human ("You got two feet, Sethe, not four" [165]). As a result, their attempted unity is nearly destroyed, and they are separated until the end of the novel.[2]

It is significant that this image of circling controls the crucial scene, for circles and circle metaphors dominate the novel. An examination of these explicit and implicit circles and their implications reveals the subtle relationships between the novel's content and its form, the paradoxical and two-edged quality of life in the novel, and the depth of the fusion and fragmentation issue.

One circle is the black neighborhood around 124 Bluestone. Comprised of other refugees of slavery and war, this neighborhood constitutes a community circle whose presence is felt throughout the novel. Personified by Stamp Paid, the community is fused together at times, as when it gathers in the circular clearing to hear Baby Suggs or when the women march on 124 Bluestone. On occasion the residents of

124 Bluestone are part of the neighborhood circle: for example, when Denver takes lessons from Lady Jones; when Denver, Paul D, and Sethe go to the carnival; or when everyone comes to the house for the feast. At such times, the community interaction appears to be healthy. For most of the novel, however, the characters in the house are fragmented from the community, even isolated from Stamp Paid when Sethe locks the door. While they are isolated they are haunted by their pasts, first by the inanimate ghost of Beloved and then by the animate Beloved, who can only be exorcised by the combined action of Sethe, Denver, and the community, actions that reintegrate 124 Bluestone with the neighborhood.

The problems confronting the characters inside the house are related to their exclusion from the community circle. That circle, however, is not always welcoming. The same people who help Denver when she seeks to rejoin the community reject Baby Suggs as a reprimand for her overreaching independence of the community, do not even warn her of schoolteacher's approach, and reject Sethe after the Misery. The community circle is therefore two-edged, capable of providing supportive unity but equally capable of causing division and alienation. One subject of the novel is the difficult process of forming a more consistently supportive community (Mohanty 56). At the very time that the community comes together for the feast at 124 Bluestone, its members' jealousy of Baby Suggs and their anger that she is overreaching contribute to its undoing. This community thus resembles the neighborhoods of Morrison's other novels, neighborhoods that both nurture her central characters but also threaten to constrict them.[3]

Another circle is families. The plot is dominated by the creation of families, the attempt to preserve them, their fragmentation, and the nostalgia for them.[4] In the novel's past, Sethe's mother (Ma'am) and Baby Suggs lose their families, Paul D envies the families he meets during his wanderings, and the family of the Sweet Home men is split up forever. Sethe's primary desire is to reunite her own family, a desire that makes her murder of her baby all the more difficult to reconcile. Paul D has no hopes of regaining his own lost family, but after circling the eastern United States (or, as he says, "walking all around this place" [46]), he is trying to settle down, to create a new family with Sethe, and thereby to find himself. Denver has the opposite journey, not from the circumference inward, but from the center outward, breaking out into "her own spiral . . . that widens rather than narrows" (Sale 49). Confined by her overprotective mother and her own agoraphobia, she tries to live by means of intimate relationships within the house—with Sethe, with the inanimate ghost, then with Beloved, whom she desperately tries to keep to herself by encircling, by "construct[ing] out of the strings she had heard all her life a net to hold" (76). Eventually excluded by Sethe and Beloved (as she had first feared she would be by Sethe and Paul D), she is forced, for her physical and psychological survival, to reenter the larger community, to move outward from the incomplete and inadequate family circle to the larger neighborhood circle.

The novel's plot also chronicles a series of attempted family circles, an oscillation between attempts to form family units and their fragmentations. It starts with the precarious family of Sethe, Denver, and the inanimate ghost of Beloved. Paul D drives out the ghost, but the potential family consisting of him, Sethe, and Denver is also unstable, primarily because Paul D and Sethe cannot yet accept their memories, cannot acknowledge the horrors of their pasts. Beloved then returns, and the competition for intimacy deepens: Paul D wants Sethe, Beloved wants Sethe, Denver wants Beloved, and Sethe wants her old family. Just below the surface of these desires lies the absent father, husband, and son, Halle. Beloved, symbolizing (among other things) the power of both Sethe's and Paul D's unaccepted memories,[5] holds the upper hand as long as these memories remain unacknowledged. Therefore, she can drive Paul D out of the house and out of the circle, and then, through her emotional hold on Sethe, she can exclude Denver and draw her circle ever more tightly around herself and Sethe.

As with the community circle, these family groups can be both healthy and destructive.[6] The loss of family is a significant part of these characters' tragedy, and their attempts to retain or remake a family reflect their desire to become spiritually and psychologically whole, to fuse at least partially their horribly fragmented selves and pasts. The novel also dramatizes, however, that family units can create additional problems, that one potential family may destroy another or may harm those it excludes. After Paul D arrives, Denver laments that "they [Paul D and Sethe] were a twosome" and that "they [Denver and Sethe] were not a twosome anymore" (13), and later Beloved claims Sethe for herself by encircling her with a shawl, to the exclusion of Paul D (130). Love can easily slide over into "horrific love" (Otten, "Horrific" 652), much like Hagar's love for Milkman becomes an "anaconda love" (*Song* 137).

These family groups usually become too intense and ingrown, isolating each group from the rest of the community and each member from him- or herself. Its members become "hand-holding shadows" (128) together, but only half-alive, in an insubstantial, unfulfilling reality. While the family of Sethe, Beloved, and Denver is temporarily balanced, they go ice-skating, holding hands "making a circle or a line" (174), but the repeated phrase is "nobody saw them falling," which, like the refrains in *Tar Baby*, underscores the scene's import.[7] Sethe and Denver are falling, not just on the ice, but as a group and as individuals. And nobody saw them, which is both a result of their isolation and a cause of their fall. Because they are isolated, too engrossed in their primary circle, too insistent on its unity, they deny themselves the necessary interaction with the community. Worse, their tightening circle forces them perilously close to a kind of hysteria. The three women's voices inside 124 Bluestone are "a conflagration of hasty voices" (172) that to Stamp Paid "wasn't nonsensical, exactly, nor was it tongues. But something was wrong with the order of the words . . ." (172). Sethe, caught up in the ring, "neither saw the prints nor heard the voices that ringed 124 like a noose" (183), like a constricting, life-threatening circle.

The "voices" of the three women, which the reader finally hears on pages 200–217, also cut two ways. On the one hand, their song is a testimony to their intimacy, to their shared sense of family, to their common lives and memories, and their three-in-one union is the most fully developed female triad in Morrison's fiction. But on the other hand, their ingrown dependencies drain away their lives. Denver is still unable to function in the outside world, Beloved becomes increasingly tyrannical and infantile, and Sethe loses her physical and emotional strength. In fact, their relationships, for all their love, are increasingly possessive.[8] The one word that Stamp Paid can make out is "mine" (172), the key word in each of their monologues:

> Sethe: "Beloved, she my daughter. She mine" (200)
> Denver: "She's mine, Beloved. She's mine" (209)
> Beloved: "I am Beloved and she is mine" (210).

And the intertwined lines of the trio end with the refrain of

> You are mine
> You are mine
> You are mine. (217)

Being "mine" or "yours" is both loving and controlling. The three characters' insistence on possessing each other underscores the destructive rivalries for affection that plague the various attempted families within 124 Bluestone. Moreover, Sethe, Denver, and Paul D are possessed (in a different sense of the word) by the ghost of Beloved, an ordeal they must pass through but not a healthy condition. In a larger sense, the novel demonstrates that no one can or should belong to anyone else and that, in fact, such possession uncomfortably resembles another form of human possession—slavery.[9]

The two-edged nature of life in this novel, simultaneously fusing and fragmenting, is further implied by other circle images. Denver's circular bower, formed by "five boxwood bushes, planted in a ring" (28), is both a safe haven and a retreat from life. An ambiguous womb image—like the tunnel in *Sula,* the cave in *Song of Solomon,* and the wells in *Jazz*—it is a metaphor, along with her fascination with the story of her birth, for her paralyzing infantilism.[10] Circles are especially ambivalent in Beloved's elliptical, imagistic references to her return to life via the Middle Passage. She sees a "round basket" (210) of flowers and then notices a "circle around [the] neck" (211) of the woman whose face she needs. But in dream-like fashion this circle becomes "the iron circle . . . around our neck" (212), an evocation of slave's collars. Perhaps the most dramatic and the most contrasting circle imagery details Sethe's near strangulation in the Clearing. As she is feeling strangled (a circle image itself), she describes the feeling as "harder, harder, the fingers moved slowly around toward her windpipe, making little circles on the way" (96). But as soon as the spell is broken, Beloved relaxes Sethe by massaging her bruised neck and throat. Hands on the throat can strangle and soothe; a circle can be destructive and constructive, confining and fulfilling.[11]

Like many novels, this one is built on repetition, which is a form of circularity. The generations of women dovetail with each other. Baby Suggs mothers Sethe in the absence of her own children, as Sethe in turn mothers her children in the absence of her mother. Sethe replaces Baby Suggs in the mother's role, which is further depicted by Sethe's replacing her in the keeping room. In turn, Sethe as mother is replaced by Denver when the latter learns to cope with the world and to provide for the family. Repetition also structures the novel in the duplication of key events. Sethe sits on the same rock in the Clearing as Baby Suggs did, and Denver and Beloved repeat the rush of children. Mr. Bodwin's arrival at the house parallels the earlier arrival of schoolteacher's posse, and Sethe's attack echoes her earlier action. Paul D arrives, leaves, and arrives again, and his "coming is the reverse route of his going" (263). Denver goes twice to Lady Jones and interacts significantly twice with Nelson Lord. The ghost of Beloved haunts Sethe and Denver, is chased away by Paul D, but returns more powerfully, and finally, through the action of Sethe, Denver, and the community, is exorcised for good.

Beloved not only presents these patterns of ambiguous circularity but also enacts them. It ends by circling back to its title word (Horvitz 157; M. Walker 46). Its telling replicates Sethe's act of circling her subject in the kitchen with Paul D: she cannot say directly what she did or why, so the narration does not tell the story directly; she says a little, then digresses, then circles back, so the narration does likewise; Paul D only catches fragments and must wait until she circles closer and closer, so readers must be content with fragments and must wait until they are told enough. The novel is like the circle Sethe spins, collecting, omitting, repeating the fragments. The novel is also like the house at 124 Bluestone Road, "where bits of news soaked like dried beans in spring water—until they were soft enough to digest" (65; Sale 44). The narrator knows the whole story, but, since the characters have trouble confronting the past, the narration must be presented in overlapping pieces.[12] Many of the pieces are "unspeakable thoughts, unspoken" (99) and hence cannot be presented directly. Since Sethe and Paul D must warily circle their painful memories, the novel must circle its subject. Just as Sethe's "brain was devious" (6), so the narration must deviate, must (as the derivation of *deviate* implies) move away from the road. In its deviousness, it uses multiple points of view—sometimes the narrator's own view but most often the thoughts and recollections of the four major characters as well as nearly all the minor ones, whose perspectives are usually provided as soon as they appear. Part of the obliqueness is the overlapping of these points of view. Like the intertwined voices of Sethe, Denver, and Beloved, the collective memories of the characters are not distinct. Even more radically than in *The Bluest Eye* and *Song of Solomon*, the *what* is insignificant compared to "the how and the why of it" (120), and these latter questions are so elusive and/or dangerous that they can be approached only indirectly.[13]

The most remarkable narrative strategy of the novel is a fuller rendition of the suspension that Morrison initiates in *Tar Baby*. The text tends to drop an unexplained fact on the reader, veer away into other matters, then circle back with more information about the initial fact, then veer away again, circle back again, and so on.[14] Sometimes the new information comes relatively soon. For example, after the novel's opening words drop one such unexplained fact ("124 was spiteful" [3]), readers are told two sentences later that "the women in the house knew it," which implies that 124 is the address of a house. Then comes new material, a circling, in the narration of Howard and Bugler's departure, which drops new unexplained facts for amplification in subsequent pages. Fifteen lines later, readers learn that "it didn't have a number then because Cincinnati didn't stretch that far," which lets them conclude that 124 is indeed a house. Sometimes the mystery is not fully explained until many pages later; for example, the three tiny lines on Beloved's forehead are first mentioned on page 51, they are referred to several more times, but their origin is not disclosed until pages 202–3. However long it takes, the same circling or spiraling strategy recurs. It is especially noticeable when the opening words of a chapter introduce a new mysterious detail, often from a point of view that is at first unidentified; for example, "It was time to lay it all down" (86), "She moved him" (114), and "That ain't her mouth" (154).

A related strategy is Morrison's lyrical repetition or near-repetition of phrases and images, such as "the hand-holding shadows on the side of the road" (128)[15] and the "little hummingbirds [that] stuck their needle beaks right through her headcloth into her hair and beat their wings" (163, 262). Especially noticeably in *Tar Baby*, this technique of image refrains, some of which act as epithets for characters (like Paul D's tobacco-tin heart), serves, like the suspension strategy, to weave a whole fabric from the disparate parts. As Maggie Sale argues, these "progressions" (45) are not the same as more conventional motifs, for they often recur in a single poetic passage. Asserting that "all experiences repeat or parallel each other" (162), Rodrigues compares this technique to the blues and demonstrates how several images (such as corn silk) reverberate in given passages and across the whole novel ("Telling").[16]

Like many elements of Morrison's fiction, this narrative strategy has affinities with African folklore and specifically with the traditional structure of oral narratives. Morrison's incorporation of African and African-American folklore has been well documented: for example, the myths of flying and the tar baby; such elements as magic, dreams, omens, and superstitions; and her emphasis on naming and places.[17]

Circularity is part of that oral tradition. Traditional African stories are usually told to an audience formed in a circle around the storyteller, or the role of storyteller shifts from person to person around the "story circle" (Finnegan 374). More significantly, the circling, spiraling, and digressive narrative pattern of *Beloved* has parallels in African folk narratives. Such narratives tend to be built on repetition of words, phrases, motifs, and stock situations and episodes. Commonly, such building blocks are not merely repeated but used in overlapping or interlocking patterns to generate a story. For example, A. M. Jones and H. Carter identify the four essential features of Tonga narratives as staging, overlapping, repetition, and synonymous expressions. Lee Haring extracts a generic pattern in which stories are comprised of traditional sequences of plot elements, such as false friendship, a contract, violation of the contract, deception, and escape. Such elements do not work in isolation but often in pairs or in sequences in which one element (such as false friendship) anticipates another (such as deception). These tales, like *Beloved*, rely upon the gradual accretion of meaning that evolves from the overlapping repetition and variation of such elements.

The typical form of the Xhosa *ntsomi*, or fanciful tale, parallels *Beloved* even more closely. Harold Scheub finds that storytellers rely upon a vast stock of "core-clichés"—stock images, characters, and episodes that can be varied to suit a particular story, audience, and occasion (39). Most stories are built upon one or more "core-images," drawn from the storyteller's repertoire and expanded to form the core of the particular story (40). The plot is developed through repetition and variation of one or more core-images in overlapping waves, much like the refrain of a song or a jazz musician's riff.[18]

Similarly, *Beloved* is developed through such core-images as "124 was spiteful" (3), "124 was loud" (169), and "124 was quiet" (239), with which its three parts begin. It is developed through the overlapping and accumulating descriptions of such images as Amy's velvet, the tree on Sethe's back, the mating turtles, and Paul D's tobacco tin. And it is developed through the iteration and reiteration of such episodes as the milking of Sethe and Sethe's murder of Beloved, and through the spiraling reiteration of larger, mythical acts such as birth, death, rebirth, quest-journeys, and the formation and disintegration of families.

Sethe and Paul D remember and relate their pasts using the same form. One word, detail, or image drops into their consciousnesses and reminds them of part of their buried past. To preserve their sanity, they have been keeping their minds in fragments, carefully partitioning off the pieces of memory that must be repressed. Cautiously, they begin to relive each memory, rethinking and sometimes retelling it bit by bit, then dropping it, only to circle back to it later, purposefully or not. The novel must be told this way, the reader must wait to hear the full story, because that is the only way characters can remember their past, and therefore it is the only way the story can be told. For example, Sethe first tells Paul D on page 10 that her daughter died, but she does not tell him (or the reader) how. Then, when she first tells him about schoolteacher's arrival at 124 Bluestone (42), she mentions going to jail but not why, to which she will return in the kitchen scene. Until Paul D sees the photograph, not only is Sethe not ready to tell him the whole story, but he is not ready to hear it: "Paul D turned away. He wanted to know more about it, but jail talk put him back in Alfred, Georgia" (42). Since neither character, the teller or the listener, can tolerate the whole truth all at once, the reader must wait. Because the characters have to be careful, have to remember their lives in fragments, the narration must be told in fragments. Form and content are synchronous, thereby forcing the reader to experience the same difficulty as the characters.

This pattern creates another two-edged sword, another paradox. Paul D and Sethe must retell and thereby acknowledge the past to free themselves from its paralyzing power, symbolized by Beloved. By telling or hearing that past, however, they risk losing their precarious sanity as well as their hopes for a new life together. Likewise, for readers the pattern cuts at least two ways. The narrative fragmentation denies readers the expected level of immediate comprehension, forcing them to wait for explanations, to recall previously narrated fragments, and to piece together the narrative's chronology. And yet, partly because of this necessity for readers' active participation, the cumulative effect of the intensive exploration of the characters' memories is profound.[19]

Beloved's exposure of the double-edged nature of circularity is especially significant in its treatment of the theme of rebirth. All four major characters undergo birth/rebirth journeys across water, journeys that thereby become symbols for birth. Beloved describes her reincarnation in terms of crossing a body of water in a ship, which invokes the Middle Passage as well as the passage of a fetus into life. Sethe's escape to the North requires two similar voyages: the birth of Denver in the waters of the Ohio River and Sethe and Denver's perilous crossing of the Ohio.[20] Paul D undergoes a similar journey of rebirth through water when he and the rest of the chain gang miraculously escape from the trench in Alfred, Georgia.[21]

These birth/rebirth journeys are part of larger thematic and formal patterns. Many features of the novel's setting are described in terms or images of death. The season in Cincinnati is usually winter, the landscape barren or frozen, the precipitation snow but never rain, the

144

creek frozen (Samuels and Hudson-Weems 122). The "life" of the chain gang in Alfred, Georgia, is metaphoric death, a *totentanz* or death dance (Samuels and Hudson-Weems 125). The patronizing white benefactors of 124 Bluestone, the Bodwins, are prematurely white-haired, suggesting that their self-serving liberalism is dead. Schoolteacher constructs a living death for the slaves at Sweet Home, forcing on them the written law that deprives them of spiritual life (Scruggs, *Sweet* 182). The house, frequently personified so that it seems to reflect the destinies of its inhabitants, is now dead, only "alive" "years ago" when neighbors came and went freely and it served as a way station for newly arrived fugitives (95).[22] The novel's preoccupation with death focuses on Beloved, whose tragic death has not been expiated. Barbara Christian claims that the Middle Passage, with its violent wrenching of Africans from their pasts and their ancestors, was an extreme violation of West African belief systems. Using John Mbiti's formulations of African belief in the continuity between life and death and the consequent presence of the recently deceased, Christian suggests that the novel's characters suffer because they are cut off from their "living dead" (Mbiti 25) and therefore that the novel is a "fixing ceremony" ("Fixing" 14) designed "to begin the process of healing that psychic wound."[23]

Against this background of death, the major characters struggle to regain life. Sethe's death image is her back—"her back skin had been dead for years" (18)—and its scar tissue embodies the suffering she endured as well as her repressed memories.[24] Paul D's dead part is his heart, replaced by the metallic tobacco tin in his chest in which he has buried his most painful memories. Denver has lived most of her life entombed within the house and yard of 124 Bluestone Road, afraid to leave the comforting yet terrifying presence of her mother. Frighteningly alone, she clings to anyone, even the inanimate ghost or any imagined other, such as her father, in the desperate attempt to confirm her own existence. When Beloved momentarily disappears, Denver suffers a brief death: "Now she is crying because she has no self" (123). When Denver does venture forth, she metaphorically passes through death into a new life: "So it was she who had to step off the edge of the world and die because if she didn't, they all would" (239). Beloved's journey is a reverse rebirth: having been denied physical life so young, she circles from death to "life" and back to death, or at least to absence. Even during her ghostly sojourn on earth, she hovers between presence and absence, for example when she vanishes in the shed (123). She also oscillates physically between wholeness and fragmentation: she dies as a baby when her neck is sliced, she regains unity on the ship when she makes "the join" with another face (213–14); as the returned young woman she worries about coming apart; and when she disappears at the end of the novel she "erupts into her separate parts" (274).

Beloved's agonizing journey epitomizes the theme of the pain of bringing anything back to life. When Amy Denver massages Sethe's feet and legs, she voices this idea—"Anything dead coming back to life hurts" (35)—and she repeats the message in another retelling of the episode: "Can't nothing heal without pain" (78). This painful restoration of Sethe's feet and legs is a "ringing note of painful but magical resurrection" (Moreland 512), which serves as a metaphor for the more complicated processes of reviving the characters' nearly dead souls. The novel's primary subject is the documentation of that process, including the accompanying pain, the necessary healers, and the essential roles of memory, storytelling, listening, and shared consciousness.

Several characters serve as healers, and each one's healing is associated with his or her pain. Paul D, although he too needs healing, has "something blessed in his manner" (17, 272) that enables him to absorb women's pain: "he had become the kind of man who could walk into a house and make the women cry" (17, 272). His empathy and patience are reminiscent of Milkman Dead after the latter's successful quest. His healing powers are exhibited by his ability to exorcise the first ghost, by his skills at repairing things (like the table that he mends "stronger than before" [64]), and by his physical and emotional tenderness in the last scene with Sethe. Paul is frequently associated with the beauty of nature, which by implication becomes a source of his healing power: he follows the blossoms to escape to the North (112) and "he could not help being astonished by the beauty of this land that was not his" (268).

Another healer is Amy Denver, who, despite her own mistreatment and vulnerability, provides physical and spiritual salvation for Sethe.

146

Amy is also associated with nature, whose webs and leaves she uses to relieve Sethe's pain (79, 83), and for whom Sethe's scars resemble a chokecherry tree in bloom (79).[25] Stamp Paid, through his role as community mediator and catalyst, tries to heal everyone. He has brought himself back from the dead by renaming himself after his wife's fatal ordeal and by constructing his contract with the world: "So he extended this debtlessness to other people by helping them pay out and off whatever they owed in misery" (185). The community women join in the healing process when they gather at 124 Bluestone and help in the final purging of the ghost. Indirectly, Beloved is also a healer, although one who simultaneously hurts as she unintentionally heals, a healer/hurter, a living dead. Since her insistent hunger for information about her and her family's past leads Sethe to unlock her repressed memories, Beloved acts as Sethe's conscience (Askeland 800, Heinze 176, Levy 115, and Samuels and Hudson-Weems 94) and even her analyst (Krumholz, "Ghosts" 400).

The principal healer is Baby Suggs. Like Amy and Stamp Paid, she surmounts her own problems, including her ruined hip, her lost children, and her near loss of self ("the desolated center where the self that was no self made its home" [140]). She helps heal the members of the community through her power of self-love, particularly through her "heart" (87, 94), the same organ that has frozen in Paul D. Even though Sethe's murder of Beloved overwhelms Baby Suggs, she "returns" to counsel Denver at her critical moment of stepping forth into the world (244).

For Baby Suggs especially, but also for the other healers, healing is most often accomplished through language. Unlike *Tar Baby*, where Nommo is lost, here the Word is usually present and nearly always therapeutic. Baby Suggs has the Call, speaking from her heart to the hearts of the rest of the community and later to Denver. Amy constantly talks while she ministers to Sethe, speaking in a voice that quiets Sethe as well as the restless fetus. By its very normality and triviality, Sethe's and Amy's "yard chat" (33) helps bring Sethe back to life. Stamp works his healing effects on the community in part by deeds but primarily by his neighborly talk. Paul D's power comes more from his empathic listening—to Sethe and to Stamp Paid—than from his talking, which often hurts rather than helps, as when he accuses Sethe of loving too much (164) and of being less than human (165).

Throughout the novel, the lack of language indicates that characters are in distress or jeopardy or both. Overwhelmed, Denver and Here Boy are driven to muteness and, in Denver's case, deafness. As a result, Denver is dependent on anyone or anything that brings her company and talk: "Anything is better than the silence" (121).[26] During her beating, Sethe is momentarily silenced when she nearly bites off part of her tongue, and Paul D is shamed by his enforced silence with the bit in his mouth. The community's silence about the approaching posse expresses its affront at the excess of the party at 124 Bluestone. The community's disapproval is further manifested by its deadening silence as Sethe is taken to jail: "No words at all" (152). In a larger sense, the novel gives "voice" to the unspoken, unwritten feelings that slave narratives could not and did not express.[27]

Sometimes words are used but are inadequate. When Sethe is circling her subject and Paul D, it is because "she knew that the words she did not understand hadn't any more power than she had to explain" (161) and in any case that she requires a listener who understands without her necessity for words: "If they didn't get it right off—she could never explain" (163). Words are also inadequate for Beloved when she tries to describe her passage from death: "how can I say things in pictures" (210). The obliqueness of Beloved's monologues (210–14), their heavy reliance on imagery, and their unconventional grammar and absent punctuation document Morrison's attempt to stretch language beyond its usual limits.[28] As far as other listeners are concerned, the "talk" among Sethe, Denver, and Beloved is beyond the limits of language. The closest outside auditor, Stamp Paid, can only detect an "undecipherable language" (198), although the privileged narrator knows that the voices, "recognizable but undecipherable to Stamp Paid, were the thoughts of the women of 124, unspeakable thoughts, unspoken" (199).

More often, though, words have a positive effect. They are used to comfort, as a "cape of sound . . . like arms to hold and steady" (152). In addition to Amy's therapeutic chatter, Sethe and Paul D enjoy each other's talk, and Denver and Beloved relish their "sweet, crazy conversations" (67). Words become food to feed the starving Beloved

(58), Nelson Lord's casual words ("Take care of yourself, Denver" [252]) become the means for her self-discovery (Rushdy, "Daughters" 585), and Ella's holler, in contrast to the heavy silence when Sethe goes to jail, releases the community energy into song in its collective purgation ritual (259, 261).[29]

Ella's healing holler is particularly significant because Ella, as Stamp Paid's female counterpart, plays a crucial and two-edged role: as upholder of community values and rescuer of fugitives. Like Sethe, she commits a form of infanticide by refusing to nurse the "hairy, white thing" (258) to which she gives birth. In one sense, she frees herself from her past (Rushdy, "Daughters" 584), a perspective that Sethe, Denver, and Paul D must and do reach. Although aware of the dangers of memory, Ella "didn't like the idea of past errors taking possession of the present. . . . The future was sunset; the past something to leave behind. And if it didn't stay behind, well, you might have to stomp it out" (256). Yet, as Paul D's eviction of the first ghost illustrates, stomping out the past doesn't always work. Moreover, Ella has made her peace by rejecting love ("she considered love a serious disability" [256]) and sex (like Alice Manfred in *Jazz* she has "a disgust for sex"), both of which are essential for Sethe's and Paul's recoveries.[30]

As in *Song of Solomon*, one particular form of words—songs—is always therapeutic in this novel, for the singer as well as the listener. Paul's power is related to his being "a singing man" (39), from the days at Sweet Home (40) and Georgia (108–9), where he survives by singing the "songs that murdered life" (221).[31] He gains this power by his former association with Sixo, whose song, even in death, celebrates his victory (229; Lawrence 197). Hi Man's leadership of the chain gang is associated with his calls of "Hiiii!" and "Hoooo!" (108) to start and end the day, with the songs in which he leads the men at work, and with the "two-step" dance he directs "to the music of the hand-forged iron" (108). Amy, besides comforting Sethe with ordinary words, sings songs of healing that mimic her own role: "Layeth she her hands upon / My dear weary little one" (81). In the first weeks of Beloved's visit, when she is docile, part of her attractiveness is her "gravelly voice and the song that seemed to lie in it" (60), and it is Sethe's recognition of her own song that Beloved hums that convinces her of the latter's identity (175). Finally, a significant part of the community women's purgation ritual is their song. In general, songs, like most words in this novel, gain their recuperative power from their ritualistic evocation of the past.

By far the most important use of words by the characters is to retell the stories of their pasts.[32] Telling and hearing each other's stories are essential because those stories are the vehicle for the release of repressed memories, for the creation of mutual trust and family bonds, and thus for the characters' revivals. Until their stories can be told and listened to, Sethe and Paul D, but especially Sethe, are prisoners of their pasts. For Sethe, who doesn't "go inside" (46) herself, "the future was a matter of keeping the past at bay" (42). For her, once a thing happens it always exists: "Where I was before I came here, that place is real. It's never going away. . . . [I]f you go there and stand in the place where it was, it will happen again" (36). It exists because she remembers it, but it exists independently; she doesn't allow Denver to go there "because even though it's all over— over and done with—it's going to always be there waiting for you." This is why Beloved, the symbol of Sethe's past, has such power over her: if that past never ceases to exist, the memory always lives, as well as the fear of the reality of that past. Sethe's word for this phenomenon is *rememory*, a combination of *memory* and *remember*, which in itself doubles the process. For her, memory is both an actual repetition of the real events and a repetition of a memory, a circling back in her mind to what was previously there both in reality and in its recall. To remember is also to re-member, that is, to put oneself back together, which is what Sethe's remembered stories finally accomplish.[33]

Sethe therefore has a compelling need to tell her story to someone. At Sweet Home, she has no one, especially no woman, to talk to, not just about caring for babies, but about anything (Samuels and Hudson-Weems 113). The only female counsel she receives is the fragmentary and confusing words of Nan, "who used different words. Words Sethe understood then but could neither recall nor repeat now" (62). She must rely on her "talk/think" (38) sessions with God, not praying but just talking (35) as she awaits "some clarifying word" (95). She is another of Morrison's characters at risk of fragmentation, needing to "piece it all back together" (22).

Paul D, so comforting a listener for the women he encounters, walls off his own emotions very carefully in his tin heart. He "protect[s] himself" (162) with his philosophy of "lov[ing] small" and "in secret" (221), because anything else would drive him crazy: "A woman, a child, a brother—a big love like that would split you wide open in Alfred, Georgia" (162). He is so vulnerable that he transfers his affections to nature, but he even "tried not to love it" (268), and his vulnerability is expressed in his obsessions with his manhood.[34] Like Sethe, he risks fragmentation, especially after the breakup of the false paradise at Sweet Home: "Without [Garner's] life each of theirs fell to pieces" (220). He is vulnerable to Beloved's power because he does not understand his own past and therefore Sethe's and Beloved's (Mohanty 65). Even though Beloved is barely part of his memory, she alone is able to unlock his tobacco tin: "he didn't hear the whisper that the flakes of rust made either as they fell away from the seams of his tobacco tin" (117). Only when Paul D relinquishes himself to the power of memory, giving himself physically to Beloved, can he release those memories, accept himself for what he is and what he has done, therefore accept Sethe for what she is and what she has done, and thereby become whole. Only then, recalling Sixo's mythic wholeness, is he finally able to recognize Sethe's true value: she is "a friend of my mind. She gather me, man. The pieces that I am, she gather them and give them back to me in all the right order" (272–73).

What Sethe and Paul D eventually find in each other is the trust to remember, and it is only through telling and retelling, circling through their horrible and, for them, shameful pasts, that healing comes: "Her story was bearable because it was his as well—to tell, to refine and tell again" (99). The promise of their future together is expressed as their equality as storytellers and listeners: "He wants to put his story next to hers" (273).

Beloved and Denver are also obsessed with storytelling and listening. For much of her visit, Beloved is starved for the stories of Sethe's life and her life: "Sethe learned the profound satisfaction Beloved got from storytelling" (58). Denver, childishly egocentric (as Beloved

151

increasingly becomes), loves to rehear and retell the story of her birth, but "hated the stories her mother told that did not concern herself" (62). Lacking the complete stories of her familial and communal pasts, she is split between her inside self, in particular her dreams about her father and her confidence in his return ("I always knew he was coming" [207]), and her "outside self," which she spent "loving Ma'am so she wouldn't kill me," protecting Beloved from Sethe, and then protecting Sethe from Beloved.

The worst bind for the survivors is that, despite their overwhelming need to share their stories, their memories are so painful and shameful that recalling or sharing them is dangerous. Not remembering can destroy one, but so can remembering too much or too fast. Everyone respects the dangers of recall: "when they met one another they neither described nor asked about the sorrow that drove them from one place to another" (53). When Beloved arrives, Paul D understands the strength it takes to tell one's story: "If she wanted them to know and was strong enough to get through the telling, she would." Even Stamp Paid has to circle widely around the subject before he can tell Paul D that he witnessed the Misery (230–35).

Because of these risks associated with memory, when characters remember and retell their past stories, they often distort the past. Sethe circles the subject of Beloved's death, Paul D doesn't tell Sethe everything he knows, and "Stamp Paid did not tell [Paul D] how [Sethe] flew" [157]). According to Barthold, "memory juxtaposes past and present, and, to varying degrees, fuses the past of personal experience with the past of a cultural exchange, underscoring the necessity of accepting, rather than attempting to escape, the past" (89). For the characters in *Beloved*, the past has been so painful, the fragmentations of self and community have been so debilitating, that the task of making those memories real by putting them into words is almost impossible.

Characters not only retell what happened when they were present but also when they were not. Stamp Paid and Paul D recount the events of the final melee at 124 Bluestone based on what they have heard, not seen. More conspicuously, Denver provides the fullest account of Sethe's encounter with Amy, of Denver's birth, and of the escape across the Ohio River, even though she has no direct memory of those events (76–85). Likewise, after Baby Suggs "told [her] all [her] daddy's things" 209), Denver invents stories about her absent but beloved father.

As the characters tell their stories about their pasts, they often conflate past and present. At any moment, a phrase or a thought can trigger memories, especially for Sethe and Paul D. Stamp Paid, trying to approach 124 Bluestone when the three women are shut inside, transposes a former visit with Baby Suggs and his present visit (176–81).[35] This dual presence of past and present becomes even more pronounced in *Jazz*, especially when Joe Trace overlays his tracking of Dorcas with his previous hunts for Wild.

Despite these potential distortions in characters' stories, Morrison insists that every character be given a voice. She privileges a Bakhtinian heteroglossia in which multiple perspectives are required. As Rodrigues puts it, "Toni Morrison turns her narrator into a Bakhtinian ventriloquist" ("Telling" 157), and Sale argues that "*Beloved* not only presents 'new' perspectives, but foregrounds the power and problematics of perspective itself; this text suggests a complex method of reading and interpreting that values multiplicity rather than codification and polemic" (42).

Just as Valerian has trouble hearing Margaret's story about abusing Michael, listening to someone else's story can be as difficult and as threatening as telling one's own.[36] Denver is thrown into near insanity upon hearing the story of Beloved's death, and she remains fearful of the outside world partly because "words could be spoken that would close your ears shut" (243). When Paul D tells Sethe about Halle's insanity, the burden is on Sethe to absorb the news without being destroyed by it: "Slowly, slowly, taking all the time allowed, Sethe moved toward the table" (68). "Carefully, carefully, she passed on to a reasonable question" (69). When it comes to the news about Beloved's death, the burden of listening shifts to Paul. Sethe anticipates his ability to hear this story, to help relieve her of it, by thinking of the secrets with which they would be able to trust each other: "The things neither knew about the other—the things neither had word-shapes for—well, it would come in time: where they led him off to sucking iron; the perfect death of her crawling already? baby" (99). But Paul, not able to hear this horror, responds by denying it (using the same repeated "No" with which Sethe refuses to return herself or her babies to slavery) and then by flight and alcohol.

In a passage that suggests the difficulties of both telling and hearing, Sethe gently opens the way for Paul D to tell about the lack of wildness in his eye:

> "You want to tell me about it?" she asked him.
>
> "I don't know. I never have talked about it. Not to a soul. Sang it sometimes, but I never told a soul."
>
> "Go ahead. I can hear it."
>
> "Maybe. Maybe you can hear it. I just ain't sure I can say it. Say it right, I mean, because it wasn't the bit—that wasn't it." (71)

After these initial revelations, Sethe worries about being able to bear Paul's memories: "if she could just manage the news Paul D brought and the news he kept to himself" (97). She becomes upset with herself for being upset: "Why now, with Paul D instead of the ghost, was she breaking up? getting scared? needing Baby? The worst was over, wasn't it?" The worst *events* are over, although Sethe's murder of Mr. Bodwin is narrowly averted, but the novel's subject is the lingering internal problems of recreating a self in the shadow of the horrors of the past. The process of that self-recovery requires the telling of one's story, the listening to one's telling, and the listening to other's similar tellings. The fragments are fused in the process: "the storyteller creates community, uniting, through narrative, the lives of the teller, the listener, and the greater world of experience from which the story is drawn" (Pérez-Torres 704).

Morrison deepens her treatment of storytelling and listening by overlapping the teller and the listener. As soon as Paul D arrives, he and Sethe's memories and minds synchronize: in pages 20–27 the point of view alternates between the two, Sethe can read Paul's thoughts ("He was not judging her" [25]), and nonverbally they share the same memory of the loose corn silk when Sethe and Halle first copulated (27). Their ability to synchronize—unlike previous Morrison couples such as Cholly and Pauline, Sula and Ajax, Milkman and Hagar, and Son and Jadine (Sitter 21)—attests to the increased focus in *Beloved* on the characters' internal lives and on "the braiding and fusing of voices and emotions" (Mohanty 61) as opposed to the gaps between them.[37]

154

Later, when Sethe realizes who Beloved is, she merges even more fully with her than with Paul D. She knows that Beloved already knows the memories so that she will be spared the pain of recalling and retelling them: "I don't have to remember nothing. I don't even have to explain. She understands it all" (183). She repeats her refrain of relief: "I can forget that . . ." (183–84). The fusion becomes explicit and mystical in Beloved's story of needing to find a face, perhaps Sethe's ("Sethe is the face I found and lost in the water under the bridge" [214]), in order to complete her passage back to life. Then, in the trio of Denver, Sethe, and Beloved, not only do all three voices blend, but Beloved expresses the unity of herself and Sethe: "You are my face; you are me" (216) and "You are my face; I am you." Denver later realizes how the two become physically similar ("it was difficult for Denver to tell who was who" [241]) and notices that they have reversed mother/child roles (250).

This blending of minds accentuates the role of the listener. Because the person remembering feels connected to or even unified with the person listening, the rememberer can communicate more freely and even nonverbally with the "listener." As in her "talk/think" sessions with God (38), Sethe thinks to and with Beloved in her internal monologues: "I went and got you a gravestone" (184) and "You know I never would a left you" (191). When Denver recreates the myth of her birth, Beloved's role as listener is crucial: "Now, watching Beloved's alert and hungry face, how she took in every word, asking questions about the color of things and their size, her downright craving to know, Denver began to see what she was saying and not just to hear it" (77). Because of Beloved's active listening, Denver "anticipated the questions by giving blood to the scraps her mother and grandmother had told her—and a heartbeat" (78). The story becomes a dialogue: "The monologue became, in fact, a duet as they lay down together," as *"the two* did the best they could to create what really happened" (emphasis added). Denver and Beloved can recreate the story because, as Sethe would say, the events are still really there, but also because the minds and the memories of the characters interpenetrate, because the novel is a collective memory. In this speakerly text, story and storyteller depend on the listener, not just as passive recipient, but as active co-creator.

Furthermore, Denver and Beloved's recreation of the story of Denver's birth replicates the recreation that is the novel itself, Morrison's imagining, doing the best she can to recreate what happened, what historical documents—such as slave narratives—say and don't say. If the minds of the teller and the listener can merge and if together the teller and listener make up the stories, the role of the reader becomes highly charged. The reader becomes Morrison's listener, necessary and participatory, and the mental interactions between Sethe and Paul D, Sethe and Beloved, and Beloved and Denver provide a model for the reader's role. Just as those minds can merge and just as those listeners can help create the story, so the reader is invited to merge with the characters' and author's minds and thereby to co-create, to "make" and "remake" (*Jazz* 229) the novel.

Many places in the text implicitly create gaps for the reader's participation. One such gap occurs just after the duet passage and just before the story of Amy and Sethe begins. In the textual space left on page 78, Denver and Beloved begin to talk/think/listen the story, and by realizing that shift in the narration, the reader joins in the reconstruction. A second such moment is when Stamp Paid introduces the women's voices in the house before the reader hears them (199). Again, there is a gap, a chapter break, to punctuate the shift in perspective and to urge the reader to participate. When the "forest" of silence "sprang up between [Sethe and Paul D]" (165), the reader is also invited to consider his or her own responses (Bell 9). Further hints for the reader's role as listener come from characters who model good listening. Ella "listened for the holes—the things the fugitives did not say; the questions they did not ask" (93; Sale 45); and Denver, perhaps a model for the author as she enthusiastically creates her fictions, is also the "ideal 'listener' " who "represents the implied community of ideal readers, the 'aural being' " (Rushdy, "Daughters" 586).

By implication, the reader becomes the listener and therefore co-creator of Paul D's two lengthiest memories. Earlier, the reader sees firsthand how Sethe coaxes Paul to release a memory about the bit and Rooster (71–73), but at that point Paul's story is brief because of the dangers for both teller and listener: "Paul D had only begun, what he was telling her was only the beginning when her fingers on his knee, soft and reassuring, stopped him. Just as well. Just as well. Saying more might push them both to a place they couldn't get back from. He would keep the rest where it belonged: in that tobacco tin in his chest where a red heart used to be" (72–73). That brief retelling *is* only the beginning, for Paul D's fuller stories of Rooster, the failed escape, and his ordeal in Alfred, Georgia, are told much more fully on pages 106–13 and 222–29. Although implicitly Sethe might be assumed to be Paul D's listener, significantly for these retellings there is no explicit character to listen. This absence of a character-listener necessitates the reader's role as the enabling listener who must adopt the model of active listening shown in other scenes by Ella, Denver, Beloved, Paul D, and Sethe. In *Jazz* this technique becomes more explicit in the long secondary narrations by Violet and Joe and in the narrator's curious relationships to the reader and the characters.[38]

Eventually the characters, and the reader, do exorcise Beloved, the past that at first they could neither ignore nor embrace, because finally they do forget: "They forgot her like a bad dream. . . . Remembering seemed unwise" (274)—and, at last, unnecessary. The novel then ends with yet another paradox when the narrator, repeating that "it was not a story to pass on," seems to agree. But by telling the story, the narrator is seemingly contradictory, for the novel *does* pass the story on. But perhaps the narrator also means not to pass on in the sense of not to pass it by, not to forget it.[39] In any case, the reader is forced to think about the story and its telling and thereby to relive the country's past horrors and to participate in the recreation of those horrors. Would it have been better not to pass it on?[40] It had to be passed on. Just as Sethe and Paul D could not pass on their memories but had to, just as Denver could not enter the world but had to, just as Sethe could not harm her children but had to, so the story could not be passed on, but had to be.

One reason for Morrison's strategies for involving the reader is the cultural sensitivity of the subject matter of *Beloved*. Since the characters must endure the painful struggle to remember and accommodate their repressed pasts, readers are asked to reconsider the traumatic past of American slavery. For Gates *Beloved* is "in many ways the Urtext of the African-American experience" (*Loose* 143). Readers must participate because this novel is about not just its characters but the

United States, and the fragmentations within the novel inscribe larger cultural divisions. If readers experience confusion, that only mirrors the dislocations felt by slaves (V. Smith, " 'Circling' " 349; Wyatt 480). The past is the South, Sweet Home, slavery; the present is the North, Cincinnati, and physical freedom but spiritual displacement. The two are divided by the temporal gap of the Civil War, which nearly split the nation in half. They are also divided by the demarcating line of the Ohio River, which symbolizes the cultural, temporal, and psychological divisions that the novel explores. As in *Uncle Tom's Cabin*, crossing the river is perilous and symbolically loaded.[41] The novel retells not only Sethe's dramatic slave narrative, but also the purchased freedom of Baby Suggs, the flight to freedom of Paul D, and the unfinished journey to the North of a social waif, Amy Denver.[42] Morrison overlays those journeys, as well as the passage into life, with the Middle Passage, whose imagery of death below decks and then rebirth into a new life of slavery further deepens and complicates the cultural and historical overtones. Morrison's dedication—"Sixty million and more"—calls attention to the larger implications of the tragedy, to *all* those who died in the African diaspora.

Beloved achieves its power not only because it addresses these cultural wounds but also because, more profoundly than Morrison's other novels, it reworks the postmodern condition. It insists that our "cultural identities . . . are defined in a way that is historically open-ended, never frozen or settled once and for all" (Mohanty 69). It delves into the recesses of its characters' souls and thereby into the American psyche, and it resists the temptations of closure. Its central figure, Beloved, can never be known: "we can name the multiplicity, but we cannot claim to know it in the sense of mastering it" (Phelan 722), for her "multiplicity transcends any story that can be told about her" (723). As a whole, this novel "creates an aesthetic identity by playing against and through the cultural field of postmodernism" (Pérez-Torres 689). In its complex discourse, it documents the continual raveling and unraveling of the fragments of experience and memory that constitute ongoing life. As Morrison says, it is about "the process by which we construct and deconstruct reality in order to be able to function in it" (E. Washington 58).

EIGHT

Make Me, Remake Me: Traces, Cracks, and Wells in *Jazz*

The postmodern tendencies in Morrison's fiction are even more explicit in *Jazz* than in her previous novels. In *Jazz,* the characters' difficulties are focused on the absence or displacement of parents and children, which, in turn, is related to the lack of satisfactory connection to the past. Such Derridean concepts as the *différance,* the trace, and the breach are especially pertinent because, in their displacement, characters tend to overemphasize either component of various binary oppositions. Joe, for example, having been deprived of his parents and therefore having had to rely solely on himself, exaggerates the importance of self, to the exclusion of anyone or anything else. Violet, on the other hand, has allowed her mother's fate to overwhelm her sense of self. The complex process of recovery that the novel documents is the movement away from such dependence on one face of an opposition and toward a healthier location within the play of oppositions. Parallel to this movement by the characters, the narrator progresses from an overreliance on her unitary self and her monologic perspective toward an open embrace of characters as well as readers. The novel depicts and simultaneously enacts the deconstructive paradigm.

By documenting the post-World War I migration from rural South to urban North, and in particular to Harlem, *Jazz* fills in another stage of Morrison's emerging fictionalization of African-American history. Each novel particularizes the lives of individuals, but each implies one or more chapters of that history. In this case, the Traces symbolize not only the millions of blacks who migrated north but also the longer history of African Americans' efforts to join the mainstream of American culture and economic life. As Leroi Jones puts it, the migration represented blacks' attempt at a "psychological realignment" with mainstream America, "a reinterpretation by the Negro of his role in this country" (96). The urban migration also repeats the earlier "migrations" of fugitive slaves and echoes the American tradition of moving on—usually West—to find a better life.

Without for the moment considering its Derridean implications, the word *trace*, Joe and Violet's last name, bears thematic weight. Like Guitar and eventually Milkman, Joe is adept at hunting, having learned the art of tracing or tracking prey from Henry LesTroy/Lestory. Good hunters follow the track of their prey by interpreting or reading its traces, the signs of its former presence. A track is also the fixed direction imposed by external forces, such as the record needle's track, the railroad tracks (which "control" the "feet" [32] of Joe, Violet, and the other North-bound migrants), and, more generally, fate: "[a faithful man near fifty] is bound to the track. It pulls him like a needle through the groove of a Bluebird record. Round and round about the town. That's the way the City spins you. . . . You can't get off the track a City lays for you" (120).

Like most of Morrison's characters, those in *Jazz* are bound to the track of northern, urban, African-American life. Lured from their rural southern roots by the promise of economic opportunity and racial liberation, they are hooked by the City's music and throbbing energy. But, like many Morrison characters, their identities are still linked to their roots in the rural South, which, no matter how devastating, remained the psychological home for migrating blacks (L. Jones 105). The track of their lives is constituted by the traces of that past, largely their memories, which paradoxically both give their present lives meaning and prevent the fulfillment of those present lives.

For Joe and Violet, as well as Dorcas and Felice, the separation from the past is figured by their loss of and need for a mother (Heinze 34; Mbalia 634). Joe, haunted by his inability to verify his mother's existence, reconstructs her in Dorcas and attempts to relive his remembered joy (his "Victory") in Vesper County.[1] For Violet, the traces of the past take the forms of her fear of repeating her mother's suicide, her inability to have her own child, and her projections of a child onto Dorcas (108–9), Felice (197), and even Golden Gray, who "lived inside [her] mind" (208). Alice Manfred is also controlled by the traces of her past, for her bitter death-in-life is associated with her husband's infidelity and her desire for revenge. Similarly, Dorcas' present is dominated by the traces of her memory of the riot-caused fire that killed her parents and burned her treasured dolls.

But *trace* carries special significance because it is one of the recurring concepts in Derrida's writing.[2] For Derrida the trace designates the play or oscillation between a presence, a thing-as-it-is, and an absence, an other. It is "the intimate relation of the living present to its outside, the opening to exteriority in general" (*Speech* 86). The trace is thus inseparable from Derrida's concept of the *différance*; both attempt to identify the indescribable gap between every pair of binary oppositions, the gap that allows them to exist, the "presence-absence" (*Of Grammatology* 71) that, never known directly, allows everything else to be comprehended. The trace is the "arche-phenomenon of 'memory' " (*Of Grammatology* 70), the play between the past and the present, the residue of the past that allows the present consciousness to exist: "the self of the living present is primordially a trace" (*Speech* 85).

Thus, like everyone, Joe Trace is a trace. He named himself because he thought that "the 'trace' [his parents] disappeared without was me" (124). His presence is only understood, only exists, in terms of the play between it and his absent parents, his absent past, and therefore his absent self. Derrida, interpreting Nietzsche, asserts that a life is a contradiction, falling as it does between the two identities of one's parents ("Otobiographies" 15). But without knowledge of either parent, Joe is denied even that location. Like Sethe's, Paul D's, and Beloved's preoccupations with their traumatic pasts, his conscious presence in the City only exists in terms of its play with, or memory of, his absent past in Vesper County. He loves Dorcas because she recalls for him that past; she is the trace of that past and the trace of himself. Her facial blemishes, "like faint hoofmarks," are the "tracks" (130) that he thinks he needs in order to renegotiate his past: "Take my little hoof marks away? Leave me with no tracks at all? In this world the best thing, the only thing, is to find the trail and stick to it." Dorcas thereby becomes a reiteration of Joe's never-acknowledged mother, Wild, and Joe's doubling of Dorcas and Wild becomes explicit in Joe's metaphor of tracking: "I tracked my mother in Virginia and it led me right to her, and I tracked Dorcas from borough to borough."

But Joe, like Sethe, is mistaken in his quest. The past cannot be reclaimed, one present cannot substitute for a lost present, one person cannot stand for another. His attempt leads to the reification of the second person, as Dorcas realizes: "Joe didn't care what kind of woman I was. He should have. I cared. I wanted to have a personality and with Acton I'm getting one" (190). Joe's love for Dorcas is the desire to possess her (Heinze 120), like Hagar's "anaconda love" for Milkman (*Song* 137) and Beloved's life-suppressing love for Sethe. Joe's quest is too self-serving. Falling into what Derrida calls the error of logocentrism or the metaphysics of presence, Joe insists on his power of self-determination. For Derrida, "there are no 'conscious' traces" (*Margins* 21), yet Joe egotistically asserts that, as opposed to his experience with Violet, he "chose" Dorcas and that she is therefore his. Similarly, he vainly recounts the seven changes in his life (123–29), as if he, his present being, could independently control his life through such choices. He assumes that he has a unitary self, that he can create and recreate that self, and that he can do so by possessing others.

None of this is meant as an indictment of Joe. Like such characters as Sethe and Paul D, he has to work through his grief for his missing mother, has to renegotiate his own past. Moreover, Joe, like Morrison's other African-American characters, is a displaced victim of the white majority, already an other, relegated to the disprivileged term of the black/white duality. Having been always already displaced into his dangerous freedom, it is inevitable for Joe to resort to displacement himself.

Joe's displacement originates with the even more radical displacement of his mother, Wild. In name and characteristics, Wild is an extreme extension of Hagar, who mentally loses herself in a "wild wilderness" (*Song* 138).[3] Except for her appearance at Joe's birth, she is known only by her absence: she simultaneously is and is not; she is "everywhere and nowhere" (179). Just as Derrida, following Heidegger, expresses this (non)existing state by placing a word under erasure, as in ~~thing~~ (*Of Grammatology* 19), she might be inscribed as ~~Wild~~. She haunts the cane fields, where a sense of her presence, a trace, is enough to generate terror and myth. When Joe attempts to find her, she (and Golden Grey) exist, not in presence, not even in fragments, but only in signs of their presence, that is in the interaction of absence and presence. Wild's presence/absence lies somewhere in the play between the signifiers (the red-winged blackbirds, her song, her human utensils and clothes) and the human being to whom those signifiers presumably point. Her presence/absence calls attention to and calls into question the usual assumptions about the privilege of presence, self, and signified.

Through Henry LesTroy/Lestory, Morrison extends these themes and the theme of parenthood. In a novel that reiterates the lack of parents, Henry's role as a father is underscored. His fatherhood is unknown both to him and Golden Grey for years, and then when his son finds him, in a quest for origins similar to Joe's quests, no father-son relationship is possible. For Golden Grey, he is a father but not a father, a ~~father~~. Henry does, however, become a surrogate father for Joe, whose birth he facilitates. Thus, Henry's fatherhood is transferred from Golden Grey, his biological son, to Joe, his surrogate son, and the transferral is completed since Golden Grey becomes in a sense Joe's (absent) stepfather through his union with Wild.[4]

In another sense Henry is the archetypal father figure, the "father" of the novel. He is "Hunter's Hunter" (166), who enjoys perfect knowledge of and union with nature. The name suggests that he is the absolute, extreme ur-hunter. Henry's bond with nature, echoed in Joe and Violet's vague longings for the health and sensibleness

(207) of their rural lives, implies his valued status. He is a *griot*, a spiritual guide, like Pilate, Circe, and Thérèse, and like them his harmony with nature corresponds with his inner harmony and fulfilled self-knowledge. In addition, his name, "Henry Lestory or LesTroy or something like that" (148), suggests that he is a synecdoche for the novel. Henry *is* the story in the sense that he has perfected the story's principal metaphor, tracking, so that he has found his role and his identity and therefore has no need for further tracking. He stands calmly in his earned selfhood, while the other characters spin around and around the track. Since such self-assurance, such presence, places Henry dangerously near, if not within, the logocentric myth, he remains on the novel's periphery.

As characters, bound by the traces, pursue the track, they are vulnerable to gaps or ruptures, for which cracks and crevices become another set of charged metaphors. Violet often loses herself in "cracks," "dark fissures in the globe light of day," "crevices one steps across all the time," "seams, ill-glued cracks and weak places beyond which is anything" (22–23). These are the "sidewalk cracks" that City women "trip" over (196), but they also suggest psychological "collapses" (24), moments of failure to cope, as when Violet suddenly sits down in the street (17), when she momentarily walks off with a baby, when Joe murders Dorcas, and when Violet stabs Dorcas's corpse. Similarly, for Golden Grey the lack of a father is "a phantom I have to behold and be held by, in whatever crevices it lies" (158).

Yet, just as circles in *Beloved* can be fulfilling and constraining, cracks and crevices are two-edged. Joe, in quest of his mother, slides through a "crevice" into her chamber of gold (183). The positive/negative mixture of the motif is reinforced by its connection to both light and dark: although fissures are normally dark, Joe's movement into absolute light, "like falling into the sun," is a direct result of his following the track through the dark crevice. Joe's fall into this womb-like cave recalls Milkman's journey into the cave near Danville: both are associated with gold, with males' quests for their ancestors, and with blinding contrasts of light and dark. In *Jazz* the paradoxical mixture of positive and negative associations for crevices is reiterated when the narrator reflects on life for blacks in the City: "the shade" (the energizing life of the City, the clicking fingers, but also the

164

"warning and the shudder") simultaneously "lurk[s]" and "hover[s] kindly" and "stretches—just there—at the edge of the dream, or slips into the crevices of a chuckle" (227).

Like the imagery of splitting in *The Bluest Eye*, this imagery of cracks and crevices is illuminated by Derrida's use of the term *breach*. Morrison's first novel foregrounds the destruction inherent in the breach, whereas here Morrison overtly stresses its double-edged quality. Cracks or breaches are disruptive, but the disruption allows us to know the entities being separated and to refocus on the gap itself and on the structure of the breaching (which is the structure of the trace, of the *différance*) and therefore to continue the constructive process of identity formation.

In *Jazz* the deepest breach is the well in which Rose Dear kills herself. This death-hole is like the "stinking hole" into which Guitar throws his candy and from whose negativity he never recovers (*Song* 227), and it is reminiscent of the tunnel that draws many of the Bottom's residents with its lure of revenge, anger, and unavailable jobs. Violet, driven almost to insanity by her mother's suicide, is haunted by the image of a well ("The well sucked her sleep" [102]) and she is even "scare[d]" by "deep holes" (223). For her the image of a well is a powerful lure, with its "limitless beckoning" (101) and its "pull" (104).

Derrida, meditating on the ontology of books, refers to "the unnameable bottomless well" (*Writing* 297), which is "the abyss" (296) as well as the center. The center is "the absence of play and difference, another name for death" (297), and the book, as a completed, enclosed entity, "was to have insinuated itself into the dangerous hole, was to have furtively penetrated into the menacing dwelling place" (297–98). For Derrida, only by repetition—also implied by the image of tracing—does one escape from this well/trap. If we return to the book, to the hole, we attain a "strange serenity" and we are "fulfilled . . . by remaining open, by pronouncing nonclosure" (298). Thus, the well is a breach, a potentially dangerous opening, abyss, or "labyrinth," but at the same time an opportunity for discovery, peace, and self-development.

In *Jazz* the well is also not merely a haunting image of death but an open image. The narrator's uncharacteristically jaunty description

165

of Rose Dear's suicide hints at this ambiguity: "And then Rose Dear jumped in the well and missed all the fun" (99). Another hint of the mixed associations of wells is Violet's sense of the well as "a place so narrow, so dark it was pure" (101). By the time Violet and Joe are reunited, the well becomes an image of secure love and generosity: "Meanwhile Violet rests her hand on [Joe's] chest as though it were the sunlit rim of a well" (225). This dual sense of the well, as a place of danger yet of awareness, is most evident when the narrator tries "to dream a nice dream for [Golden Grey]" (161):

> I want him to stand next to a well dug quite clear from trees so twigs and leaves will not fall into the deep water, and while standing there in shapely light, his fingertips on the rim of stone, his gaze at no one thing, his mind soaked and sodden with sorrow, or dry and brittle with the hopelessness that comes from knowing too little and feeling too much (so brittle, so dry he is in danger of the reverse: feeling nothing and knowing everything). There then, with nothing available but the soaking or the brittleness, not even looking toward the well, not aware of its mossy, unpleasant odor, or the little life that hovers at its rim, but to stand there next to it and from down in it, where the light does not reach, a collection of leftover smiles stirs, some brief benevolent love rises from the darkness and there is nothing for him to see or hear, and there is no reason to stay but he does. For the safety at first, then for the company. Then for himself—with a kind of confident, enabling, serene power that flicks like a razor and then hides. (161)

At the rim of the well—another circle—Golden Grey, like Violet and Joe, can enjoy the play, the life, between and among ultimate dichotomous forces: life/death, light/dark, self/other, humanity/nature, solitude/plenitude, presence/absence. So the well is necessary even if it is a death-hole, even if fear of it may paralyze. Like the breach, the well is salutary and serene, not something to embrace, for embracing the other is no answer, but something to stand in relation to, an opening into *différance*, a trace.

Like Derrida's insistence on repetition as the way to avoid closure, the narrator's dream of Golden Grey's ideal relationship with the well includes the sense of endless repetition: "But he has felt it now, and it may come again. No doubt a lot of other things will come again: doubt will come, and things may seem unclear from time to time.

But once the razor blade has flicked—he will remember it, and if he remembers it he can recall it. That is to say, he has it at his disposal" (161). Once in the mind, the scene or act becomes not mere presence but productive combination of presence and absence, becomes not mere work to be consumed but text to be endlessly reread.[5]

Despite the felicity of this remembered paradisiacal scene by the well, the narrator grows to the realization that the well too must be rejected: "I started out believing that life was made just so the world would have some way to think about itself, but that it had gone awry with humans because flesh, pinioned by misery, hangs on to it with pleasure. Hangs on to wells and a boy's golden hair; would just as soon inhale sweet fire caused by a burning girl as hold a maybe-yes maybe-no hand. I don't believe that anymore. Something is missing there. Something rogue. Something else you have to figure in before you can figure it out" (228). Whether it be lovely (the golden hair), scary (the well), or ambiguously lovely/scary (the fire), holding on to anything—the past, the unitary self, another being—is dangerous, dangerously static, dangerously death-like. The well must be rejected, for rogueness—the unpredictable, the uncentered, the undeterminable, the free—is required.

Through its narration *Jazz* explores this rogueness and its implied insistence on blurred distinctions. The main narrator, first-person but not a character in the fictional world, thereby straddles the conventional dichotomy between third-person (external) narrators and first-person (internal) narrators.[6] The dichotomy is further compromised by the characters' long, first-person monologues in which they take over the narrating function, and by the narrator's tendency to move inconspicuously in and out of their minds, for example in the long chapter in which Violet sits with her malt in the drugstore but mentally ranges over her whole life (89–114).[7]

Since Morrison wants to "fret the pieces and fragments of memory" (E. Washington 58), in this novel she frets out distinctions by creating a narrator who is paradoxically both knowledgeable and unreliable/limited. From the opening sentence ("Sth, I know that woman"), the narrator emphasizes her knowledge with phrases like "I know" (63, 119, 152, 154), "I have seen" (35, 36, 59, 67), "I see" (143), "I could see" (195), and "I could hear" (196).[8] She often

167

speaks in the present tense to emphasize the direct, firsthand nature of her knowledge, and she asserts that she has known the whole story in advance and that as she narrates she still can "see" the characters (226). Although readers may doubt such assertions, her knowledge is verified throughout the novel by the consistency between her assertions and the characters' first-person accounts.[9]

By casting her as a first-person narrator, however, Morrison moves the narration from the hypothetical "omniscient" to somewhere between knowledgeable and not knowledgeable. As Rodrigues argues, she must be both detached and involved, neither objective nor omniscient but not completely subjective either, in order for readers to understand the significance of the story ("Experiencing" 748). The narrator often alludes to what she does not know: how Violet's affair ended (5), what Joe whispered to Dorcas at Alice Manfred's luncheon (71), what Joe's tears were for (221). She admits to relying on what other people knew or thought (57, 166, 179), and she is quite explicitly and admittedly a gossip, who, when she doesn't know, speculates. Her admissions of limited knowledge do not silence her and are often followed by such phrases as "but I *do* know" (5, 17, 137). If opinions are divided, she gives hers (118); if she doesn't have access to a character's mind, "[she] can tell" by their manner (49); and if she lacks direct knowledge, she speculates by resorting to conditional verb tenses: "It had to be" (140); "It must have been" (173). Her sense of Joe and Violet is "caught midway between was and must be" (226), caught in the play between past tense and conditional tense, between fact and speculation. "For [her] they are real," but the nature of that reality, somewhere between the narrator's imagination and the "actual" reality of the novel's world, remains open. Instead of a conventional narration, this fugal text presents fragments, bits and pieces of information, which, like a jazz performance or a musical score, ask readers to "set aside Cartesian logic" (Rodrigues, "Experiencing" 734), to respond with their complete selves rather than merely their intellects.

Three passages call special attention to the narrator's sense of her role and purposes. Near the beginning of the novel, she says that she survives the City by being secretive and by "watch[ing] everything and everyone and try[ing] to figure out their plans, their reasonings, long before they do" (8). Later she knows that it is "risky . . . trying to figure out anybody's state of mind. But worth the trouble if you're like me—curious, inventive, and well-informed" (137). And near the end she acknowledges that she "invented stories about [the characters]," that she "took every opportunity I had to follow them, to gossip about and fill in their lives," and that she was immersed in "meddling" and "finger-shaping" (220). She is well-informed, and/or/but she must *try* to figure things out, but "try" and "fill in" suggest that her figuring may not always be accurate and that, by her own admission, her biases have affected her narration.

The narrator's biases undermine her reliability. Dazzled by the City's music, its "unbelievable sky" (35), its springtime (117), and its "sweetheart weather" (195), she admits that it distorts her feelings: "A city like this one makes me dream tall and feel in on things" (7), and the City has resulted in her "liv[ing] a long time, maybe too much, in my own mind" (9). She worries that "it can make you inhospitable if you aren't careful, the last thing I want to be."

Yet that is what has happened to her. She has been deceived by the "artful City" (118) into wanting to see, and therefore into seeing, more problems than actually exist. She overemphasizes the negative in Golden Grey, not merely describing him as "a hypocrite" (154), but judgmentally laying on the criticism: "He is lying, the hypocrite." And she revels in asserting her own superiority: "He thinks his story is wonderful, and that if spoken right will impress his father with his willingness, his honor. But I know better." Since an external narrator *should* know better, such protestations at first ring false. A few pages later after reporting Golden's anguish, the narrator realizes her mistake: "What was I thinking of? How could I have imagined him so poorly?" (160). This unreliability then becomes explicit: "I have been careless and stupid and it infuriates me to discover (again) how unreliable I am." Again? Yes, the narrator has been unreliable before and will be again, for example when she dates Dorcas's funeral as both seven and eight years after the armistice (9–10) and when she describes Golden Grey's shirt first as white (147) and then yellow (158). Her admission of unreliability and the numerous examples of it undermine her credibility, and yet her willingness to revise also suggests her recognition of the dangers of asserting one-dimensional "truths," of appropriating all author-ity to herself, of shutting off continuing investigation. In her revision of Golden Grey's story, she reenvisions herself and her roles, shifting from a monologic to a dialogic perspective.[10]

Like her exaggeration of Golden Grey's weakness, the narrator also signifies on the reader by mispredicting, from the beginning, further disaster for Joe and Violet: "It promised to be a mighty bleak household" (6); "A host of thoughtful people looked at the signs . . . and believed it was the commencement of all sorts of destruction" (9). Her biases lead her to proclaim, unreliably, that a second murder takes place: "Violet invited [Felice] in to examine the record and that's how that scandalizing threesome on Lenox Avenue began. What turned out different was who shot whom" (6). Already knowing that no one else actually is shot, she is conscious of her unreliability and therefore of her manipulations of the reader. Because of her premonition of disaster, based on her desire to believe that the worst will happen, she retains the pose of being taken aback when Joe and Violet recover. Since Felice will be an instrument in that recovery, "she makes [the narrator] nervous" (198) and she "mak[es] me doubt my own self."

This self-doubt becomes overt when the narrator ultimately confesses:

> So I missed it altogether. I was sure one would kill the other. I waited for it so I could describe it. I was so sure it would happen. That the past was an abused record with no choice but to repeat itself at the crack and no power on earth could lift the arm that held the needle. I was so sure, and they danced and walked all over me. Busy, they were, busy being original, complicated, changeable—human, I guess you'd say, while I was the predictable one, confused in my solitude into arrogance, thinking my space, my view was the only one that was or that mattered. I got so aroused while meddling, while finger-shaping, I overreached and missed the obvious. (220)

The narrator thus commits the same logocentric mistake that the characters commit. In her solitude, her privileged selfhood, she thinks that only she knows, that only her perceptions have truth, or at least that her view and her imagination are superior. She privileges self over other, present over past, her narration of events (the *sjuzet* or discourse) over the events themselves (the *fabula* or story). Morrison thereby suggests that such privileging, as well as the insistence on the distinctions that inevitably lead to the privileging, is suspect. The pattern is similar to the other novels: artificial categories—for example, narrators, individuals, and races—reflect metaphysical simplification and the closure of death. Neither fusion nor fragmentation is adequate; instead, one must recognize and enter the indeterminate and vital play within the plurality/unity.

When she realizes each of her major errors, the narrator's self-correcting wish is to move into physical closeness with the characters. To make up for overly criticizing Golden Grey, she says, "I want to dream a nice dream for him, and another of him. Lie down next to him, a wrinkle in the sheet, and contemplate his pain and by doing so ease, diminish it" (161). Similarly, after misinterpreting Felice, Joe, and Violet, she "want[s] to be in a place already made for me, both snug and wide open" (221), and that place is "in the peace left by [Wild] who lived [in the chamber of gold] and scared everybody." She wants to enter the characters' world and to exist there peacefully, in intimate communion with the characters: "[Wild] has seen me and is not afraid of me. She hugs me. Understands me. Has given me her hand. I am touched by her. Released in secret." By the conventional distinctions between external narrator and characters, this cannot happen. It cannot and yet it does: the narrator does enter the characters' space even as she remains outside it. Morrison insists on this because, wary of conventional distinctions, she blurs the distinctions, pushes beyond them, plumbs the *différance*.

The *différance*, in this case the presumed gap between narrator and characters, is further teased out by the characters' tendency to share the narrator's role. Like her, they are compulsive talkers: they must tell their individual stories in their monologues, Joe and Violet must talk all night when they first meet (105), Violet and Alice find mutual comfort in endless conversations, and Dorcas wants a lover whom she can talk about. Characters also imitate the narrator by recreating or "narrating" scenes through memory, as when Joe struggles fiercely to remember "every detail of that October afternoon" (28) when he met Dorcas. Like the narrator, they also project themselves mentally into events they did not experience: Dorcas pictures the burning of her dolls (60–61), Violet imagines Joe and Dorcas at the Mexico nightclub (94–96), and Joe constructs a reconciliation scene with Dorcas (183). Neither characters nor narrator are limited by the usual constraint of being present at the scenes they describe.

The most remarkable conflation of the narrator's and a character's mental projections occurs when the narrator relates Golden Grey's encounter with Wild. The narrator's knowledge is expressed as what she envisions: "I see him in a two-seat phaeton" (143). But Golden's experience is reported with the same metaphor: he thinks that "what he is running from is not a real woman but a 'vision' " (144). Furthermore, his action to help the unconscious Wild is triggered by his inward vision of himself *not* helping her: "He does not see himself touching her, but the picture he does imagine is himself walking away from her a second time, climbing into his carriage and leaving her a second time" (145). Since the scene *is* a vision, a vision of the narrator's, the doubling of the metaphor further calls into question the traditional distinctions between narrator and character and between their ways of knowing.

The narrator doubles the doubling when, without warning, she re-imagines and retells the same scene (150–55). This "double-take" re-reports the scene with slightly different details from the first version; the fireplace, for example, is now "clean, set for a new fire" (152) whereas in the first telling it "has a heap of ash" (147). The discrepancies, and the mere fact of the juxtaposition of two competing accounts by the same narrator, calls into question the status of each account and of the narrator's accounting in general. Such an unraveling of the means of narrative transmission calls attention to the narrative and therefore to the act of reading, thereby reminding readers of their roles and requiring their active participation, much like the invitational gaps in the text of *Beloved*. This telling/retelling is an explicit "return to the book," a testimony to the necessity of repetition.

The distinction between characters and narrator is also blurred when the characters assume the narrator's traditional role by inventing personality traits of other characters. Unnamed characters make up stories about Wild (165–67), Alice muses over the personalities of Joe (73) and Violet (75), and, most notably, Violet "invent[s]" a

172

"personality" for Dorcas (28). Later in her "deep-dreaming," that made-up personality becomes intermingled with her miscarried baby as she imagines Dorcas to be "a girl young enough to be that daughter" (108–9), and when Felice appears Violet repeats the projection, thinking of Felice as "another true-as-life Dorcas" (197).

Two further examples reinforce this pattern of blurred character/narrator distinctions. Malvonne not only gossips but actually intervenes in others' lives. Since "her interest lay in the neighborhood people" (41), she opens their letters and tries to write helpful responses. In both respects she thereby replicates the narrator, who "watch[es] everything and everyone and tr[ies] to figure out their plans, their reasonings, long before they do" (8). Thus, the character Malvonne, a present third-person gossip, doubles the narrator, an absent first-person gossip. The second example occurs in a single passage. After Violet has refound herself at the end of the novel, she tells Felice, "What's the world for if you can't make it up the way you want it?" (208). This appears to be one lesson Violet has learned, one part of what it takes to gain and retain a viable identity in Morrison's fictional world. At the same time the power to make up the world as you want it describes the role of the narrator, thus implying that success in both roles is indistinguishable.

In addition to the blurring between narrator and characters, the presumed gap between narrator and reader is called into question and radically diminished. Just as the narrator imagines physical embraces with Golden Grey and later with Wild, she ends the novel by projecting physical intimacy with the reader. After describing Joe and Violet's new love (222–25) and then recalling a tender moment from their Virginia past (225–26), the narrator extrapolates their love to lovers in general (226–29). But the narrator, isolated in her peculiar role neither within the characters' world nor physically in the readers', cannot participate directly in human relationships, so, in the extraordinary closing paragraphs, she laments her isolation: "I envy them their public love. I myself have only known it in secret, shared it in secret" (229). Her secret love is for the reader: "*That I have loved only you, surrendered my whole self reckless to you and nobody else.*" Like any lover she wants hers to reciprocate: "*That I want you to love me back and show it to me.*" She imagines that she is the book and there-

173

fore that the reader holds her: "*That I love the way you hold me, how close you let me be to you. I like your fingers on and on, lifting, turning.*" The reader's act of reading the book becomes the basis for the narrator's imagined love affair: "*I have watched your face for a long time now, and missed your eyes when you went away from me. Talking to you and hearing you answer—that's the kick.*"[11] Or, as Derrida writes: "The beyond of the closure of the book is neither to be awaited nor to be refound. It is *there*, but out there, *beyond*, within repetition, but eluding us there. It is there like the shadow of the book, the third party between the hands holding the book, the deferral within the now of writing, the distance between the book and the book, that other hand" (*Writing* 300).

The narrator of *Jazz* uses italics because she "can't say that aloud" (229) cannot erase the barrier, cannot actually see and feel the reader. She can dream across the barrier, and thus Morrison can adumbrate the *différance*, but the reader remains separate. Still, the narrator urges the reader to share in the dream, in the play: "If I were able I'd say it. Say make me, remake me." If the reader actively participates, participates in the (re)making of the novel, then the narrator/reader relationship exists and the absolute distinction between the two is dissolved. Only by repeating the book can we avoid its potential dead end: "the return to the book does not enclose us within the book" (Derrida, *Writing* 294). The book, any book, must be remade, must be "ceaselessly begun and taken up again on a site which is neither in the book nor outside it" (298), because in that "repetition," that "bottomlessness of infinite redoubling" (296), or tracing, what disappears is "the self-identity of the origin," the deadening lack of play of self, presence, and origin. Once again, the image of tracing is instructive. To trace is to copy, to double, and thus to avoid the death-like closure of completion, thereby allowing for endless readings, endless reader participation, endless versions of the text. Since to trace is also to write, to make physical marks on a blank surface, to set in motion the continuing flux of meaning (Miller 6–8), author, narrator, characters, and reader are theoretically fused.

In closing, the narrator reaches even farther toward the reader to imagine physical intimacy: "You are free to do it and I am free to let you because look, look. Look where your hands are. Now." This lyrical evocation of loving contact between narrator and reader is antici-pated by the narrator's references to the reader throughout the novel. She narrates as though she were talking directly to the reader, and she often includes the reader in her talk: "Close up on the tops of buildings, near, nearer than the cap you are wearing" (35); "Think how it is, if you can manage, just manage it" (63); and "Can you see the fields beyond, crackling and drying in the wind?" (153).

As these invocations of the reader suggest, the narrator's rhetoric often resembles spoken rather than written language, as if the narra-tor were gossiping over the back fence with her neighbor. The initial "word" of the novel implants this sense of orality. "Sth" is not a word but a sound, the sound of sucking one's teeth while talking, which is reiterated by the woman in the Dumfrey women's building (19), by Alice Manfred (84), and in *Beloved* by Ella (185). In all these cases the sound, along with the appropriate body language, expresses each woman's disapproval of someone's behavior. In *Beloved*, however, the narrator describes the sound somewhat differently when Stamp Paid overhears the voices of Sethe, Denver, and Beloved: "They had be-come an occasional mutter—like the interior sounds a woman makes when she believes she is alone and unobserved at her work: a *sth* when she misses the needle's eye; a soft moan when she sees another chip in her one good platter; the low, friendly argument with which she greets the hens. Nothing fierce or startling. Just that eternal, pri-vate conversation that takes place between women and their tasks" (172).

This startling first word/sound enters at least two gaps. It begins the oral quality of the prose, a quality continued throughout by refer-ences to the reader and by numerous colloquial words and expres-sions, such as "Good luck and let me know" (5), "hincty" (143), and "quiet as it's kept" (17).[12] It also suggests at least two ways of per-ceiving the narrator's activity. On the one hand, the narrator is like the other women, gossiping and sucking her teeth in disapproving exaggeration of their problems; but on the other hand, by the impli-cations of the passage from *Beloved*, her discourse, like Claudia's, is also her solitary ruminations to herself.

This play between written and oral language begins with the nov-el's epigraph. The passage from "The Thunder: Perfect Mind," one of

175

the texts in the collection known as the Nag Hammadi library (Robinson), juxtaposes orality ("the name of the sound") and inscription ("the sign of the letter"). Like *Jazz*, "Thunder" is a "revelation discourse" narrated by a presumably female figure (MacRae 295), who combines both genders ("I am the bride and the bridegroom") and who transcends worldly limitations (MacRae 296). Like Morrison's narrator, the narrator of "Thunder" is contradictory: "I am strength and I am fear," "I am the union and the dissolution." Both narrators both know and do not know ("For I am knowledge and ignorance"), are self-deprecatory and accusatory ("I am shame and boldness"), are sympathetic and antagonistic ("I am compassionate and I am cruel"), and are present and absent ("on the day when I [am far away] from you, [I am close] to you." Both speak words that can be heard but not fully comprehended: "I am the hearing that is attainable to everyone and the speech which cannot be grasped."[13]

For Derrida, a principle error of traditional Western thought is its opposition between speech and writing and its privileging of the former. Morrison necessarily approaches this dualism from the perspective of a genre in which writing is privileged, and thus, by calling attention to the oral elements in its language, her novel's rhetoric compensates for that privileging, inscribes the *différance*, and thereby enacts an alternative to the either/or trap of the old metaphysics.

Unlike the emphasis on fragmentation in *The Bluest Eye*, *Sula*, and *Tar Baby*, *Jazz* privileges fusion. Characters become whole again: Violet unites *that* Violet and herself (92); Violet, Joe, and Felice do put their lives together (Rodrigues, "Experiencing" 749), in contrast to Morrison's earlier fragmented characters; and Alice Manfred regains control of her identity. Joe and Violet are reunited as a couple, forming a new family with Felice and their new bird. Simultaneously, they find harmony with their community in New York, harmony and community that they did not even know they missed since leaving Vesper County. At the same time, the narrator, initially isolated from the characters in her haughtiness, comes in from the cold to loving and generous reciprocity with them, as conventional boundaries between narrator and characters and between narrator and reader are breached.

In *Jazz* Morrison "constructs jazz possibilities out of the (post)-

modernist, dispersed chaos" (Werner, *Playing* 301). By not insisting on definite meanings (Rodrigues, "Experiencing" 750); by unraveling single-voiced authority into multi-voiced sensibilities; by blending written, oral, and musical forms; by demonstrating how past and present can be reconciled; by celebrating African-American adaptations to modern, urban life, *Jazz* is postmodern in the most positive senses.

NINE

What's the World For If You Can't Make It Up the Way You Want It?

Beset with the inversions, displacements, and fragmentations of a racialized society, Morrison's characters have few viable options for developing fulfilled identities. One such option, however, is storytelling. Characters' social and psychological health is dependent on their ability to articulate the stories of their pasts or to invent stories that parallel or reconstruct their own lives, and sometimes on their ability to listen sympathetically to others' stories. Storytelling and story-listening enable the characters to transcend fixed, dead-end positions and instead to engage in the reconstructive processes of ongoing fusion and fragmentation.

Such beneficial effects are a commonplace of Euro-American psychology and African and African-American oral traditions. As William Carlos Williams puts it, "Their story, yours, mine—it's what we all carry with us on this trip we take, and we owe it to each other to respect our stories and learn from them" (qtd. in Coles 30). The West African belief in the power of the spoken word literally to create that which is uttered implies that, until uttered, the events of one's life, and therefore one's very self, do not exist. Through the interactive speaking and listening of the story circle, individual and community achieve mutual integration and fulfillment, and individual, community, and universe are connected (Bell xi). Based on the African heritage, the African-American oral tradition continues the privileging of individual/group interconnectedness through storytelling and listening. Call and response, signifying, and testifying/witnessing are complex forms of the interaction between storyteller and listener, individual and group.

Such forms represent attempts to cope with the historical and enduring problem of identity formation. Storytelling provides authenticity to one's self (V. Smith, *Self-Discovery* 2), and, along with borrowing information from others' stories, it is central to the quest for identity (Kubitschek 21). As bell hooks argues, the move from silence to speech is an essential act for the oppressed and exploited, an act that transforms the self from object to subject by unloosening "the liberating voice" (*Talking Back* 15). Similarly, Keith Byerman stresses the importance in African-American literature of the quest for voice, for authority over the narrative, and he contrasts the use of words to dehumanize with the power of words to liberate (6).

In Morrison's fiction, characters who cannot or do not tell their stories tend to fail—to die, to flee, to remain fixed in static, monologic, unfulfilling lives. Conversely, characters who voice their own stories find as much integration and satisfaction as Morrison's world permits, and the ability to listen with care and absorption usually coincides with this storytelling power: "Her characters understand why they are and what their lives mean when they can tell stories about how they came to be" (V. Smith, *Self-Discovery* 122).

Especially in Morrison's first three novels, many characters are virtually mute, unable to invent or tell any stories. Pecola Breedlove is the extreme case, as she falls from passive, monosyllabic responses into psychotic, mute withdrawal. Other women are almost inarticulate. Helene Wright is determined to repress her colorful past and her daughter's creativity, allowing only conformity to middle-class values. For both mother and daughter (until Nel's recovering epiphany at the end of the novel), such denial freezes identity formation in a

179

single stance, a narrow fragment, and thereby precludes the open play that verbal articulation allows. Hannah Peace, although seemingly content with her chosen nonconformity, also never voices her story and thus also remains static. Like Helene and Nel, she also expresses no interest in hearing anyone else's story. In *Song of Solomon* Reba and Hagar suffer blindly, despite Pilate's influence, partly because they are not articulate about their lives or interested in anyone else's. Reba drifts almost silently from lover to lover and contest to contest. Hagar, unable to express her desires either to her family or to Milkman, drives herself more and more narrowly into self-defeating and primarily silent actions—first her monthly hunts for Milkman, then her sadly insane shopping spree, and finally her loss of the will to live.

Men, especially in the first two novels, are reduced to near silence and disinterest. Cholly Breedlove suffers almost the same silence as Pecola. Driven from meaningful relationships with others, he speaks only to curse and he listens to no one. Other men in Morrison's first book, such as Mr. Henry and Soaphead Church, tend to prey on women and girls but rarely to speak. In *Sula*, Shadrack, shocked like Cholly out of verbal communication with others, survives only through symbolic acts, such as National Suicide Day and the military order of his cabin. Males' dominant mode in *Sula* is silent escape: through death (Plum, Chicken Little), mental incapacity (Shadrack, the deweys, Tar Baby), or physical flight (BoyBoy, the four Irish boys, Jude, Ajax). Cut off from their own and others' stories, the men have no enduring community or family functions and therefore cannot engage in significant identity development.

Other Morrison characters are unable to tell their stories fully or articulately but do make a momentary breakthrough. Sula, trying to create her own life, cannot sustain the effort partly because she never learns how to tell her story and never finds the right listener. Like Cholly or Shadrack, she replaces telling and listening with actions, which become increasingly futile and self-defeating. But she does sense the need to tell her story, as, too little and too late, her last moment of consciousness is the urge to communicate: "Wait 'til I tell Nel" (149). Nel also lacks voice and audience, in her case because of her repression of self and of her responsibility for her actions. Like

Sula, she has a momentary epiphany, a "fine cry, loud and long" in which her deepest feelings are finally expressed, but her release comes many years too late. Margaret Street, also a victim of self-repression, is fortunate to have Ondine tell her story, after which she finds her own voice and is relieved to tell and retell her abuse of Michael. Ondine herself does "tell it" (178), finally unburdening herself of the secret, but the release does not enable her to overcome her long-developed bitterness. In *Jazz* Dorcas similarly represses the terror of the fire in East St. Louis that destroyed her dolls. Reduced to an object in Joe's story, she realizes her need for a boyfriend she can talk about, but, like Pecola, she passively accepts silence, which literally leads to her death.

Pauline Breedlove, Ruth and Macon Dead, and Jadine Childs struggle to tell their stories by expressing their inner lives, but their efforts remain fragmentary and unsuccessful. Pauline, like Sula endowed with artistic sensibilities and without an appropriate medium, allows her voice and her self to be subsumed by Hollywood images. She partially tells her story, but, significantly, her first-person narration is presented only in disconnected paragraphs. Similarly, Ruth and Macon, locked in a no-win feud with each other, release some of their repressed feelings in fragmentary stories of their pasts. Although these bits and pieces help their son, they come too late for Ruth or Macon, much like Sula's and Nel's momentary and belated breakthroughs. Jadine hears and rationally understands the stories of the characters around her, but she does not care to listen to such stories, and she therefore remains confused by them as well as by the voices of the mythic women who remind her of her racial and gender betrayals. Repressing others' stories and the pasts they intimate, and unable to reconcile these conflicting claims on her, she cannot frame her own story.

As all these characters struggle to find and maintain viable identities, their fragmentary efforts to tell their stories parallel their fragmented lives. As their selves are displaced by alien stereotypes, their stories are shunted aside, silenced. Fusion of self through participation in the ongoing play of plurality-in-unity is elusive, just as their own stories are only partially articulated in momentary bits and pieces.

181

Although not telling one's story is always harmful, telling it is not necessarily a panacea. For some characters, the obstacles are simply too great: Pauline, Ruth, and Macon do recall parts of their pasts, but the confining patterns of their lives have already been determined. For others, telling their story is not therapeutic because they are too dogmatic and monologic. Helene and Geraldine harp on the one theme of their stories: conformity. Eva similarly insists too rigidly on the absolute rightness of her own actions and tries to use her stories of her own life and her invented lives of others, such as the deweys and Tar Baby, to justify her tyranny. Likewise, Golden Grey tries to use the story of his mixed-blood parentage to gain revenge on his father. Still others adopt a single-stranded story that justifies their own existence but is invalidated by the novel's discourse. Soaphead Church creates a bizarre argument defying God's flawed creation and conveniently providing cover for his own immorality. Guitar Bains, despite having told the story of his father's death and his mother's humiliation and despite listening to Hagar's plight, does not resolve his own feelings about his past and thus is seduced into the Seven Days' "story," which provides him with a theory to rationalize his violent anger. Valerian Street adopts the myth of white, patriarchal, hegemonic privilege and thereby uses his inherited power to suppress his buried feelings and to blind himself to his own familial tragedy. Borrowing his status from his employers, Sydney and Ondine similarly adopt the myth of the urban house Negro, which they use to justify their presumed status above that of lower-class blacks.

Out of harmony with themselves and their communities, these characters with their monolithic, egotistic stories usually do not listen empathetically to others' stories. Often, they are presented in pairs of characters, who have the opportunity to hear each other's stories but who cannot or do not: Nel and Sula, after subconsciously dreaming the same dream, stop listening to each other; the narrator of *The Bluest Eye* reports Pauline's and Cholly's past lives, but they have long since stopped talking to each other; and Ruth and Macon can tell fragments of their stories to Milkman but not to each other. Unable or unwilling either to allow diversity into their stories or to tolerate that diversity in others, such characters remain stuck on their single notes.

Other characters are forced to listen, but the stories they are told are dull or unbearable. Milkman is initially bored by the stories he hears from Macon, Ruth, and Guitar. Valerian finds Margaret's story of abusing Michael impossible to accept, so, like Pecola who finds life itself unlivable, he mentally retires from reality. This difficulty of speaking and hearing the unspeakable dominates *Beloved*, driving Halle into insanity, forcing Denver into temporary muteness and prolonged agoraphobia, and nearly destroying Sethe and Paul D. Psychic survival depends upon working through such painful and threatening impasses toward a healthier engagement with the complexities of one's past, one's family, and one's community, and the multifarious but healing stories associated therewith.

Characters who do listen tend to be those who also articulate their own stories and thus not only survive but recover. Several female triads, such as the prostitutes and Aunt Jimmy's friends in *The Bluest Eye*, provide mutual and harmonious support by constituting small communities of listeners. Claudia MacTeer, although unsure of her discoveries, hears all the stories, tries desperately to save Pecola, and then reconstructs the others' stories into her own. Milkman Dead, bored at first, nevertheless absorbs the competing stories of those around him. For the wrong reasons, he stumbles upon the clues that lead him to reassemble the lost story of his family and thus himself, which he retells to himself, Sweet, his parents, and Pilate. Pilate herself is Morrison's first *griot*, who helps form Milkman's character by her lifestyle but also by her stories, as she exemplifies empathic love through attentive listening and talking. Another such *griot* is Thérèse, who tells not so much her own story as others'. She bridges the commonplace and the mythical, the human and the natural, largely through the stories she invents. She makes the world up the way she wants it, convincing Son to accept her version of his mythical role. In the first four novels, Claudia (to an extent), Milkman, Pilate, and Thérèse transcend their fragmented milieus and achieve stable selfhood largely because of their skills as storytellers and listeners.

In Morrison's fifth and sixth novels, the powers of storytelling and listening are especially prominent. Beloved, denied a voice and any participation in her own life, illustrates the destructiveness of demanding, judgmental listening. Like those characters who insist on telling their own stories to fulfill their selfish requirements, she uses Sethe's guilt to devour Sethe with her demands to hear her story. But for other characters in *Beloved*, storytelling and story-listening are essential for mental health. Ella has no patience for keeping silent, preferring to let the truth out and get on with life. Stamp Paid knows and tells his own story, renames himself accordingly, hears everyone else's story, and becomes the neighborhood's healer and an exemplary witness/testifier. He risks telling Sethe's story to Paul D, which temporarily sidetracks Paul and exiles Stamp from 124 Bluestone, but which proves to be a therapeutic communication. Paul D is the perfect listener, but he has bottled up his own unspeakable story, and until he can retell it he is not ready to hear Sethe's story and therefore is not ready to resume his own course of identity development. Paul D and Sethe function like the female triads, in turn telling and listening, retelling and re-listening, in bits and pieces, until the unspeakable and unrememberable stories are told and heard so that their inner lives can resume.

The community suffers a similar repression after Baby Suggs gives up serving as its *griot*. In her sermons, she tries to give voice to the community's needs to tell its various stories, but she cannot carry their collective burdens. Without her voice, the community stops listening, therefore becoming static and fragmented, only to become unstuck when the community women, led by Ella, rediscover their voice, their responsibility, their role, and thereby their identity.

Denver amply illustrates the theme of recovery through finding one's voice. Like Pecola she is struck dumb, in her case by the unbearable story of her mother's actions. Within 124 Bluestone, she creates a mental life by retelling the almost mythic stories of her mother's journey to Cincinnati and especially of her own birth. Still, despite her powers of storytelling and listening, the stories become too ingrown and finally destructive, so Denver, with the help of Baby Suggs's "story," extricates herself and rescues herself and her mother by telling her new story to the community.

Sethe and Paul D mutually enact the paradoxical pain and necessity of voicing and hearing their repressed stories. Until they build the trust in themselves and in each other to endure this process of re-memberment, they cannot love, cannot live, cannot be whole. But having found that trust and that courage, they can exorcise their demons, can put their stories next to each other's (273), and thereby can reengage with life.

In *Jazz* the recuperative powers of telling and listening are equally pervasive. The horrific deeds that must be explained and from which the Traces must recover are associated with the Traces' failures to communicate. Violet lapses into silence, unable to come to grips with her mother's suicidal silence and her own inability to have children. Joe, martyred by this withdrawal of Violet, withdraws into his memories of Vesper County and his lost mother through his reification of Dorcas. In parallel fashion, Alice Manfred represses her anger over her unfaithful husband, expressing it not in words but in her insistence on rigidly conservative moral and sexual behavior. For all these characters, telling their stories and listening to others' stories leads to recovery. Violet and Alice, in their strange alliance, help heal each other. Both Joe and Violet are granted long internal monologues in which they voice and revoice their own stories. After her identity crisis, Violet verbally reconstructs her life and listens patiently to Alice and others, so that she gains author-ity over her self and life. She thereby reaches a position much like Morrison's, when she rhetorically asks Felice, "What's the world for if you can't make it up the way you want it?" (208). Although Dorcas never tells her story, her double, Felice, steps forward to tell hers, which releases Joe and Violet from their impasse.

At the same time that the characters recover through telling and listening, the narrator of *Jazz* enacts a similar recovery. At first, she is convinced of her own truth, anxious to use her story to victimize the characters through gossip. But as she invents their world, she is changed by it. She learns to listen to them, to empathize with them, to love them. Correspondingly, she learns humility, learns that her own versions aren't the only ones and aren't necessarily accurate. Along with this maturity, she develops a deeper relationship with the reader. If listening is crucial for her own role as storyteller, then she appreciates the reader's role as listener and, presumably, shared storyteller. There are, finally, no real differences between author, characters, narrator, and reader.

Morrison's theme of the necessity of storytelling and listening can be summarized by tracing the quests for *nommo* throughout the six novels. In *The Bluest Eye*, Claudia seeks the source of the dolls' voices and in the process gains her own voice, while conversely Cholly and Pauline attempt but fail to find their voices or to hear anyone else's, and Pecola even more absolutely retreats into silence. In *Sula*, in an environment characterized by the misuse and absence of *nommo*, Sula and Nel commune silently as girls but are unable to verbalize that union or to further the creation of their own identities by telling or hearing each other's stories. In *Song of Solomon*, Milkman transcends a similarly negative environment and, guided by Pilate's powers, achieves psychic, social, and metaphysical union through his discovery of *nommo*. In *Tar Baby*, *nommo*/Nommo is literally lost in American society, as Jadine and Son, as well as everyone except Thérèse, flounder in disharmony, seeking vainly for healthy identities, meaningful places, satisfying futures, and their own life-stories. In *Beloved*, recovery through *nommo* is represented through Denver's successful journey from muteness to storytelling and listening and finally to confident emergence into selfhood and community, through Sethe's and Paul D's painful reconstructions of the past and their psyches, and through the therapeutic examples of Baby Suggs, Stamp Paid, and the community women. And in *Jazz*, Joe, Violet, and Alice Manfred similarly lose and then slowly regain *nommo*, a process that is mirrored in the replacement of Dorcas by Felice and that is paralleled by the narrator's recovery from the language of abuse to the language of healing.

The overt development of the narrator's and reader's roles in *Jazz* makes explicit a pattern that is implied in Morrison's previous novels. In each of them, the narration grants some characters room to tell their stories and invites the reader into active participation. Characters are increasingly allowed to speak in the first person, are given extensive internal monologues, and/or are permitted long stretches of dialogue. Readers are presented with problems, not solutions; the novels are texts, not works; at issue is not the *what*, but the *how* and the *why*.

All this points to a major impact of Morrison's fiction: the necessity for each participant in a novel—author, characters, narrator, and reader—to tell his or her story and to listen actively and empathetically to others. As Morrison's stories urge this, they enact it, for through her fiction she tells her own story and urges others to tell theirs. Her fiction calls us to listen, to tell our stories, to make up our worlds the way we want to.

Morrison's treatment of storytelling and listening exemplifies the theme of dangerous freedom. From the startling Dick-and-Jane passage that opens her first novel to the extreme implications of "make me, remake me" with which *Jazz* ends, Morrison risks her authority, her freedom to create. She places her characters in social and psychological situations in which they, like her, confront the dangers implicit in their own freedom. Displaced from their pasts, their psyches, their families, their communities, and mainstream American culture, her characters in varying degrees embrace, abdicate, or equivocate about the freedom they are granted. Simultaneously, Morrison's novels both allow and force readers to experience their own dangerous freedom. Because the novels require so much of readers, because they leave such tantalizing holes and spaces, they both disturb and liberate readers. Since Morrison exercises her authority *and* yields unusual degrees of control to characters, narrators, and readers, readers in turn are invited to exercise unusual degrees of power, to stretch their imaginations, and therefore to experience vicariously the dangers and the freedoms of the author and the characters.

Such overlapping among the novels' participants also enable the novels to enact the pattern of fusion and fragmentation. Conventional distinctions among author, narrators, characters, and readers are not completely erased but ambiguously blurred. The participants are separate but united. The novels' forms thus mirror the emphasis on fusion and fragmentation that their plots unfold: individuals, families, communities, African-American culture, and American culture are shown to be complex entities that are at once multiple and single, divided and unified, fragmented and fused.

For all participants in Morrison's fiction, a postmodern perspective is required. The old either/or logic does not suffice. Just as Morrison holds solutions in abeyance, patiently ravels and unravels the *how* and the *why*, and works through complex processes of pluralism-in-unity, so characters gradually and often painfully re-member their

187

lives, reassemble themselves by re-calling their pasts, and thereby re-gain the strength to accept the challenges of their dangerous free-dom. Similarly, readers must enter into the *différance*, must experience as well as understand the texts, must replace the old either/or logic with a more fluid and open perspective that allows for full immersion and active participation. Because Morrison's fiction generates such responses, it compels readers toward insights into African-American and American cultures and into the paradoxical and crucial role of African Americans in American culture. More significantly, her fic-tion has the power to expand the souls of all readers by inviting them into the recesses of other souls-in-process, by requiring them to re-work the traumas and dilemmas those other souls endure, and by challenging them to know, accept, and keep open their own danger-ous freedom.

1. The Puzzle of the One-and-the-Many

1. Many words (such as *syzygy, concrescence, heterogeneity, hybridity, multifari-ousness, heteromorphism,* and *divarication*) help identify the idea of the one-and-the-many, but, as Michael Kammen says of *syzygy* (89), these words are ugly (and/or, I would add, too long). I borrow my title phrase from Sacvan Bercovitch: "The American way is to turn potential conflict into a quarrel about fusion or fragmentation" (*Rites* 373) and "to varying degrees, this strategy of fusion through fragmentation informs the entire course of American literary criticism" ("Afterword" 420).

2. Claude Lefort implies the connection between democracy and postmodern thinking: "democracy is instituted and sustained by the *dissolution of the markers of certainty*. It inaugurates a history in which people experience a fundamental indeterminacy as to the basis of power, law and knowledge, and as to the basis of relations between *self* and *other* at every level of social life" (19).

3. Much the same could be said for any marginalized group.

4. In *Lure and Loathing*, Gerald Early collects essays by twenty African Americans reflecting on racial double-consciousness.

5. Robert Stepto affirms that African-American culture values the both/and, or "modal," perspective in contrast to the Euro-American either/or, Cartesian one (*From* xiii). In developing his theory of Signifyin(g), Henry Louis Gates invokes the power of the "double-voiced" tradition in African-American culture, that is, that black culture is distinct from white culture and that the differences are based on doubleness, on "repetition and revision, or repetition with a signal difference" (*Signifying* xxiv).

6. Despite cultural variations among the slave-originating regions of West Africa, Levine claims that there is enough common ground on which to gen-

eralize (*Black Culture* 4), and John Mbiti generalizes about the unity of African religions and philosophy.

7. Lawrence Hogue also substantiates this dialectical reversal, that white America needed the African-American other (24). According to Gates, race is the ultimate trope of difference, and blacks began their existence in America as "veritable deconstructions . . . of all that Western culture so ardently wished itself to be" ("Trope" 321). Byerman adds that the interdependence works both ways, that blacks and whites define themselves in terms of the other and that race is both a unifying force in American culture and a divisive one (3).

8. Arthur Schlesinger sees "the curse of racism" as "the great failure of the American experiment, the glaring contradiction of American ideals and the still crippling disease of American life" (14). Philip Fisher defines transparency—a sense of openness, intelligibility, and uniformity—as the key ingredient in the theoretical "undamaged social space" of American culture ("Democratic" 85), and then asserts that slavery was "the fundamental denial of transparency within American experience."

9. In addition to call and response, Morrison's fiction also uses written equivalents of other oral forms, such as signifying, witnessing, and testifying.

10. For example, Ellison asserts that Negro music blends European and African music and therefore exemplifies America's pluralism even before pluralism became a doctrine (*Shadow* 255).

11. Jones shows how this process involved the combination of Western regularity and African nonregularity (31), the fusion of the European focus on the individual performer and the African focus on the group's performance (66), the blending of African and Western rhythms (66), the adaptation of Western instruments (75), and the appropriation of white pianistic techniques (114). For Hartman jazz synthesizes on many levels not merely African and European elements, but melody and rhythm, past and present, soloist and ensemble, composer and performer (10), and musicians and listeners (73).

12. This is a widely reported phenomenon; see, for example, Levine, *Black* 242.

13. Similarly, Antonio Benítez-Rojo claims that jazz, like the literature of the Caribbean, requires a dialogic, polyrhythmic approach that unravels traditional binary oppositions, not into convenient syntheses but "into insoluble differential equations" (26).

14. Roger Abrahams makes a similar connection between deconstruction and the African-American oral tradition. In call and response, testifying, and black speech, he argues, oppositions are tolerated as ever-present contraries,

and the lack of closure leads to broader cultural affirmation. Like Hegel's concept of *aufheben*, a simultaneous negating and affirming, the oral tradition, and by extension African-American culture, asserts its simultaneous independence and interdependence (82–83).

15. Bell goes so far as to say that technique became more important than message (337). In contrast, in his otherwise insightful history of twentieth-century African-American literature, Michael Cooke claims that black writers have not been interested in formal innovation (3).

16. Examples include Toni Cade Bambara's *The Salt Eaters*, Charles Gaines's *A Gathering of Old Men*, Paule Marshall's *Praisesong for the Widow*, Gloria Naylor's *Bailey's Cafe*, Ntozake Shange's *Sassafras, Cypress and Indigo*, Alice Walker's *The Color Purple*, and John Henry Wideman's *Reuben*.

2. Morrison's Novels as Texts, Not Works

1. Barbara Hill Rigney analyzes the dyad or doubling that occurs in pregnancy and childbirth as a crucial element in Morrison's fiction (*Voices* 46–50).

2. Barbara Christian notes the crucial relationship between the characters' mythical pasts and their present lives (*Black Feminist* 62); Rigney discusses the importance of history in Morrison's fictional world (*Voices* 61–75); Valerie Smith traces the link between self-knowledge and acceptance of the past (*Self-Discovery* 122–53); and Susan Willis argues that "For Morrison, everything is historical" (90).

3. Both Dixon (*Ride* 141–43) and Rigney (*Voices* 62) comment on the symbolic significance of Ohio in Morrison's geography.

4. Examples of such dualities are good and evil (McKay 420, 423; Parker 253; Tate 129), male and female (B. Jones, "Interview" 148; Ruas 231, 239), the nest and adventure (Tate 122), reality and nonreality (Bakerman, "Seams" 60), and presence and absence (Morrison, "Unspeakable" 210).

5. Morrison comments on the open-endedness of her fiction in B. Jones ("Interview" 135), Ruas (232, 236), Morrison ("Rootedness" 341), and Morrison ("Unspeakable" 226, 229). For Morrison's parallels between her fiction and jazz, see LeClair (28) and McKay (429). For parallels with traditional African-American cultural forms, see Morrison ("Memory" 388–89). Morrison stresses the absent over the present in her fiction in Bakerman ("Seams" 59), McKay (429), Morrison ("Rootedness" 341), and Stepto (" 'Intimate' " 218).

6. Commentators on Morrison's form have noticed its puzzling qualities: for example, Elliott Butler-Evans stresses the "ideological ruptures and dissonance" (63) of the novels; Cynthia Davis notes the need for a shifting point of view because any individual viewpoint is too limited (336–37); Rigney

191

compares Morrison's "circular, diffuse" structures (*Voices* 31) to French feminists' theories of feminine writing (31–33); and Linda Wagner notes the intentional misdirection, the fragments, and the "method of moving a story on several fronts simultaneously" (203).

7. Charles Johnson admires Morrison's prose, in particular its musical and mythical elements (101–3).

8. Christian refers to "the mythic quality of [Morrison's] novels," particularly in the central presences of nature and characters' ancestors ("Layered" 496).

9. Denise Heinze notes that "Morrison avoids the polarization of black and white humanity" (9).

3. The Break Was a Bad One: The Split World of *The Bluest Eye*

1. Other critics have discussed additional dimensions of inversion: Vanessa Dickerson notes that Cholly's hatred of Darlene inverts his previous desire to protect her (112, 116), Bessie Jones and Audrey Vinson describe the novel as an inversion of fairy tale patterns (25–33), Terry Otten argues that the novel reverses the usual values of good and evil (*Crime* 8–25), and Roberta Rubenstein points out that the stereotyped white family depicted in the Dick-and-Jane primer is inverted in the Breedloves (127).

2. Such linkages lie behind Barbara Christian's description of the novel's structure as a musical or dance composition, in which, as in a blues or a jazz piece, form is achieved through the repeated sounding of chords (*Black Women* 144, 152).

3. Christian (*Black Women* 145–46) discusses Pauline's preoccupation with color.

4. Rubenstein equates Pauline's physical deformity with Cholly's emotional one (144).

5. The unrelenting consequences of the deformations of Pauline's body—her limp and her missing tooth—are examples of Karen Sanchez-Eppler's thesis that the lives of slaves and women are determined by their physical differences from white males. Similarly, Rubenstein hypothesizes that the mutilations of the body reveal the problematics of identity formation (230–32), and Barbara Rigney claims that marked bodies in Morrison's fiction are like hieroglyphics providing "clues to a culture and a history more than to individual personality" (*Voices* 39).

6. As Rubenstein points out, both Pecola in her menstruation and Cholly in his defecation "soil themselves" (149–50).

7. Madonne Miner asserts that Soaphead figuratively rapes Pecola by using her wish to express his own anger at God (97).

8. Christian contends that all of Morrison's novels are "bracketed by war" ("Layered" 489).

9. Otten comments on the opposition between Soaphead's God and the watermelon-splitting father (*Crime* 22).

10. Otten notes that the disintegration of the primer's text foreshadows Pecola's annihilation and rejection (*Crime* 8), and Valerie Smith sees a parallel between the jumbled words of the primer and the inverted values implicit in Geraldine's family (*Self-Discovery* 129).

11. For more on the breach, see Derrida (*Margins* 18) and Peggy Kamuf (41n).

12. Morrison has said that she added Claudia and her sister Frieda because she needed "a bridge" between the Breedloves and the reader, which would give "a playful quality to [the Breedloves'] lives, to relieve the grimness" (Ruas 220).

13. Susan Willis goes so far as to call Claudia "the author's alter ego" (88).

14. In Morrison's *Playing in the Dark*, she argues for the reverse—that white Americans also defined themselves against the African-American other.

4. Shocked into Separateness: Unresolved Oppositions in *Sula*

1. Maureen T. Reddy sees *Sula* as an "anti-war novel" (30).

2. In addition to Morrison's comments on the opening sentence of the novel ("Unspeakable" 221–24), Susan Sniader Lanser analyzes the covert revelation of the narrator's values in the opening section of *Sula* (234–38).

3. For discussions of the good/evil issue, see Keith Byerman (200), Robert Grant (93–94), Terry Otten (*Crime* 29), and Philip Royster ("Priest" 164).

4. In addition to the critics cited above on the good versus evil issue, others have noted additional oppositions: Barbara Lounsberry and Grace Ann Hovet conclude that the novel circles around the "dialectical poles" of new and old modes of perception (129); Karen Stein shows how characters' names contrast with their identities; Marianne Hirsch argues that *Sula* constructs oppositions, such as those between watch and help, self-reliance and care, and mother and artist (*Mother/Daughter* 182–83); and Byerman explains how Sula tries to escape the dialectic between a controlling social order and its negation (192).

5. I follow Lanser's reasoning that an unmarked narrator be assigned the same gender as the author (167).

6. Hirsch notes the sparseness of maternal dialogue (*Mother/Daughter* 179), but none of the characters is allowed many words.

7. For example, Houston Baker, Jr., points out that the novel begins in the present, delves into the detailed past, and returns to the present ("When" 254); Barbara Christian argues that the novel's structure appears to be neat and chronological but is characterized by the intertwining of past and present (*Black Women* 155); Lounsberry and Hovet document the prevalence and significance of circle images (129); McDowell details the novel's unsettlingly fluid portrayal of time (" 'self' " 86); Chikwenye Ogunyemi notes that "the novel is circular like a medallion" ("*Sula*" 132); Catherine Rainwater claims that the novel's "circular narrative pattern" suggests repetition but no "completeness or closure" (102–3); and Linda W. Wagner notes that the frequency of circle imagery suggests that life in this novel does not follow "a linear, progressive pattern" (199). Morrison characterizes *Sula* as "more spiral than circular" (Tate 124).

8. See Tate (129) and Parker (253); Otten discusses this issue in both interviews (*Crime* 28–29).

9. Hirsch discusses the impossibility of Nel and Sula repeating their mothers' plots (*Mother/Daughter* 185), and Rigney emphasizes the importance of mother-daughter "dyads" in the novel (*Voices* 49).

10. Barbara Smith claims that *Sula* is a lesbian novel because of its "critical stance toward the heterosexual institutions of male/female relationships" (175), but the novel calls into question *all* relationships, not just heterosexual ones.

11. If merged they would have been one whole person (Bakerman, "Failures" 549); their emotional connections transcend all divisive forces (Gillespie and Kubitschek 44); they share a telepathic communication (Grant 99); they represent "a kind of psychological symbiosis (Rubenstein 135); and they are doubles (McDowell, " 'self' " 81). Morrison states that each contains something of the other (Stepto, " 'Intimate' " 216) and that "they complement each other" (Parker 253).

12. See Diane Gillespie and Missy Dehn Kubitschek for a detailed application of research on female psychology and female relationships to *Sula* and in particular to Sula and Nel's relationship (40–44).

13. Baker (*Workings* 142), Byerman (195), and Spillers (199) note Eva's goddess-like qualities.

14. See Gillespie and Kubitschek (25), Lounsberry and Hovet (128), and Rigney (*Voices* 89) for discussions of the diminishment of the males.

15. Rigney argues that *Sula* is about absence and that relationships are attempts by characters to fill empty spaces (*Voices* 23).

16. I am indebted here to McDowell, who argues that Nel essentially belongs to the town, having given over her sense of self and her sexuality to

community standards. As a result, "Nel fits [Thomas] Docherty's description of the type of character who is 'fixed and centered up on one locatable ego,' blocking 'the possibility of authentic response, genuine sentiment'" (" 'self' " 84).

17. Gillespie and Kubitschek define the grey ball as "Nel's submerged needs" (32) and as "an extreme of repression" (33), and Reddy calls it "a physical manifestation of her own feelings, which she is afraid to examine" (38).

18. The birthmark has attracted considerable attention. Hirsch (*Mother/Daughter* 182) and Gloria Wade-Gayles (192) note that it associates Sula with both the feminine and the masculine, Henderson (127) and Susan Willis (101) see it as a mark of inferiority or stigma, and Dorothy Lee relates it to Sula's "passion for experience" ("Quest" 352). But the most common reading is that it suggests the openness of interpretations of Sula's identity; see Baker (*Workings* 156), Byerman (198–99), Lounsberry and Hovet (128, 129), and Rigney (*Voices* 38). Henderson also argues that its multiple meanings become "symbols of opposition and ambiguity" which "evoke the qualities of permanence and mutability . . . the meaning and valence of which changes with the reading and the reader" (130).

19. Byerman argues that Sula probes the negative effects of "social oppression, victimization, and social order" and that she tries to escape from them, but he concludes that Sula's attempt fails (192).

20. Shadrack's distorted but verifying vision of himself recalls Morrison's statement that she "thought of *Sula* as a cracked mirror, fragments and pieces we have to see independently and put together" (LeClair 28).

21. Vashti Crutcher Lewis (92) and Willis (102) also see Shadrack's "Always" as indicative of the bond between Sula and Shadrack, whereas Baker (*Workings* 149) argues that its assertion of a benevolent cosmic design is absurdly comic. Ashraf Rushdy (" 'Rememory' " 308) finds the word in the primal scenes of both Sula and Nel, Sula on her deathbed when she wonders "Who was it that had promised her a sleep of water always?" (149) and Nel when her mother turns to custard on the train and "she resolved to be on guard—always" (22).

22. Lawrence Hogue shows how *Sula* reflects African-American experience in America, in particular how residents of the Bottom, paralleling African Americans as a whole, survive by creating a flexible, infinitely expandable neighborhood (143–44).

23. Leo Marx's *The Machine in the Garden* is a classic statement of this issue.

24. Both of Baker's treatments of *Sula* underscore the ironic inversions of the place of African Americans ("When"; *Workings* 136–61).

25. This form is also radically ironic since slave narratives were written for whites and their content was often controlled by whites.

26. See Bellah et al. (144–46), Jehlen (139), and R. Lewis (111).

27. Sula has been compared to Bigger Thomas (Barthold 109), Ellison's invisible man and Wright's Cross Damon in *The Outsider* (Christian, *Black Feminist* 54), Melville's Ishmael (Heinze 82), and, in considerable detail, Janie Starks (Spillers).

28. Critics have focused on the Bottom as representative of African Americans: Baker ("When" *Workings* 136–61), Butler-Evans (86), Montgomery (128), and Reddy (31, 43). Willis sees Shadrack's imagined deformation of his hands as a representative marker for the displacing effects of white culture on African Americans (102).

5. Putting It All Together: Attempted Unification in *Song of Solomon*

1. Much of the criticism on *Song of Solomon* has addressed how it explores the past by paralleling and modifying several mythic patterns. Most frequently cited is the hero's quest, or monomyth, as developed by Otto Rank and Joseph Campbell: see Michael Awkward (" 'Unruly' " 491–94), Kimberly Benston, Gerry Brenner, Peter Bruck, Jane Campbell, Cynthia Davis, Genevieve Fabre, Leslie Harris (70–74), and Dorothy Lee ("*Song*"). Besides the parallels with classical Western mythology, critics have noticed the links with Christian traditions, obviously in the title, and in such characters' names as Pilate, Ruth, First Corinthians, and Lena (see especially Lee, "*Song*" 66–67). In addition, analogues have been found in Gullah folklore (Blake), African-American folktales (Brenner), African cultural forms (Skerritt; O'Shaughnessy), and African epics (Krumholz, "Dead" 563–66).

2. I agree with Barbara Christian, for whom the watermark connects Ruth's past and present (*Black Feminist* 61), and with Charles Scruggs, for whom it symbolizes her buried life ("Nature" 325). For Lee, the watermark stands for Ruth's blemished life ("*Song*" 66), for Wilfred Samuels and Clenora Hudson-Weems it suggests her flawed existence (56), and for Susan Willis it represents Macon's rejection of Ruth (90).

3. Jane Campbell, arguing for the importance of ancestor worship in Milkman's quest to regain his lost African heritage, notes that Ruth and Pilate "maintain posthumous relationships with their fathers" (145). Similarly, Barbara Hill Rigney points out that characters in *Song of Solomon* resurrect their fathers and seek meaning in the legends of the past (*Voices* 65).

4. Without specifically identifying this figure as Jake, Terry Otten suggests

196

that he reveals Milkman's contact with the spiritual power of the past (*Crime* 54).

5. Valerie Smith also notes the prevalence of flashbacks and discusses the importance of the characters' storytelling (*Self-Discovery* 135–50).

6. Deborah Guth focuses on Milkman's symbolic process of reading, a process that for her determines the novel's structure: "The plot of this novel of restoration is thus the transformative act of reading itself" (580).

7. Milkman thereby extends Nel's brief excursion to the South, in which she is entranced by her grandmother but is prevented from absorbing a lasting influence from her and the lost past she represents.

8. See Bonnie Barthold for a thorough discussion of these cultural distinctions.

9. Morrison has said that this novel, unlike her first two, is not circular: "*Song of Solomon* is different. I was trying to push this novel outward; its movement is neither circular nor spiral. The image in my mind for it is that of a train picking up speed" (Tate 124).

10. This payoff echoes the hollow promise of "$40 and a mule," which was made to African Americans after the Civil War.

11. As Melissa Walker points out, this novel takes place during the most violent years of the civil rights era, almost exactly those years that are omitted from *Sula* (140–41).

12. For discussions of the political implications of the novel, see Barthold (181–83), Ralph Story (149–58), Melissa Walker (129–46), and Willis (316).

13. Melissa Walker argues for the parallelism between Guitar and Malcolm X on the one hand and Milkman and King on the other, even going so far as to suggest that King's initials, MLK, are an abbreviation of "Milkman" (142–43).

14. Morrison's fascination with the Till case is also evident in her play, *Dreaming Emmett*.

15. Tommy's speech is reminiscent of Sula's list of the transformation of racial attitudes that will take place before she is loved: "when Lindbergh sleeps with Bessie Smith . . . " (*Sula* 145–46).

16. Rigney asserts that characters in this novel, such as Milkman and Pilate, are often defined by what they are not (*Voices* 24–25).

17. See Samuels and Hudson-Weems for a discussion of Pilate as self-creator (61–63) and trickster and *griot* (77), and see Valerie Smith for Pilate's contrasts with Macon and her circular sense of time ("*Song*" 279–81).

18. As Gay Wilentz claims, Pilate is the culture bearer, in communion with her father and therefore with her ancestral heritage (88). Marilyn Sanders Mobley similarly finds that Pilate is an effective guide because she mediates between the present and the past, this world and the next (*Folk* 114).

19. Several commentators—Otten (*Crime* 46), Philip Royster ("Milkman's" 419), and Rigney (*Voices* 33)—have described the novel as a *bildungsroman*. The tendency is to see Milkman between varying pairs of characters rather than as the object of a wider battle. Barthold (179), Susan Blake (78), and Valerie Smith (*"Song"* 280–81) place him between Pilate and Macon, whereas Ann Imbrie (482) says that he stands between Guitar's political stance and Pilate's humanist one, and Otten (*Crime* 50) positions him between the two dialectical poles of Guitar and Macon. Royster more broadly sees Milkman trying to resolve the opposing world views of Macon, Pilate, and Guitar ("Milkman's" 427). Another possible descriptor for the novel is *prufungsroman*, a novel of examination and trial.

20. Imbrie points out that Milkman's hometown is "primeval" (6), and Denise Heinze sees Shalimar as "a ritual ground" (140).

21. See Davis (336–37), Fabre (108), and Scruggs ("Nature" 316) for similar positions on this point.

22. In contrast to my view, Leslie Harris sees Milkman's childhood as a mythic time, followed by his alienation at around age thirty and then his quest (70).

23. This alienating image echoes James Baldwin's similar experience of moving opposite a crowd (*Notes* 95).

24. Benston even argues that Milkman's preoccupation with things behind him prepares him for appreciating Pilate's apprehension of what lies behind the apparent (100n).

25. Joyce Wegs associates Milkman's inappropriate urination with his "negative dominion" of others, that is, with "his self-concern, his indifference to others, and his childishness" (218). Milkman's errant urination also echoes Henry Porter's pissing down on people in his anger and alienation.

26. For similar formulations, see Awkward ("Unruly" 491) and Valerie Smith (*"Song"* 281–83).

27. Jane Campbell also comments on the implications of merging in the song (146).

28. Krumholz analyzes the significance of darkness as a figure for the liminal state in which Milkman "is initiated into his own blackness" as a new way of seeing and reading ("Dead" 560–62).

29. Fabre sees the prevalence of death as a metaphor for the Dead family and for the condition of African Americans (111).

30. I am indebted here to Guth (583) and Krumholz ("Dead" 562–63).

6. Everyone Was Out of Place: Contention and Dissolution in *Tar Baby*

1. For reasons different from those I develop, Malin Lavon Walther views *Tar Baby* as a transitional novel, marking the end of Morrison's critique of Eurocentric aesthetics (146–47).

2. Roberta Rubenstein states that "divisions operate simultaneously between families and generations" (141), and Sandra Pouchet Paquet agrees that the novel "focuses on the unresolved conflict between characters whose values appear to be irreconcilable" (501). Other critics have pointed out such dualities as the garden ("l'arbe") and the cross ("croix") (B. Jones, "Garden" 118), village values and city values (Scruggs, *Sweet* 176), African-American and Euro-American mythic sensibilities (Werner, "Briar" 161), and fraternity versus industry (Werner, "Briar" 165).

3. In discussing her reactions to readers and critics of her novels, Morrison invokes *nommo*: "I sometimes know when the work works, when *nommo* has effectively summoned, by reading and listening to those who have entered the text" ("Unspeakable" 229).

4. Morrison says that she deliberately sought an isolated setting in which the characters would be placed under duress (McKay 417).

5. Bessie Jones argues that the island is an ambiguous Garden of Eden, both pre- and postlapsarian ("Garden" 117–18), whereas Terry Otten sees it as a clearly fallen Eden (*Crime* 63).

6. Since Gideon and Thérèse are privileged by the narrator's rhetoric, their refusal to enter the house devalues it.

7. "Going crazy" is an interesting motif in Morrison's novels. It usually coincides with increased mental clarity for the "crazy" character, for example Pecola or Sethe. Similarly, in *Tar Baby* the craziness of the Christmas dinner leads to a restructuring of roles within the household and to Jadine and Son's increased clarity about their relationship.

8. Marilyn Sanders Mobley connects these contentions with Jadine's conflicts and with Morrison's dilemma in depicting them ("Narrative" 285), and, without referring to the epigraph, Peter B. Erickson suggests that the novel reveals "an authorial self-division that Morrison does not fully acknowledge" (304n).

9. James Coleman notes that Jadine often misperceives (67), Rubenstein claims that characters are enslaved by appearances (130), and Judylyn Ryan argues that vision is problematic and contested (602–7).

10. For the idea of the household as a microcosm, see Denise Heinze (142), Karla Holloway ("African" 118), Bessie Jones ("Garden" 122), and Craig Werner ("Briar" 156–57).

11. Ryan also notes that the house resembles a plantation (600), and Evelyn Hawthorne (102) and Holloway ("African" 120) remark that the Childs function like house slaves.

12. Byerman calls Valerian an "insubstantial confection" (210), Rigney argues that the fake flavors of candy suggest his questionable masculinity (*Voices* 86), and Ryan notes that his name echoes that of a sleep-inducing drug (600).

13. Werner shows that Valerian has constructed an elaborate myth of safety into which he unsuccessfully retreats ("Briar" 158–60).

14. Heinze asserts that even after the household coup Margaret, Sydney, and Ondine remain locked in the old system (90).

15. According to Werner, Sydney and Ondine are caught in a double bind of African-American and Euro-American sensibilities and resort to various masking techniques in their unsuccessful attempt to balance the two ("Briar" 157, 161).

16. For Heinze, Jadine has "almost a sociopathic disinterest" in others (145), and for Eleanor Traylor she suffers from the "disease of disconnection" (146).

17. Rubenstein notes that all the characters are enslaved by appearances or by false images of selfhood (130).

18. Werner focuses on the characters' attempts to create safety for themselves ("Briar" 157–66), attempts that stem, I suggest, from their nearly paralyzing fears.

19. For Butler-Evans, Son is the disruptive primitive other (159), for Byerman he reveals other characters' insecurities (208), for B. Jones he shatters everyone's delusions ("Garden" 121), for Kubitschek he exposes contradictions (130), for Otten he forces self-confrontation in the others (*Crime* 65), for Paquet he is the catalyst (509), and for Traylor he dissolves pretensions (142).

20. Although Angelita Reyes denies that Son is a trickster (197), Trudier Harris (*Fiction* 119–21), Paquet (513), and Werner ("Briar" 164) feel that he is.

21. Cynthia Edelberg sees Son as a savior figure, healing and forgiving others (232); Jones compares his truth, honesty, freedom, and hope to Christ's ("Garden" 121); and Rubenstein finds him Christlike when he becomes "the scapegoat for the internal contradictions of a cultural group" (159). For Otten, however, he is not Christ but the serpent in the garden, the ambiguous criminal/hero (*Crime* 69–70), and for Samuels and Hudson-Weems he is a black Messiah, representing African values in opposition to Jadine's European ones (85).

22. Ryan compares Jadine's and Son's mutual rescue attempts to stereotypical rescue narratives (602).

23. Aloneness also tastes good for Sula and Pilate, but they are better able to create their own identities.

24. Coleman states that both Jadine and Son retreat to their refuges of safety and security (68).

25. Jadine's choice has elicited considerable debate. Some critics blame

her for her lack of wholeness (Mobley, "Narrative" 289), for retreating to the white world (Coleman 68), and for accepting her status as an object (Byerman 213; Rigney, *Voices* 58–59). Others see her more positively, trying to construct her own identity (Butler-Evans 157) or pursuing a quest for identity like such male characters as Milkman (Paquet 512). Still others note that her choice of white culture derives from her upbringing, which did not inculcate in her the values and tradition of her African-American heritage. For them, she is split between Euro-American and African-American cultures, "lost in a state of liminality" (Samuels and Hudson-Weems 79), caught in the "implications of psychological and cultural boundary-straddling" (Rubenstein 141), and trapped between gender and race in unresolved duality (Otten, *Crime* 78–79).

26. Erickson argues that Jadine is a rare example of Morrison's intolerance for one of her characters (301), and Mobley ("Narrative" 285) and Traylor (149) make the connection between the dedication and Jadine.

27. Both T. Harris (*Fiction* 148) and Hawthorne (105) point out this image.

28. Morrison suggests this initial reading of the myth: "So I just gave these characters parts, Tar Baby being a black woman and the rabbit a black man. I introduced a white man and remembered the tar. The fact that it was made out of tar and was a black woman, if it was made to trap a black man—the white man made her for that purpose. That was the beginning of the story" (Ruas 226).

29. Byerman (209), T. Harris (*Fiction* 119), and Holloway ("African" 127) contend that Son and Jadine are tar babies for each other.

30. Mobley delineates two contradictory implications of the tar baby myth—a sense of entrapment and more positive connotations ("Narrative" 290), Rubenstein finds that the tar baby is whatever overwhelms one's ego boundaries (158), Melissa Walker concludes that the tar baby references are ambivalent much like the dialectics of African-Americanism (197–98), and Werner argues that Morrison is attracted by the multiplicity implicit in the tar baby tales and their endless interpretations ("Briar" 155–56).

31. Paquet notes the "unfinished dialogue" and the "unresolved conflict" between Son and Jadine (501), Melissa Walker finds that the novel "ends in ambiguity" (196) and "with the tension of unfinishedness" (197), and Werner stresses the "new beginnings" for Son and Jadine ("Briar" 165–66). For Morrison's comments on the openness of "lickety-split" at the novel's very end, see McKay (424–25).

32. Other examples of refrains include "he had not followed the women (114–17, 119), "she couldn't shake it" (223, 225), "no time for dreaming" (250–51), and "it was all mixed up" (257–58).

201

33. I allude to the idea of "thick description," a phrase that Clifford Geertz borrows from Gilbert Ryle (Geertz 6).

7. Anything Dead Coming Back to Life Hurts: Circularity in *Beloved*

1. Scruggs agrees that *Beloved* marks a thematic shift for Morrison, asserting that in the first four novels "the splitting off of individuals from a local culture by the power and attraction of a market-driven mass culture is a major source of conflict" and that in contrast characters in *Beloved* address the problem of finding a usable past (*Sweet* 177).

2. In addition to my previous discussion of the symbolism of Sethe's circling Paul D, see Guth (585), Krumholz ("Ghosts" 406–7), Rigney (*Voices* 33), Rodrigues ("Telling" 158), and V. Smith ("Circling" 349).

3. See, for example, Barbara Lounsberry and Grace Ann Hovet's analysis of the Bottom's role in *Sula*.

4. Emily Budick (122, 131), Heinze (92–93), and Rigney (" 'Story' " 230) emphasize the failures of families in *Beloved*.

5. In addition to the past and all slaves, which many commentators suggest, a dazzling diversity of other signifieds have been offered for Beloved, such as the beast of Revelation (Bowers 68), the collective unconscious (Heinze 95), the reader's ghost (Krumholz, "Ghosts" 400), and the *syuzhet* (Finney 31). One can only conclude that she/it is an open symbol, "a composite symbol" (Otten, *Crime* 83) who/that is "too complex to be catalogued and contained" (Krumholz, "Ghosts" 401) and who/that "escapes any comprehensive, coherent account" (Phelan 714).

6. Others have noted the two-edged nature of maternal love as a paradoxical force within the novel's families: Linda Anderson (139), Karen Baker-Fletcher (633), Deborah Horvitz (158), Liz Huron, Susan Jaret McKinstry (267), Rigney (" 'Story' " 231–32), Wilfred D. Samuels and Clenora Hudson-Weems (105), and Judith Thurman (176).

7. According to Samuels and Hudson-Weems, "the passage allows us to capture the momentum of the uncontrolled turbulence of their relationship as it rollercoasters under the impetus of forces over which they seem to have no control" (121).

8. Critical emphasis on this plurality-in-unity is divided: Anderson (140) and Bell (13) focus on the fusion of the three identities; David Lawrence (196), McKinstry (267, 271), Rigney (" 'Story' " 233), and Barbara Schapiro (202) stress the consequent loss of individuality; closer to my position, Krumholz sees it as a "ritual of mergence and possession" ("Ghosts" 404),

and Jane Wyatt analyzes it as both identity confusion (480) and achievement of pre-oedipal oneness (481).

9. For discussions of the connection between possessive love and slavery, see Horvitz (160–61), Kubitschek (169), Lawrence (196), McKinstry (264, 271), Samuels and Hudson-Weems (109), Thurmon (180), and Wyatt (482).

10. Rigney analyzes the simultaneous attraction and danger of maternal space throughout Morrison's fiction (*Voices* 16–20).

11. As Otten asserts, "In this complex scene, Morrison exposes Beloved's dual nature" (*Crime* 85).

12. Baker-Fletcher refers to the novel's form as bits and pieces (631), Trudier Harris writes that it proceeds "associatively" (*Fiction* 172), Rodrigues refers to its accumulation of meaning ("Telling" 161), Scruggs points out that readers don't need to know all the missing bits (*Sweet* 187), and Deborah Ayer Sitter describes the novel's form as fragmented (20).

13. T. Harris (*Fiction* 171) and Mobley ("Different" 194) make similar points about the importance of how and why in this novel.

14. Rodrigues describes the form as "a mode of telling that involves delay, repetition, and a slow but controlled release of information" ("Telling" 159). As Rosellen Brown puts it: "What Morrison manages is a continual heaving up of images and specific memories like stones, only to have them disappear and resurface again and yet again, each time more deeply embedded in the jagged landscape of relationships" (418–19).

15. For iterations of this image, see pages 47, 132, 173, and 182.

16. Another level of this technique of overlapping is Morrison's insertion of characters from one novel into another novel, such as the brief appearances of Baby Suggs in *Sula* and Dorcas in *Tar Baby*.

17. See, for example, Blake, Norris Clark, T. Harris (*Fiction*), Hovet and Lounsberry, and V. Lewis.

18. According to Janheinz Jahn, African narratives rely heavily on repetition and more specifically on "variation of the repetition, unity in the diversity" (166).

19. As D. Keith Mano points out, the "allusive, oblique" narrative form enables Morrison to avoid the excessive melodrama that a more straightforward form would have produced (55).

20. Scruggs points out that, according to Saint Augustine, the name *Seth* (the masculine form of *Sethe*) means resurrection (*Sweet* 185).

21. Samuels and Hudson-Weems emphasize Paul D's repeated burials and rebirths in and from the wooden tomb/trench in Georgia (Samuels and Hudson-Weems 125) and the church basement (133).

22. Scruggs asserts that the house, first in an undefined, unnumbered

space and then in a space defined by the white society, "recapitulates the slave's experience in the New World" (*Sweet* 185–86).

23. Mbiti describes the horror that results when the living dead are forgotten: they "are in effect excommunicated, their personal immortality is destroyed, and they are turned into a state of non-existence. And this is the worst possible punishment for anyone" (26).

24. Wyatt sees Sethe's back as "not her own," but instead "a tablet on which the slave masters have inscribed their code" (478).

25. For Samuels and Hudson-Weems, Amy is a "resurrectress," a healer like Pilate, and a "*curandera*" (115).

26. Since Denver first abandons language and then reenters it and later its social order, Wyatt extrapolates that she lives out the unspeakable story of Sethe's infanticide (482).

27. Samuels and Hudson-Weems limit this voicing to women: "What Morrison also unearths at the excavation site is the silenced voice of the black slave woman" (97).

28. Horvitz notes that Beloved's language breaks conventional barriers just like her existence and behavior (162), and Wyatt discusses the flouting of the rules of language in the novel (474).

29. Rodrigues sees Ella's holler as an "elemental cry" ("Telling" 165), and Bowers calls it a "primal sound" (71) that is associated in the text with the quasi-biblical first sound: "in the beginning was the sound" (*Beloved* 259).

30. Lori Askeland views Ella as "scarred" in her rejection of love, which leads to her and the community's rejection of Baby Suggs's love (798), and Scruggs argues that community wholeness is not achieved until both Ella and Stamp Paid revise their positions to accept Sethe (*Sweet* 180).

31. In contrast, Samuels and Hudson-Weems regard Paul's work songs as a reflection of the chaos within him (130).

32. Storytelling in *Beloved* has been described as a survival strategy (Holloway, "*Beloved*" 518), a means to power (T. Harris, *Fiction* 166), a link between survival and power (Levy 114), and a means of self-development (Schapiro 208). Both Denver (Kubitschek 175) and Sethe (Scruggs, *Sweet* 189) need to become storytellers. Furthermore, storytelling is a communal effort (Kubitschek 175), and it is "the form as well as the substance" of the novel (T. Harris, *Fiction* 172). See also Joseph T. Skerritt, Jr., for an analysis of storytelling in *Song of Solomon* and generally in Morrison's fiction.

33. Henry Louis Gates, Jr., mentions the pun (*Signifying* 172), and numerous critics of *Beloved* have remarked upon it.

34. For discussions of Paul D's manhood problems, see Heinze (112), Samuels and Hudson-Weems (127, 129), Scruggs (*Sweet* 196–98), and especially Sitter.

35. Writing about the "subliminal" life of *Beloved*, Morrison asserts that there is "no time because memory, pre-historic memory, has no time" ("Unspeakable" 229).

36. Budick (134), T. Harris (*Fiction* 164), Sale (42), and Scruggs (*Sweet* 198) agree on the importance of listening in this novel.

37. Sitter describes how Sethe and Paul D's "minds merge orgasmically" in their shared memory of the corn silk, and Satya Mohanty refers to the "fused memory" of the two characters (58). See also Rodrigues for praise of this "epithalamium" ("Telling" 157).

38. Trudier Harris (*Fiction* 171) and Melissa Walker (40) note that Morrison asks for the reader's active participation, and Sale (43) refers to the call and response pattern that invokes that participation. Heinze (180), Krumholz ("Ghosts" 396), Phelan, and Rodrigues ("Telling" 166) assert that the reader experiences an emotional release similar to the characters'.

39. Many critics have commented on this phrase, including its potential ambiguity.

40. Baker-Fletcher asks this question and adds, "Whether or not *Beloved* should have been written is an ethical question in itself" (632).

41. Both Askeland (787–88) and Eileen Bender (130, 134–36) elucidate parallels between the two novels.

42. Bowers (64), Mobley ("Different" 191), and Samuels and Hudson-Weems (95) point out similarities between *Beloved* and slave narratives.

8. Make Me, Remake Me: Traces, Cracks, and Wells in *Jazz*

1. Joe's reconstruction echoes Cholly's blind desire to repeat his union with Polly when he rapes his daughter, and is similar to Sethe's and Beloved's mutual attempts to resurrect versions of their own past selves in each other.

2. Whether or not the allusion to Derrida is deliberate may have to wait for a future interview with Morrison, but, as outlined in chapter 2, her previous statements about her work attest to the postmodern tenor of her thinking.

3. Both characters, but especially Wild, suggest "the wild zone or 'female space' " (Showalter 262) that Edwin Ardener theorizes in "Belief in the Problem of Women" and "The 'Problem' Revisited" (discussed in Showalter 261–63).

4. Golden Grey's name suggests his dual role: he is radiant but drab, white but colorless, symbolically rich and poor. In Black English, "grey" is a derogatory term for whites.

5. In addition to Roland Barthes's "From Work to Text" (74–79), see also his *S/Z* (10–16) for his thoughts on rereading.

6. In Gerard Genette's terms this narrator is simultaneously "extradiegetic" and "intradiegetic" (228–29).

7. Commentators agree on the narration's strange mixtures: for Paula Eckard it blends various voices (13), for Dorothea Drummond Mbalia it is a hybrid ("half character, half omniscient narrator" [624]) and "a bridge between first-person and third-person narration" (635), for Rodrigues it is contradictory and changeable ("Experiencing" 749), and for Craig Werner it is "elusive" as "it shifts shapes almost continually" (*Playing* 296). The peculiarities of the narration lead Eckard to equate the narrator with jazz ("jazz is the essential narrator" [11]) and Rodrigues to equate the narrator with the speaker of the epigraph, "the feminine immanence of the divine" ("Experiencing" 749).

8. For me, as for many readers, this strange narrator seems female. The narrator's gender, however, is never clearly indicated, which reinforces my point about Morrison's blurring of conventional distinctions. Eckard claims that the "narrator is at once both male and female" (13), and Gates asserts that "it [Morrison's narrator] is neither male nor female; neither young nor old; neither rich nor poor. It is *both* and *neither*" ("Review" 54).

9. Seymour Chatman contends that a primary source of narratorial authority evolves from the narrator's overlap with the characters. When the narratorial stance or value system is consistent with that of the characters, especially when "the narrator possesses not only access to but an unusual affinity or 'vibration' with the character's mind, the narrator's authority is increased" (207).

10. Mbalia argues similarly that the narrator grows during her telling of the Golden Grey episode, replacing "self-confidence, arrogance, and objectivity" with "regret, humility, and subjectivity" (637–38). Heinze likewise asserts that the narrator realizes that Golden Grey's hypocrisy in shaping a story to suit himself applies to her story and that "to understand Golden Grey the narrator must deconstruct herself" (184).

11. By punning on *dilation,* Barthes alludes to this erotic dimension of reading when he asserts that "the Text is dilatory" ("From" 76). Similarly Antonio Benítez-Rojo articulates the "reciprocal seductions" of text and reader: "With each reading the reader seduces the text, transforms it, makes it his own; with each reading the text seduces the reader, transforms him, makes him its own" (23).

12. In commenting on "Quiet as it's kept" in the opening line of *The Bluest Eye,* Morrison calls it "speakerly" and refers to its " 'back fence' connotation, its suggestion of illicit gossip" ("Unspeakable" 218). The mixed spoken/written quality of the rhetoric of *Jazz* continues the emphasis in Morrison's fic-

tion on the oral tradition of African-American folklore. As Trudier Harris shows (*Fiction*), Morrison's previous novels reveal this interest in the form of narrator-as-storyteller; in the use of folk tales, jokes, superstitions, and other kinds of folklore; and in the emphasis on such "oral" features as music.

13. Werner also notes the similarities between the speaker of the epigraph and the novel's narrator (*Playing* 301–2), and Rodrigues goes so far as to equate the two ("Experiencing" 748–49).

WORKS CITED

Abrahams, Roger. *Talking Black*. Rowley, MA: Newberry House, 1976.

Anderson, Linda. "The Re-Imagining of History in Contemporary Women's Fiction." *Plotting Change: Contemporary Women's Fiction*. Ed. Linda Anderson. London: Edward Arnold, 1990. 128–41.

Asante, Molefi Kete. *The Afrocentric Idea*. Philadelphia: Temple UP, 1987.

Askeland, Lori. "Remodeling the Model Home in *Uncle Tom's Cabin* and *Beloved*." *American Literature* 64 (1992): 785–805.

Awkward, Michael. *Inspiriting Influences: Tradition, Revision, and Afro-American Women's Novels*. New York: Columbia UP, 1989.

———. "Roadblocks and Relatives: Critical Revision in Toni Morrison's *The Bluest Eye*." *Critical Essays on Toni Morrison*. Ed. Nellie Y. McKay. Boston: G. K. Hall, 1988. 57–67.

———. " 'Unruly and Let Loose': Myth, Ideology and Gender in *Song of Solomon*." *Callaloo* 13 (1990): 482–98.

Baker, Houston A., Jr. *Blues, Ideology and Afro-American Literature*. Chicago: U of Chicago P, 1984.

———. "There Is No More Beautiful Way: Theory and the Poetics of Afro-American Women's Writing." *Afro-American Literary Study in the 1990s*. Ed. Baker and Patricia Redmond. Chicago: U of Chicago P, 1989. 135–55.

———. "When Lindbergh Sleeps with Bessie Smith: The Writing of Place in Toni Morrison's *Sula*." *Toni Morrison: Critical Perspectives Past and Present*. Ed. Henry Louis Gates, Jr., and K. A. Appiah. New York: Amistad, 1993. 236–60.

———. *Workings of the Spirit: The Poetics of Afro-American Women's Writing*. Chicago: U of Chicago P, 1991.

Baker-Fletcher, Karen. "Fierce Love Comes to Haunt." Rev. of *Beloved*. *Commonweal* 6 Nov. 1987: 631–33.

Works Cited

Bakerman, Jane S. "Failures of Love: Female Intuition in the Novels of Toni Morrison." *American Literature* 52 (1981): 548–54.

———. "The Seams Can't Show: An Interview with Toni Morrison." *Black American Literature Forum* 12 (1978): 56–60.

Bakhtin, M. M. *The Dialogic Imagination*. Trans. Caryl Emerson and Michael Holquist. Austin: U of Texas P, 1981.

Baldwin, James. *Nobody Knows My Name: More Notes of a Native Son*. New York: Dial, 1961.

———. *Notes of a Native Son*. Boston: Beacon, 1955.

Bambara, Toni Cade. *The Salt Eaters*. New York: Random House, 1981.

Barthes, Roland. "From Work to Text." *Textual Strategies: Perspectives in Post-Structuralist Criticism*. Ed. Josue V. Harari. Ithaca, NY: Cornell UP, 1979. 73–82.

———. *Image-Music-Text*. Trans. Stephen Heath. New York: Hill and Wang, 1977.

———. *S/Z*. Trans. Richard Miller. New York: Hill and Wang, 1974.

Barthold, Bonnie J. *Black Time: Fiction of Africa, the Caribbean, and the United States*. New Haven, CT: Yale UP, 1981.

Beauvoir, Simone de. *The Second Sex*. Trans. H. M. Parshley. New York: Knopf, 1957.

Bell, Bernard W. "*Beloved*: A Womanist Neo-Slave Narrative; or Multivocal Remembrances of Things Past." *African American Review* 26 (1992): 7–16.

Bellah, Robert N., Richard Madsen, William M. Sullivan, Ann Swidler, and Steven M. Tipton. *Habits of the Heart: Individualism and Commitment in American Life*. New York: Harper and Row, 1985.

Bender, Eileen T. "Repossessing *Uncle Tom's Cabin*: Toni Morrison's *Beloved*." *Cultural Power/Cultural Literacy*. Ed. Bonnie Braendlin. Tallahassee: Florida State UP, 1991. 129–42.

Benítez-Rojo, Antonio. *The Repeating Island: The Caribbean and the Postmodern Perspective*. Trans. James Maraniss. Durham, NC: Duke UP, 1992.

Benston, Kimberly W. "Re-Weaving the 'Ulysses Scene': Enchantment, Post-Oedipal Identity, and the Buried Text of Blackness in Toni Morrison's *Song of Solomon*." *Comparative American Identities: Race, Sex, and Nationality in the Modern Text*. Ed. Hortense J. Spillers. New York: Routledge, 1991. 87–109.

Bercovitch, Sacvan. "Afterword." *Ideology and Classic American Literature*. Ed. Sacvan Bercovitch and Myra Jehlen. Cambridge: Cambridge UP, 1986. 418–42.

———. *The Rites of Assent*. New York: Routledge, 1993.

Berret, Anthony J. "Toni Morrison's Literary Jazz." *College Language Association Journal* 32 (1989): 267–83.

210

Works Cited

Blake, Susan. "Folklore and Community in *Song of Solomon*. *Melus* 7 (1980): 77–82.

Bowers, Susan. "*Beloved* and the New Apocalypse." *Journal of Ethnic Studies* 18.1 (1990): 59–77.

Brenner, Gerry. "*Song of Solomon*: Rejecting Rank's Monomyth and Feminism." *Critical Essays on Toni Morrison.* Ed. Nellie Y. McKay. Boston: G. K. Hall, 1988. 114–24.

Brown, Rosellen. "The Pleasure of Enchantment." Rev. of *Beloved. The Nation* 17 Oct. 1987: 418–21.

Bruck, Peter. "Returning to One's Roots: The Motif of Searching and Flying in Toni Morrison's *Song of Solomon.*" *The Afro-American Novel since 1960.* Ed. Bruck and Wolfgang Karper. Amsterdam: B. R. Gruner, 1982. 289–305.

Budick, Emily Miller. "Absence, Loss, and the Space of History in Toni Morrison's *Beloved.*" *Arizona Quarterly* 48 (1992): 117–38.

Butler, Robert James. "Open Movement and Selfhood in Toni Morrison's *Song of Solomon.*" *Centennial Review* 28–29 (1984–85): 58–75.

Butler-Evans, Elliott. *Race, Gender, and Desire: Narrative Strategies in the Fiction of Toni Cade Bambara, Toni Morrison, and Alice Walker.* Philadelphia: Temple UP, 1989.

Byerman, Keith. *Fingering the Jagged Grain: Tradition and Form in Recent Black Fiction.* Athens: U of Georgia P, 1985.

Campbell, Jane. *Mythic Black Fiction: The Transformation of History.* Knoxville: U of Tennessee P, 1986.

Campbell, Joseph. *The Hero with a Thousand Faces.* New York: Methuen, 1953.

Carby, Hazel. *Reconstructing Womanhood: The Emergence of the Afro-American Woman Novelist.* New York: Oxford UP, 1987.

Chatman, Seymour. *Story and Discourse: Narrative Structure in Fiction and Film.* Ithaca, NY: Cornell UP, 1978.

Christian, Barbara. *Black Feminist Criticism: Perspectives on Black Women Writers.* New York: Pergamon, 1985.

———. *Black Women Novelists: The Development of a Tradition, 1892–1976.* Westport, CT: Greenwood, 1980.

———. "Fixing Methodologies: *Beloved.*" *Cultural Critique* 24 (1993): 5–15.

———. "Layered Rhythms: Virginia Woolf and Toni Morrison." *Modern Fiction Studies* 39 (1993): 483–500.

Clark, Norris. "Flying Black: Toni Morrison's *The Bluest Eye, Sula,* and *Song of Solomon.*" *Minority Voices* 4.2 (1980): 51–63.

Coleman, James. "The Quest for Wholeness in Toni Morrison's *Tar Baby.*" *Black American Literature Forum* 20 (1986): 63–73.

Coles, Robert. *The Call of Stories: Teaching and the Moral Imagination.* Boston: Houghton Mifflin, 1989.

211

Works Cited

Collins, Patricia Hill. *Black Feminist Thought: Knowledge, Consciousness, and the Politics of Empowerment.* New York: Routledge, 1990.

Cone, James H. *The Spirituals and the Blues.* Maryknoll, NY: Orbis, 1992.

Cooke, Michael G. *Afro-American Literature in the Twentieth Century: The Achievement of Intimacy.* New Haven, CT: Yale UP, 1984.

Cross, William E., Jr. *Shades of Black: Diversity in African-American Identity.* Philadelphia: Temple UP, 1991.

Davis, Cynthia A. "Self, Society, and Myth in Toni Morrison's Fiction." *Contemporary Literature* 23 (1982): 323–42.

Derrida, Jacques. *Margins of Philosophy.* Trans. Alan Bass. Chicago: U of Chicago P, 1982.

———. *Of Grammatology.* Trans. Gayatri Chakravorty Spivak. Baltimore: Johns Hopkins UP, 1974.

———. "Otobiographies: The Teaching of Nietzsche and the Politics of the Proper Name." Trans. Avital Ronell. *The Ear of the Other: Otobiography, Transference, Translation.* Lincoln: U of Nebraska P, 1985.

———. *Speech and Phenomena.* Trans. D. B. Allison. Evanston, IL: Northwestern UP, 1973.

———. *Writing and Difference.* Trans. Alan Bass. Chicago: U of Chicago P, 1978.

De Weever, Jacqueline. *Mythmaking and Metaphor in Black Women's Fiction.* New York: St. Martin's, 1991.

Dickerson, Vanessa D. "The Naked Father in Toni Morrison's *The Bluest Eye.*" *Refiguring the Father: New Feminist Readings of Patriarchy.* Ed. Patricia Yaeger and Beth Kowalski-Wallace. Carbondale: Southern Illinois UP, 1989. 108–27.

Dittmar, Linda. " 'Will the Circle Be Unbroken?' The Politics of Form in *The Bluest Eye.*" *Novel* 23 (1990): 137–55.

Dixon, Melvin. "Like an Eagle in the Air: Toni Morrison." *Modern Critical Views: Toni Morrison.* Ed. Harold Bloom. New York: Chelsea House, 1990.

———. *Ride Out the Wilderness.* Urbana: U of Illinois P, 1987.

Docherty, Thomas. *Reading (Absent) Character: Toward a Theory of Characterization in Fiction.* Oxford: Clarendon, 1983.

Du Bois, W. E. B. *The Souls of Black Folk.* New York: Penguin, 1989.

DuPlessis, Rachel Blau. "For the Etruscans." *The New Feminist Criticism.* Ed. Elaine Showalter. New York: Pantheon, 1985. 271–91.

Early, Gerald, ed. *Lure and Loathing: Essays on Race, Identity, and Ambivalence of Assimilation.* New York: Penguin, 1993.

Eckard, Paula Gallant. "The Interplay of Music, Language, and Narrative in Toni Morrison's *Jazz.*" *College Language Association Journal* 38 (1994): 11–19.

Works Cited

Edelberg, Cynthia. "Morrison's Voices: Formal Education, the Work Ethic, and the Bible." *American Literature* 58 (1986): 217–37.

Ellison, Ralph. *Going to the Territory*. New York: Random House, 1987.

———. *Invisible Man*. New York: Random House, 1952.

———. *Shadow and Act*. New York: Vintage, 1972.

Erickson, Peter B. "Images of Nurturance in *Tar Baby*." *Toni Morrison: Critical Perspectives Past and Present*. Ed. Henry Louis Gates, Jr., and K. A. Appiah. New York: Amistad, 1993. 293–307.

Fabre, Genevieve. "Genealogical Archaeology or the Quest for Legacy in Toni Morrison's *Song of Solomon*." *Critical Essays on Toni Morrison*. Ed. Nellie Y. McKay. Boston: G. K. Hall, 1988. 105–13.

Fauset, Jesse Redmon. *Plum Bun*. Boston: Beacon, 1990.

Finnegan, Ruth. *Oral Literature in Africa*. Oxford: Clarendon, 1970.

Finney, Brian. "Temporal Defamiliarization in Toni Morrison's *Beloved*." *Obsidian II* 5 (1990): 20–36.

Fisher, Philip. "Democratic Social Space: Whitman, Melville, and the Promise of American Transparency." *The New American Studies*. Ed. Fisher. Berkeley: U of California P, 1991. 70–111.

———. "Introduction." *The New American Studies*. Ed. Fisher. Berkeley: U of California P, 1991. vii–xxii.

Foucault, Michel. *Madness and Civilization: A History of Insanity in the Age of Reason*. Trans. Richard Howard. New York: Random House, 1965.

Gaines, Ernest J. *The Autobiography of Miss Jane Pittman*. New York: Bantam, 1971.

———. *A Gathering of Old Men*. New York: Knopf, 1983.

Gates, Henry Louis, Jr. *Figures in Black: Words, Signs, and the "Racial" Self*. New York: Oxford UP, 1987.

———. *Loose Canons: Notes on the Culture Wars*. New York: Oxford UP, 1992.

———. Review of *Jazz*. *Toni Morrison: Critical Perspectives Past and Present*. Ed. Gates and K. A. Appiah. New York: Amistad, 1993. 52–55.

———. *The Signifying Monkey: A Theory of African-American Literary Criticism*. New York: Oxford UP, 1988.

———. "The Trope of a New Negro and the Reconstruction of the Image of the Black." *The New American Studies*. Ed. Philip Fisher. Berkeley: U of California P, 1991. 319–45.

Geertz, Clifford. *The Interpretation of Cultures*. New York: Basic, 1973.

Genette, Gerard. *Narrative Discourse: An Essay in Method*. Trans. Jane E. Lewin. Ithaca, NY: Cornell UP, 1980.

Gillespie, Diane, and Missy Dehn Kubitschek. "Who Cares? Women-Centered Psychology in *Sula*." *Black American Literature Forum* 24 (1990): 21–48.

Works Cited

Grant, Robert. "Absence into Presence: The Thematics of Memory and 'Missing' Subjects in Toni Morrison's *Sula.*" *Critical Essays on Toni Morrison.* Ed. Nellie Y. McKay. Boston: G. K. Hall, 1988. 90–103.

Grossman, Allan. "The Poetics of Union in Whitman and Lincoln: An Inquiry Toward the Relationship of Art and Polity." *The American Renaissance Reconsidered.* Ed. Walter Benn Michael and Donald E. Pease. Baltimore: Johns Hopkins UP, 1985. 175–92.

Guth, Deborah. "A Blessing and Burden: The Relation to the Past in *Sula, Song of Solomon,* and *Beloved.*" *Modern Fiction Studies* 39 (1993): 575–96.

Haring, Lee. "A Characteristic African Folktale Pattern." *African Folklore.* Ed Richard M. Dorson. Bloomington: Indiana UP, 1972. 165–79.

Harris, Leslie. "Myth as Structure in Toni Morrison's *Song of Solomon. Melus* 7 (1980): 69–76.

Harris, Trudier. *Fiction and Folklore: The Novels of Toni Morrison.* Knoxville: U of Tennessee P, 1991.

———. "Reconnecting Fragments: Afro-American Folk Traditions in *The Bluest Eye.*" *Critical Essays on Toni Morrison.* Ed. Nellie Y. McKay. Boston: G. K. Hall, 1988. 68–76.

Hartman, Charles. *Jazz Text: Voice and Improvisation in Poetry, Jazz, and Song.* Princeton, NJ: Princeton UP, 1991.

Hawthorne, Evelyn. "On Gaining the Double-Vision: *Tar Baby* as Diasporean Novel." *Black American Literature Forum* 22 (1988): 97–107.

Heinze, Denise. *The Dilemma of "Double-Consciousness": Toni Morrison's Novels.* Athens: U of Georgia P, 1993.

Henderson, Mae Gwendolyn. "Speaking in Tongues: Dialogics, Dialectics, and the Black Woman Writer's Literary Tradition." *Reading Black, Reading Feminist: A Critical Anthology.* Ed. Henry Louis Gates, Jr. New York: Meridian, 1990. 116–42.

Hirsch, Marianne. "Maternal Narratives: 'Cruel Enough to Stop the Blood'." *Reading Black, Reading Feminist: A Critical Anthology.* Ed. Henry Louis Gates, Jr. New York: Meridian, 1990. 415–30.

———. *The Mother/Daughter Plot: Narrative, Psychoanalysis, Feminism.* Bloomington: Indiana UP, 1989.

Hogue, Lawrence. *Discourse and the Other: The Production of the Afro-American Text.* Durham, NC: Duke UP, 1986.

Holloway, Karla F. C. "African Values and Western Chaos." Holloway and Stephanie A. Demetrakopoulos. *New Dimensions of Spirituality: A Biracial and Bicultural Reading of the Novels of Toni Morrison.* New York: Greenwood, 1987. 117–30.

———. "*Beloved*: A Spiritual." *Callaloo* 13 (1990): 516–25.

Works Cited

Homans, Margaret. " 'Her Very Own Howl': The Ambiguities of Representation in Recent Women's Fiction." *Signs* 9 (1983): 186–205.

hooks, bell. *Ain't I a Woman: Black Women and Feminism*. Boston: South End, 1981.

———. *Talking Back: thinking feminist, thinking black*. Boston: South End, 1989.

Horvitz, Deborah. "Nameless Ghosts: Possession and Dispossession in *Beloved*." *Studies in American Fiction* 17 (1989): 157–67.

House, Elizabeth. "The 'Sweet Life' in Toni Morrison's Fiction." *American Literature* 56 (1984): 181–202.

Huron, Liz. "It Won't Let Go." Rev. of *Beloved*. *The Listener* 29 Oct. 1987: 28.

Hurston, Zora Neale. *Their Eyes Were Watching God*. New York: Lippincott, 1937.

Imbrie, Ann E. " 'What Shalimar Knew': Toni Morrison's *Song of Solomon* as a Pastoral Novel." *College English* 55 (1993): 473–90.

Irigaray, Luce. "The Power of Discourse and the Subordination of the Feminine." *The Irigaray Reader*. Ed. Margaret Whitford. Oxford: Basil Blackwell, 1991. 118–27.

———. "Volume without Contours." *The Irigaray Reader*. Ed. Margaret Whitford. Oxford: Basil Blackwell, 1991. 53–60.

Jahn, Janheinz. *Muntu: An Outline of the New African Culture*. Trans. Marjorie Grene. New York: Grove, 1961.

Jameson, Fredric. *Postmodernism, or, The Cultural Logic of Late Capitalism*. Durham, NC: Duke UP, 1991.

Jehlen, Myra. "The Novel and the American Middle Class." *Ideology and Classic American Literature*. Ed. Sacvan Bercovitch and Jehlen. New York: Cambridge UP, 1986. 125–44.

Johnson, Barbara. *A World of Difference*. Baltimore: Johns Hopkins UP, 1987.

Johnson, Charles. *Being and Race*. Bloomington: Indiana UP, 1988.

Johnson, James Weldon. *The Autobiography of an Ex-Coloured Man*. New York: Knopf, 1927.

Jones, A. M., and H. Carter. "The Styles of a Tonga Historical Narrative." *African Language Studies* 8 (1967): 113–20.

Jones, Bessie W. "Garden Metaphor and Christian Symbolism in *Tar Baby*." Jones and Audrey L. Vinson. *The World of Toni Morrison: Explorations in Literary Criticism*. Dubuque, IA: Kendall/Hunt, 1985. 115–26.

———. "An Interview with Toni Morrison." Jones and Audrey L. Vinson. *The World of Toni Morrison: Explorations in Literary Criticism*. Dubuque, IA: Kendall/Hunt, 1985.

Jones, Bessie W., and Audrey L. Vinson. *The World of Toni Morrison: Explorations in Literary Criticism*. Dubuque, IA: Kendall/Hunt, 1985.

Works Cited

Jones, Leroi (Amiri Baraka). *Blues People: Negro Music in White America*. New York: Morrow Quill, 1963.

Kammen, Michael. *People of Paradox*. Ithaca, NY: Cornell UP, 1990.

Kamuf, Peggy, ed. *A Derrida Reader: Between the Blinds*. New York: Columbia UP, 1991.

Krumholz, Linda. "Dead Teachers: Rituals of Manhood and Rituals of Reading in *Song of Solomon*." *Modern Fiction Studies* 39 (1993): 551–74.

———. "The Ghosts of Slavery: Historical Recovery in Toni Morrison's *Beloved*." *African American Review* 26 (1992): 395–408.

Kubitschek, Missy Dehn. *Claiming the Heritage*. Jackson: UP of Mississippi, 1991.

Lacan, Jacques. *Ecrits: A Selection*. Trans. Alan Sheridan. New York: Norton, 1977.

Lanser, Susan Sniador. *The Narrative Act: Point of View in Prose Fiction*. Princeton, NJ: Princeton UP, 1981.

Lawrence, David. "Fleshly Ghosts and Ghostly Flesh: The Word and the Body in *Beloved*." *Studies in American Fiction* 19 (1991): 189–201.

LeClair, Thomas. " 'The Language Must Not Sweat': A Conversation with Toni Morrison." *New Republic* 184 (21 Mar. 1981): 25–29.

Lee, Dorothy H. "The Quest for Self: Triumph and Failure in the Works of Toni Morrison." *Black Women Writers (1950–1980)*. Ed. Mari Evans. Garden City, NY: Anchor, 1984. 346–50.

———. "*Song of Solomon*: To Ride the Air." *Black American Literature Forum* 16 (1982): 64–70.

Lefort, Claude. *Democracy and Political Theory*. Trans. David Macey. Cambridge, England: Polity, 1988.

Levine, Lawrence. *Black Culture and Black Consciousness*. New York: Oxford UP, 1977.

———. *Highbrow/Lowbrow: The Emergence of Cultural Hierarchy in America*. Cambridge: Harvard UP, 1988.

Levy, Andrew. "Telling *Beloved*." *Texas Studies in Literature and Language* 33 (1991): 114–23.

Lewis, R. W. B. *The American Adam: Innocence, Tragedy, and Tradition in the Nineteenth Century*. Chicago: U of Chicago P, 1955.

Lewis, Vashti Crutcher. "African Tradition in Toni Morrison's *Sula*." *Phylon* 48 (1987): 91–97.

Lounsberry, Barbara, and Grace Ann Hovet. "Principles of Perception in Toni Morrison's *Sula*." *Black American Literature Forum* 13 (1979): 126–29.

MacRae, George W. Introduction to "The Thunder: Perfect Mind." *The Nag Hammadi Library in English*. Gen. ed. James M. Robinson. 3rd ed. San Francisco: Harper and Row, 1988.

Works Cited

Mano, D. Keith. "Poignant Instant, Stubborn Evil." Rev. of *Beloved*. *National Review* 4 Dec. 1987: 54–55.

Marx, Leo. *The Machine in the Garden: Technology and the Pastoral Ideal in America*. London: Oxford UP, 1964.

———. "Pastoralism in America." *Ideology and Classic American Literature*. Ed. Sacvan Bercovitch and Myra Jehlen. New York: Cambridge UP, 1986. 36–69.

Mbalia, Dorothea Drummond. "Women Who Run with Wild: The Need for Sisterhoods in *Jazz*." *Modern Fiction Studies* 39 (1993): 623–50.

Mbiti, John. *African Religions and Philosophy*. 2nd ed. Oxford: Heinemann, 1989.

McDowell, Deborah E. "New Directions for Black Feminist Criticism." *The New Feminist Criticism*. Ed. Elaine Showalter. New York: Pantheon, 1985. 186–99.

———. "The 'self and the other': Reading Toni Morrison's *Sula* and the Black Female Text." *Critical Essays on Toni Morrison*. Ed. Nellie Y. McKay. Boston: G. K. Hall, 1988. 77–90.

McKay, Nellie Y. "An Interview with Toni Morrison." *Contemporary Literature* 24 (Winter 1983): 413–29.

McKinstry, Susan Jaret. "A Ghost of An/Other Chance: The Spinster-Mother in Toni Morrison's *Beloved*." *Old Maids to Radical Spinsters: Unmarried Women in the Twentieth-Century Novel*. Ed. Laura L. Doan. Urbana: U of Illinois P, 1991. 259–74.

Melville, Herman. *Moby-Dick*. Ed. Harrison Hayford and Hershel Parker. New York: Norton, 1967.

Miller, J. Hillis. *Ariadne's Thread: Story Lines*. New Haven, CT: Yale UP, 1992.

Miner, Madonne. "Lady No Longer Sings the Blues: Rape, Madness, and Silence in *The Bluest Eye*." *Modern Critical Views: Toni Morrison*. Ed. Harold Bloom. New York: Chelsea House, 1990. 85–100.

Mobley, Marilyn Sanders. "A Different Remembering: Memory, History, and Meaning in Toni Morrison's *Beloved*." *Modern Critical Views: Toni Morrison*. Ed. Harold Bloom. New York: Chelsea House, 1990. 189–200.

———. *Folk Roots and Mythic Wings in Sarah Orne Jewett and Toni Morrison: The Cultural Functions of Narrative*. Baton Rouge: Louisiana State UP, 1991.

———. "Narrative Dilemma: Jadine as Cultural Orphan in *Tar Baby*." *Toni Morrison: Critical Perspectives Past and Present*. Ed. Henry Louis Gates, Jr., and K. A. Appiah. New York: Amistad, 1993. 284–92.

Mohanty, Satya P. "The Epistemic Status of Cultural Identity: On *Beloved* and the Postcolonial Condition." *Cultural Critique* 24 (1993): 41–80.

Monson, Ingrid. "Doubleness and Jazz Improvisation: Irony, Parody, and Ethnomusicology." *Critical Inquiry* 20 (1994): 283–313.

Works Cited

Montgomery, Maxine Lavon. "A Pilgrimage to the Origins: The Apocalypse as Structure and Theme in Toni Morrison's *Sula.*" *Black American Literature Forum* 23 (1989): 127–37.

Moreland, Richard C. " 'He Wants to Put His Story Next to Hers': Putting Twain's Story Next to Hers in Morrison's *Beloved.*" *Modern Fiction Studies* 39 (1993): 501–26.

Morrison, Toni. *Beloved*. New York: Knopf, 1987.

———. *The Bluest Eye*. New York: Pocket Books, 1972.

———. *Dreaming Emmett*. Performed 4 January 1986 by the Capital Repertory Theater, Albany, New York.

———. *Jazz*. New York: Knopf, 1992.

———. "Memory, Creation, and Writing." *Thought* 59 (1984): 385–90.

———. *Playing in the Dark: Whiteness and the Literary Imagination*. Cambridge: Harvard UP, 1992.

———. "Rootedness: The Ancestor as Foundation." *Black Women Writers (1950–1980): A Critical Evaluation*. Ed. Mari Evans. Garden City, NY: Anchor/Doubleday, 1984. 339–45.

———. *Song of Solomon*. New York: Signet, 1978.

———. *Sula*. New York: Bantam, 1975.

———. *Tar Baby*. New York: Signet, 1981.

———. "Unspeakable Things Unspoken: The Afro-American Presence in American Literature." *Modern Critical Views: Toni Morrison*. Ed. Harold Bloom. New York: Chelsea House, 1990. 201–30.

Murray, Albert. *The Omni-Americans: New Perspectives on Black Experience and American Culture*. New York: Outerbridge and Dienstfrey, 1970.

Naylor, Gloria. *Bailey's Cafe*. New York: Vintage, 1993.

Nisenson, Eric. *Ascension: John Coltrane and His Quest*. New York: St. Martins, 1993.

Ogunyemi, Chikwenye Okonjo. "Order and Disorder in Toni Morrison's *The Bluest Eye.*" *Critique: Studies in Modern Fiction* 19 (1977): 112–20.

———. "*Sula*: 'A Nigger Joke.' " *Black American Literature Forum* 13 (1979), 131–33.

O'Shaughnessy, Kathleen. " 'Life Life Life Life': The Community as Chorus in *Song of Solomon.*" *Critical Essays on Toni Morrison*. Ed. Nellie Y. McKay. Boston: G. K. Hall, 1988. 125–33.

Otten, Terry. *The Crime of Innocence in the Fiction of Toni Morrison*. Columbia: U of Missouri P, 1989.

———. "Horrific Love in Toni Morrison's Fiction." *Modern Fiction Studies* 39 (1993): 651–68.

Page, Philip. "Circularity in Toni Morrison's *Beloved.*" *African American Review* 26 (1992): 31–39.

218

Works Cited

Paquet, Sandra Pouchet. "The Ancestor as Foundation in *Their Eyes Were Watching God* and *Tar Baby*." *Callaloo* 13 (1990): 499–515.

Parker, Betty J. "Complexity: Toni Morrison's Women—An Interview Essay." *Sturdy Black Bridges: Visions of Black Women in Literature*. Ed. Roseann P. Bell, Parker, and Beverly Guy-Sheftall. New York: Anchor/Doubleday, 1979. 251–57.

Pérez-Torres, Rafael. "Knitting and Knotting the Narrative Thread—*Beloved* as Postmodern Novel." *Modern Fiction Studies* 39 (1993): 689–708.

Phelan, James. "Toward a Rhetorical Reader-Response Criticism: The Difficult, the Stubborn, and the Ending of *Beloved*." *Modern Fiction Studies* 39 (1993): 709–28.

Pullin, Faith. "Landscapes of Reality: The Fiction of Contemporary Afro-American Women." *Black Fiction: New Studies in the African American Novel Since 1945*. Ed. A. Robert Lee. New York: Barnes, 1980. 173–203.

Rainwater, Catherine. "Worthy Messengers: Narrative Voices in Toni Morrison's Novels." *Texas Studies in Literature and Language* 33 (1991): 96–113.

Rank, Otto. *In Quest of the Hero*. Princeton, NJ: Princeton UP, 1990.

Reddy, Maureen T. "The Tripled Plot and Center of *Sula*." *Black American Literature Forum* 22 (1988): 29–45.

Reyes, Angelita. "Politics and Metaphors of Materialism in Paule Marshall's *Praisesong for the Widow* and Toni Morrison's *Tar Baby*." *Politics and the Muse*. Ed. Adam J. Sorkin. Bowling Green, OH: Bowling Green State UP, 1989. 179–205.

Rigney, Barbara Hill. " 'A Story to Pass On': Ghosts and the Significance of History in Toni Morrison's *Beloved*." *Haunting the House of Fiction: Feminist Perspectives on Ghost Stories by American Women*. Ed. Lynette Carpenter and Wendy K. Kolmar. Knoxville: U of Tennessee P, 1991. 229–35.

———. *The Voices of Toni Morrison*. Columbus: Ohio State UP, 1991.

Roberts, John W. *From Trickster to Badman: The Black Folk Hero in Slavery and Freedom*. Philadelphia: U of Pennsylvania P, 1989.

Robinson, James M., gen. ed. *The Nag Hammadi Library in English*. 3rd ed. San Francisco: Harper and Row, 1988.

Rodrigues, Eusebio L. "Experiencing *Jazz*." *Modern Fiction Studies* 39 (1993): 733–54.

———. "The Telling of *Beloved*." *Journal of Narrative Technique* 21 (1991): 153–69.

Royster, Philip. "A Priest and a Witch Against the Spiders and the Snakes: Scapegoating in Toni Morrison's *Sula*." *Umoja* n.s. 2 (1978): 149–68.

———. "Milkman's Flying: The Scapegoat Transcended in Toni Morrison's *Song of Solomon*." *College Language Association Journal* 24 (1982): 419–40.

Works Cited

Ruas, Charles. *Conversations with American Writers*. New York: Knopf, 1985.

Rubenstein, Roberta. *Boundaries of the Self: Gender, Culture, Fiction*. Urbana: U of Illinois P, 1987.

Rushdy, Ashraf H. A. "Daughters Signifyin(g) History: The Example of Toni Morrison's *Beloved*." *American Literature* 64 (1992): 567–97.

———. " 'Rememory': Primal Scenes and Constructions in Toni Morrison's Novels." *Contemporary Literature* 31 (1990): 300–323.

Ryan, Judylyn. "Contested Visions/Double-Vision in *Tar Baby*." *Modern Fiction Studies* 39 (1993): 597–622.

Sale, Maggie. "Call and Response as Critical Method: African American Oral Traditions and *Beloved*." *African American Review* 26 (1992): 41–50.

Samuels, Wilfred D., and Clenora Hudson-Weems. *Toni Morrison*. Boston: Twayne, 1990.

Sanchez-Eppler, Karen. "Bodily Bonds: The Intersecting Rhetorics of Feminism and Abolition." *The New American Studies*. Ed. Philip Fisher. Berkeley: U of California P, 1991. 228–59.

Schapiro, Barbara. "The Bonds of Love and the Boundaries of Self in Toni Morrison's *Beloved*." *Contemporary Literature* 32 (1991): 194–210.

Scheub, Harold. "The Technique of the Expansible Image in Xhosa *Ntsomi*-Performances." *Forms of Folklore in Africa*. Ed. Bernth Lindfors. Austin: U of Texas P, 1977. 37–63.

Schlesinger, Arthur M., Jr. *The Disuniting of America: Reflections on a Multicultural Society*. New York: Norton, 1992.

Scruggs, Charles. "The Nature of Desire in Toni Morrison's *Song of Solomon*." *Arizona Quarterly* 38 (1982): 311–35.

———. *Sweet Home: Invisible Cities in the Afro-American Novel*. Baltimore: Johns Hopkins UP, 1993.

Shange, Ntozake. *Sassafras, Cypress, and Indigo*. New York: St. Martin, 1982.

Showalter, Elaine. "Feminist Criticism in the Wilderness." *The New Feminist Criticism: Essays on Women, Literature, and Theory*. New York: Pantheon, 1985. 243–70.

Sitter, Deborah Ayer. "The Making of a Man: Dialogic Meaning in *Beloved*." *African American Review* 26 (1992): 17–30.

Skerritt, Joseph T., Jr. "Recitation to the *Griot*: Storytelling and Learning in Toni Morrison's *Song of Solomon*." *Conjuring: Black Women, Fiction, and Literary Tradition*. Ed. Marjorie Pryse and Hortense J. Spillers. Bloomington: Indiana UP, 1985. 192–202.

Smith, Barbara. "Toward a Black Feminist Criticism." *The New Feminist Criticism*. Ed. Elaine Showalter. New York: Pantheon, 1985. 168–85.

Smith, Valerie. "Black Feminist Theory and the Representation of the

'Other'." *Changing Our Own Words: Essays on Criticism, Theory, and Writing by Black Women*. Ed. Cheryl A. Wall. New Brunswick, NJ: Rutgers UP, 1989. 38–57.

———. " 'Circling the Subject': History and Narrative in *Beloved*." *Toni Morrison: Critical Perspectives Past and Present*. Ed. Henry Louis Gates, Jr., and K. A. Appiah. New York: Amistad, 1993. 342–55.

———. *Self-Discovery and Authority in Afro-American Narrative*. Cambridge: Harvard UP, 1987. 122–54.

———. "*Song of Solomon*: Continuities of Community." *Toni Morrison: Critical Perspectives Past and Present*. Ed. Henry Louis Gates, Jr., and K. A. Appiah. New York: Amistad, 1993. 274–83.

Smitherman, Geneva. *Talkin' and Testifyin': The Language of Black America*. Detroit: Wayne State UP, 1986.

Spiller, Robert. "The Cycle and Its Roots." *Toward a New American Literary History*. Ed. Louis J. Budd, Edwin H. Cady, and Carl L. Anderson. Durham, NC: Duke UP, 1980. 3–21.

Spillers, Hortense. "A Hateful Passion, A Lost Love." *Feminist Issues in Literary Scholarship*. Ed. Shari Benstock. Bloomington: Indiana UP, 1981. 181–207.

Stein, Karen. " 'I Didn't Even Know His Name': Names and Naming in Toni Morrison's *Sula*." *Names: Journal of the American Name Society* 28 (1980): 226–29.

Stepto, Robert B. *From Behind the Veil: A Study of Afro-American Narrative*. Urbana: U of Illinois P, 1979.

———. " 'Intimate Things in Place': A Conversation with Toni Morrison." *Chant of Saints: A Gathering of Afro-American Literature, Art, and Scholarship*. Ed. Michael S. Harper and Stepto. Urbana: U of Illinois P, 1979. 213–29.

Stockton, Kathryn Bond. "Heaven's Bottom: Anal Economics and the Critical Debasement of Freud in Toni Morrison's *Sula*." *Cultural Critique* 24 (1993): 81–118.

Story, Ralph. "An Excursion into the Black World: The 'Seven Days' in Toni Morrison's *Song of Solomon*." *Black American Literature Forum* 23 (1989): 149–58.

Sundquist, Eric. *To Wake the Nations: Race in the Making of American Literature*. Cambridge: Harvard UP, 1993.

Tate, Claudia. "Toni Morrison." *Black Women Writers at Work*. New York: Continuum, 1989. 117–31.

Thurman, Judith. "A House Divided." Rev. of *Beloved*. *New Yorker* 2 Nov. 1987: 175–80.

Traylor, Eleanor W. "The Fabulous World of Toni Morrison: *Tar Baby*." *Critical Essays on Toni Morrison*. Ed. Nellie Y. McKay. Boston: G. K. Hall, 1988. 135–49.

Works Cited

Varenne, Herve. "Introduction." *Symbolizing America*. Ed. Varenne. Lincoln: U of Nebraska P, 1986. 1–9.

Wade-Gayles, Gloria. *No Crystal Stair: Visions of Race and Sex in Black Women's Fiction*. New York: Pilgrim, 1984.

Wagner, Linda. "Toni Morrison: Mastery of Narrative." *Contemporary American Women Writers: Narrative Strategies*. Ed. Catherine Rainwater and William J. Scheick. Lexington: UP of Kentucky, 1985. 191–204.

Walker, Alice. *The Color Purple*. New York: Harcourt Brace, 1982.

Walker, Melissa. *Down from the Mountaintop: Black Women's Novels in the Wake of the Civil Rights Movement, 1966–1989*. New Haven, CT: Yale UP, 1991.

Wallace, Michele. *Black Macho and the Myth of the Superwoman*. New York: Dial, 1979.

———. "Variations on Negation and the Heresy of Black Feminist Creativity." *Reading Black, Reading Feminine*. Ed. Henry Louis Gates, Jr. New York: Meridian, 1990. 52–67.

Walther, Malin Lavon. "Toni Morrison's *Tar Baby*: Re-Figuring the Colonizer's Aesthetics." *Cross-Cultural Performances: Differences in Women's Re-Visions of Shakespeare*. Ed. Marianne Novy. Urbana: U of Illinois P, 1993. 137–49.

Washington, Elsie B. "Toni Morrison Now." *Essence* 18 (Oct. 1987): 58, 136–37.

Washington, Mary Helen. "Introduction." *Black-Eyed Susans: Classic Stories by and about Black Women*. Ed. Washington. New York: Anchor, 1975. ix–xxxii.

———. "I Sign My Mother's Name: Alice Walker, Dorothy West, Paule Marshall." *Mothering the Mind*. Ed. Ruth Perry and Martine Watson Brownley. New York: Holmes and Meier, 1984. 142–63.

———. "Teaching *Black-Eyed Susans*: An Approach to the Study of Black Women Writers." *All the Women Are White, All the Blacks Are Men, But Some of Us Are Brave*. Ed. Gloria T. Hull, Patricia Bell Scott, and Barbara Smith. Old Westbury, NY: Feminist, 1982. 208–17.

Wegs, Joyce M. "Toni Morrison's *Song of Solomon*: A Blues Song." *Essays in Literature* 9 (1982): 222.

Werner, Craig H. "The Briar Patch as Modernist Myth: Morrison, Barthes, and Tar Baby As-Is." *Critical Essays on Toni Morrison*. Ed. Nellie Y. McKay. Boston: G. K. Hall, 1988. 150–67.

———. *Playing the Changes: From Afro-Modernism to the Jazz Impulse*. Urbana: U of Illinois P, 1994.

Wideman, John Henry. *Reuben*. New York: Vintage, 1987.

Wilentz, Gay. *Binding Cultures: Black Women Writers in Africa and the Diaspora*. Bloomington: Indiana UP, 1992.

Willis, Susan. *Specifying: Black Women Writing the American Experience*. Madison: U of Wisconsin P, 1987. 83–109.

Works Cited

Woolf, Virginia. *A Room of One's Own*. New York: Harcourt Brace, 1929.

Wright, Richard. *Eight Men*. Cleveland: World, 1961.

———. *Native Son*. New York: Harper, 1940.

———. *The Outsider*. New York: Harper, 1953.

Wyatt, Jane. "Giving Body to the Word: The Maternal Symbolic in Toni Morrison's *Beloved*." *Publications of the Modern Language Association* 108 (1993): 474–88.

INDEX

Abrahams, Roger, 13, 17 n14
Absence, 10, 32, 35, 62, 65, 72 n15, 91–92,
146, 159, 161–63, 166–67, 176
Adesanya, Adebayo, 11
African-American culture, 4, 9–25,
187–88; deconstructive qualities, 16;
double-consciousness in, 9–10; identity
search, 22–23, 80, 160; nigrescence,
104–06; past, 15, 18–22, 29, 87, 157–
58, 160; place, 16–18, 79, 89, 121; pluralistic, 12–13, 31, 51–52, 56, 90; reaction to dominant culture, 12–13, 35, 58,
79, 162
African-American literature, 17–25
African philosophy and culture, 10–12;
oral narratives, 142–43; spoken word,
11–12, 42, 109, 178–79
Ajax (Albert Jacks) (S), 28, 63, 65, 67–68,
71–72, 74, 100, 154, 180
Alfred, Georgia (B), 133, 144–45, 149,
151, 157
Alice Manfred (J), 149, 161, 168, 171–72,
175–76, 185–86
Alienation, 9, 29, 44, 50, 52, 95, 97
Alma Estée (TB), 109, 124, 128
Ambiguity, 26, 32, 34, 187; in BE, 41,
57–58; in S, 65, 81–82; in SOS, 84, 96,
104, 106; in TB, 109, 123, 128, 130; in
B, 139; in J, 167. See also Open-endedness
American culture: agrarian ideal, 78;
equality, lack of, 52, 123; microcosm of,
111; past, 29; pluralistic, 4–6, 17, 31,
36, 51–52, 77, 90, 106, 158, 187–88; racial tensions in, 10, 12, 27–28, 51, 59,
77, 89–92, 111, 121
Amy Denver (B), 143, 146–49, 152, 156

Ancestors: in SOS, 86, 88, 97, 100–05; in
TB, 118, 128; in J, 164
Artists, 47–48, 73, 116–17, 123
Asante, Molefi Kete, 11–12
Askeland, Lori, 147
Assimilation: in BE, 52, 56; in S, 62, 68,
70, 81–82; in SOS, 90, 93; in TB, 125
Aunt Jimmy (BE), 39, 42, 45–47, 183
Aunt Rosa (TB), 126
Awkward, Michael, 20–21, 49, 56

Baby Suggs (B), 28, 70, 135–36, 140, 153,
158; healer, 143, 184, 186
Bains, Mr. (SOS), 30, 86, 89
Baker, Houston A., Jr., 10, 15–18, 22, 24–
25, 68, 70, 75, 79
Bakhtin, M. M., 7, 32, 55, 153
Baldwin, James, 12, 22
Bambara, Toni Cade, 23–24
Barthes, Roland, 7–8, 32, 55
Barthold, Bonnie, 11, 18, 22–23, 85, 101,
152
Beauvoir, Simone de, 9
Bell, Bernard, 22–23, 156, 179
Bellah, Robert N., et al., 5
Beloved, 28–31, 33–34, 36, 107, 131–58,
186; circularity, 134–40; circularity of
form, 140–43; death imagery, 144–46;
healing and healers, 146–50; narration,
134, 140–44, 148, 153, 156–57; storytelling and listening, 151–57
Beloved (B), 27–28, 30, 34, 36, 66, 70,
134, 136–41, 149–50, 156, 175; between death and life, 145–46, 148, 155;
healer, 147; listener, 151–52, 155, 157,
183; possessive of Sethe, 93, 151–52,
162; power over Paul D, 151; symbol of

Index

Double-consciousness: in African-American culture, 9–10, 20, 22, 35; in feminist theory, 9; in *BE*, 59; in *S*, 79–80; in *SOS*, 97, 104; in *TB*, 117
Du Bois, W. E. B., 9–10, 52, 81
DuPlessis, Rachel, 9
Dyads. *See* Paired entities
Dysfunctionality, 37, 48, 114

Edelberg, Cynthia, 110, 124
Elegiac, 61–62, 83
Ella (*B*), 149, 156–57, 175, 184
Ellison, Ralph, 3, 5, 10, 12, 14–15, 22, 48, 62, 80
Eloe (*TB*), 29, 117, 124–26, 128, 132
Epithets, 118, 131–32, 134, 142
Erickson, Peter, 112, 118
Ernie Paul (*TB*), 126
Eva Peace (*S*), 27, 30, 63–64, 66, 68, 70–71, 73, 182

Fabre, Genevieve, 96, 101
Family, 4, 28, 183, 187; in *BE*, 44–46; in *SOS*, 84–85; in *TB*, 28, 109–22, 124; in *B*, 136–39, 143
Fathers, 45–46, 67, 71, 87 *n*3, 113, 137, 145, 152–53, 163
Fauset, Jesse Redmon, 80
Fear, 99, 102, 106, 118–29, 124, 161
Felice (*J*), 161, 170–71, 173, 176, 185–86
Female triads, 44–46, 66, 85, 138, 183
Feminist theory, 8–9, 21
Finnegan, Ruth, 142
First Corinthians Dead (*SOS*), 94, 101–02
Fisher, Philip, 5, 12 *n*8, 80
Fishers, the (*BE*), 39, 42, 46, 50–51
Flying, 67–68, 71, 97, 100, 106
Form: of African-American fiction, 23–25; of Morrison's novels, 4, 32 *n*6, 187; of *S*, 63; of *SOS*, 87–89, 96; of *B* and *J*, 133–34; of *B*, 140–44; of *J*, 164. *See also* Narration
Foucault, Michel, 117
Fragmentation. *See* Fusion
Freddie (*SOS*), 86, 99
Freedom, 27, 38, 43, 48–49, 61–62, 73–74, 81–82, 123, 129, 144, 158, 163, 187–88
Freud, Sigmund, 55
Frieda MacTeer (*BE*), 40, 42, 44, 50
Fusion and fragmentation, 3; in African-American culture, 10, 12–13, 17–18, 23; in black feminist theory, 20; in blues

and jazz, 13–16; in Morrison's fiction, 25, 28–29, 32, 34–35, 134, 174, 178, 181, 185–87; in *BE*, 37, 43, 45, 47–49, 53, 55–59; in *S*, 60–61, 65–66, 68–69, 74, 83; in *SOS*, 84–85, 88–89, 92, 95–97, 99–101, 104–06; in *TB*, 108, 118, 121, 123–27, 131; in *B*, 134, 136–37, 140, 143–44, 146, 151–52, 154–55, 158; in *J*, 167, 171, 174, 176; in postmodern theories, 6–9, 11

Gaines, Ernest, 80
Garner, Mr. (*B*), 151
Gates, Henry Louis, Jr., 5, 10 *n*5, 21–22, 79, 81, 158
Geraldine (*BE*), 30, 43–44, 46, 50–52, 70, 182
Ghosts, 86–87, 100, 113, 136, 140, 145–47, 149, 163
Gideon (*TB*), 110–12, 117, 119, 121–24
Golden Grey (*J*), 29, 91, 161, 163–64, 166, 169–73, 182
Grant, Robert, 63, 65
Grief, 61–62, 83, 162
Griot, 92, 117, 128–29, 164, 183–84
Grossman, Allan, 5
Guitar Bains (*SOS*), 31, 85–86, 88, 90, 94–96, 99–100, 106, 119, 123, 165, 182; influence over Milkman, 93, 96, 98, 104; vengeful, 91, 103, 105
Guth, Deborah, 74, 92, 100

Hagar Dead (*SOS*), 66, 85–86, 98–100, 154, 183; deprived, 91; inarticulate, 180; lost, 163; influence on Milkman, 93, 98; possessive love for Milkman, 93–94, 103, 138, 162
Halle (*B*), 29, 137, 154, 183
Hannah Peace (*S*), 63, 66–68, 70, 180
Haring, Lee, 142–43
Harris, Trudier, 51, 117, 127
Hartman, Charles, 14, 16–17
Hawthorne, Evelyn, 118
Healers, 146–50
Heidegger, Martin, 163
Heinze, Denise, 64, 96, 147, 162
Helene Wright (*S*), 27, 63, 67–68, 70, 73, 179–80, 182
Henderson, Mae, 20, 74, 76
Henry LesTroy/Lestory (*J*), 29, 160, 163–64
Henry, Mr. (*BE*), 42–43, 180
Here Boy (*B*), 148

Index

Index

Mother/daughter relationships, 20, 63, 66–67, 85, 137 n6, 140, 145, 155, 159, 161

Muhammad, Elijah (*SOS*), 90

Multiplicity: in African-American cultural forms, 13–17, 32; in African-American fiction, 23–24; in Morrison's fiction, 26, 28, 30–31, 34; in postmodern theories, 35; in *BE*, 54–55, 59; in *S*, 65; in *SOS*, 96; in *TB*, 116, 126, 130, 132; in *B*, 134, 141, 153, 158

Murray, Albert, 5, 15–17

Myth: in Morrison's fiction, 29; in *BE*, 40; in *SOS*, 84 n1, 96, 106–07; in *TB*, 108–09, 113, 118, 125, 128–30, 132; in *B*, 151, 155

Nadel, Alan, 16

Nan (*B*), 150

Narration, 4; in Morrison's fiction, 31–32, 186; in *BE*, 42, 53–59; in *S*, 63; in *SOS*, 87–89, 96, 104; in *TB*, 111, 131; in *B*, 134, 140–44, 148, 153, 156–57; in *J*, 164–77. *See also* Form

Narrator of *Jazz*, 31, 34, 64, 157, 159, 164–66, 175–76; confessions, 169–70; critical, 169–70; dream for Golden Grey, 166–67, 171; errors, 169–70; loving, 173–76; purposes, 168–69, 171; recovery, 185; relationship to reader, 173–75; unconventional, 167–68, 176; visions, 172

National Suicide Day (*S*), 64, 71, 180

Naylor, Gloria, 21

Nel Wright (*S*), 28–30, 36, 56, 63, 66, 68, 92, 100, 179–80; balances self and other, 72–73, 76; lacks voice and audience, 180–82, 186; relationship with Sula, 68–69, 77, 82

Nelson Lord (*B*), 140, 149

Nietzsche, Friedrich, 161

Night women (*TB*), 116–17, 124–25, 127, 130

Nisenson, Eric, 14–15

Nommo, 11–12, 42, 109, 186

Nommo (*TB*), 109, 186

North, 4, 17, 29–30, 33, 46, 51, 102, 109, 146, 158, 160

"Not" and "no," 91–92, 154

Ogunyemi, Chikwenye, 44

Ohio, 29, 37, 57, 144, 158

Old Man (*TB*), 126

Ondine Childs (*TB*), 112, 114–16, 119–23, 127, 181–82

Open-endedness: in African-American cultural forms, 15–16, 32; in African-American fiction, 23–24; in Morrison's fiction, 26–27, 30, 32, 34, 36, 188; in *BE*, 57–58; in *S*, 65, 74–75, 77; in *SOS*, 106; in *TB*, 130; in *B*, 137 n5, 158; in *J*, 165, 174. *See also* Ambiguity

Oral tradition: in African-American culture, 17 n14, 21, 179; in African cultures, 11, 13; in Morrison's fiction, 32, 176 n12

Orality, 23–24, 175

Oscillation. *See* Play

Otten, Terry, 56, 138

Paired entities, 27–28, 61, 63, 82, 108

Paquet, Sandra Pouchet, 132

Pariahs, 44, 51, 61, 74, 76, 82, 123, 129

Paul D (*B*), 27–29, 36, 82, 88, 109, 118, 133, 135–41, 148–50, 152, 156, 158, 186; healer, 146, 149; listener, 153–54, 157, 184; memory, 143–44, 151–53; storyteller, 153, 156–57, 183; tobacco-tin heart, 142–43, 145, 147, 151

Pauline Breedlove (*BE*), 27–28, 30, 39–42, 44–48, 50–52, 55, 70, 88, 154; as narrator, 53, 181–82, 186

Past: in African-American culture, 15, 18–22; in Morrison's fiction, 29–30, 33, 183, 186–88; in *S*, 62; in *SOS*, 84, 86–88, 92, 94, 100, 102–03; in *TB*, 109, 112, 124, 126–27; in *B*, 132–34, 136–37, 143–44, 149–54, 157; in *J*, 159, 161–62, 167, 173

Pecola Breedlove (*BE*), 28, 30–31, 33, 37, 39, 42, 43, 74, 100, 113, 183; internal dialogue, 53–54; scapegoat, 43–45; silent, 179, 186; split personality, 49–52; symbol of African Americans, 52

Pérez-Torres, Rafael, 154, 158

Phelan, James, 158

Pilate Dead (*SOS*), 27, 30, 34, 49, 66, 73, 81, 85–89, 95, 100–01, 103, 106, 116, 180; *griot*, 92, 99, 164, 183; influence on Milkman, 93–94, 99, 186; lack of navel, 92; love, 94, 183

Play: in Morrison's fiction, 35, 180–81; in *BE*, 43, 59; in *S*, 75; in *B*, 137, 158; in *J*, 159, 161–63, 165–66, 168, 171, 174–75

Playing in the Dark, 12, 58 n14

Plum Peace (*S*), 67, 71, 180

Index

Index

231